THE INFLUENCE
OF EXISTENTIALISM
ON INGMAR BERGMAN

An Analysis of the Theological Ideas
Shaping a Filmmaker's Art

Charles B. Ketcham

Studies in Art and **Religious** Interpretation
Volume 5

The Edwin Mellen Press
Lewiston/Queenston

Library of Congress Cataloging-in-Publication Data

Ketcham, Charles B.
    The influence of existentialism on Ingmar Bergman.

    (Studies in art and religious interpretation ; v. 5)
    Bibliography: p.
    1. Bergman, Ingmar, 1918-   --Criticism and interpretation.
2. Moving-pictures--Plots, themes, etc. 3. Religion in motion
pictures. 4.Existentialism in motion pictures. I. Title. II. Series.
PN1998.A3B46635 1985   791.43'0233'0924   85-28429
ISBN 0-88946-556-8

This is volume 5 in the continuing series
Studies in Art and Religious Interpretation
Volume 5 ISBN 0-88946-556-8
SARI Series ISBN 0-88946-956-3

The Edwin Mellen Press   The Edwin Mellen Press
Box 450   Box 67
Lewiston, New York   Queenston, Ontario
USA   14092   CANADA   L0S 1L0

Printed in the United States of America

This book is dedicated to my students
in "The Theology of Contemporary
Film," without whose sight and
insight this book could not have been
written; and to my colleague Kate
Wayland-Smith wihout whose
collaboration and lectures, freely
given and free, this course would
have been sorely diminished.

Special thanks must be accorded to Andrew T. Ford, Provost of Allegheny College, for his financial support and personal encouragement; Karen Myers for her superb typing, Janice Cutshall for her gracious undertaking of the demanding task of manuscript preparation, and Joyce Ketcham for her incredible patience and understanding.

I wrote silences, I wrote the night. I
recorded the inexpressible. I fixed
frenzies in their flight.
Arthur Rimbaud
A <u>Season</u> <u>in</u> <u>Hell</u>

We live in a time of religious and theological confusion. The nature and ground of faith-claims have yet to be clarified for a hi-tec world whose contours are electronically established by the binary order of computers. All traditional aspects of Western culture are being called into question. Consequently, when the trumpets of the Church, Synagogue, and Temple sound an uncertain note or any number of loud, distant notes at once, there are many who are hesitant to follow, even though they may long to; they are listening for the compelling and clear prophetic voice out of the wonderland-world of technology. In such times, other searchers for religious truth, e.g. poets, painters, novelists, musicians, film-makers, propheticaly do emerge to make their artistic contributions. One of the greatest of these contemporaries is the Swedish film director Ingmar Bergman. He is an artist whose gifts for creating and writing scripts are matched by his genius for innovative and imaginative visual production. Bergman's holistic approach gives a unique power and focus to his work and permits us to study his contributions both from the screen and from. the respective published texts. This present study utilizes both sources for the analysis of his work.

Although Bergman would never label himself a religious prophet, he would acknowledge a deep and abiding interest in the religious question, even though he ostensibly says that he wants to rid himself of it. In responding to film-maker and critic Jonas Sima's question, "After your trilogy and your new films, do you think you could succumb again to a religious 'flood-tide' in your film-making?", Bergman responds: "No one is safe from religious ideas and

confessional phenomena. Neither you nor I. We can
fall victim to them when we least expect it. It's
like Mao 'flu', or being struck by lightning. You're
utterly helpless. Exposed...As I see it today, any
relapse is utterly out of the question. But I can't
say it's out of the question tomorrow."[1]

Bergman's demur is not meant to be conquettish or
cute. It comes, rather, from Bergman's awareness of
the radical timefulness of human existence, of its
fractured discontinuity as opposed to its faceted
predictability. It is the response of one who, since
the late 1940s, has been a contributor to the
existential critique of culture. From Bergman's
writings and films, it is obvious that the
existentialism with which he is most familiar is that
of Sartre and Camus. Bergman realizes that both
existential nihilism and existential faith claim to go
to the heart of life, to cut through the
superficialities of daily routines which parade
themselves as substantive. The human urgency which
both nihilism and religion share would seem to defy
any radical separation of them in Bergman's mind; both
lend themselves to cinematic expression just because
they are concerned with basic human anxiety and hope.

Bergman knows that left to our inauthentic selves,
to the soul-searching levels of the media soap operas
and commerical religion, we avoid asking the probing
and disturbing questions. We don't ask ourselves by
what practices, ideas, or myths we have been brought
to this point of vacuous self-awareness; we neglect to
search for the human face behind the technological
features of our pseudosophisticated, plastic way of
life; we tune our ears to an electronic world lest
"human voices wake us and we drown."

But to ask the questions, to listen, and especially to search the human face are just what Bergman does do with great skill and integrity. No cinema director in the world pays such attention to or takes such exquisite care exploring faces than Bergman, for it is here that the human drama of existence is mirrored most intimately, most tellingly: "There are many film makers who forget that the human face is the starting point in our work. To be sure, we can become absorbed by the esthetic of the picture montage, we can blend objects and still lifes into wonderful rhythms, we can fashion nature studies of astonishing beauty, but the proximity of the human face is without doubt the film's distinguishing mark and patent of nobility...In order to give the greatest possible power to the actor's expression, the movement of the camera must be simple and uncomplicated...We must also consider that the actor's finest means of expression is in his eyes."[2]

It is the contention of this study that in his search for reality, integrity, and meaning, Bergman participates cinematically in the existential revolt against the entrenched ideology of Western traditionalism. Religiously, Bergman finds the magical and superstitious reliance upon the salvific powers of the classical dogmas, doctrines, and practices of the Church to be spiritually stultifying. Analogously for him, the demand for progress and the imposition of the logic of technology stifle the personal and professional creativity apotheosized by secular humanism. As the son of a Lutheran pastor and as an artistically creative member of an increasingly secularized society, Bergman is affronted by the hypocrisy and superficiality he finds in both sacred and secular claims to interpret reality. Consequently, he has turned to existentialism which is a radical method of acknowledging life in terms of one's existence rather than one's essence, one's individuality rather than one's commonality, one's choices rather than one's conformity.

To follow Bergman through his cinematic quest with sensitivity and imagination is not to assure oneself of an understanding of existentialism; it is to have participated in it. Many, I am sure, have made this journey without realizing that they were participating in a recognizable and historic transition, the ending of an era. The result is exciting yet concurrently distressing. One no longer feels "at home" in the old surroundings, with the old structures, with the old ecclesiastical forms and formulations. We are disturbed that we understand the philosopher William Barrett when he writes: "It is evident that anyone who has passed through the depths of modern experience and strives to place religion in relation to that experience is bound to acquire the label of heretic."[3] Obviously, the force of such a statement is exerted against the present inadequate and popularized teaching of the Church rather than against religion per se. It is a situation which leaves many of us in an awkward position, for we find ourselves labeled "heretic" by the very religious community whose vitality and viability we are struggling to save.

Bergman's early films superficially toy with the ideas of doubt, despair, and death--those now all-too-familiar themes of the existential revolt--but

it is not until he formally poses the question of the
existence of God in his film The Seventh Seal that the
existential journey begins in earnest. It is for this
reason that this allegorical film, produced in 1956,
is still listed as one of his finest, although many
film critics have found his later works more mature
thematically and more excellent technically. Our
present study begins with the film The Seventh Seal
and ends with the film Autumn Sonata. I should have
said "pauses" rather than "ends," for Bergman's
journey is not any more complete than ours. Two
subsequent films, From the Life of the Marionettes
(1980) and Fanny and Alexander (1982), have been
released. The former is an intensified study of the
destructive power of human isolation and is considered ·
in this text as a contribution in depth rather than
direction. The latter is a delightful divertissement,
a recapitulation of traditional themes, but without
angst or theological depth.

One further preliminary question needs brief
exploration: how legitimate is it to translate the
genre of films into literary form for critical study?
Many film critics are quite adamant about the
impossibility of any such direct translation--the
denotation of words cannot possibly do justice to the
connotations of moving pictures, the nuances and
complexities of audio-visual art. The aesthetic
experiences may have points of emotional and
intellectual similarity, but the genres can never be
confused for one another or considered aesthetic
equivalents. In his "Introduction" to Four
Screenplays, Bergman himself seems adamant about the
point: "Film has nothing to do with literature; the
character and substance of the two art forms are

usually in conflict. This probably has something to
do with the receptive process of the mind. The
written word is read and assimilated by a conscious
act of the will in alliance with the intellect; little
by little it affects the imagination and the
emotions. The process is different with a motion
picture. When we experience a film, we consciously
prime ourselves for illusion. Putting aside will and
intellect, we make way for it in our imagination. The
sequence of pictures plays directly on our
feelings."[5]

Accepting such differences in genre as inherent, I
believe it is possible to give a literary or
theological critique of cinema art so long as one
acknowledges, in the beginning, the limitations of
that critique, both in purpose and scope. To come to
"Bergman-the-cinematic-theologian" would be to
prostitute both cinema and academic theology, but to
see what "Bergman-the-cinema-director," as a concerned
artist, has to tell us about religion and the Church
is most instructive and legitimate. Unfortunately,
because of the amount of material available to us
through interviews with Bergman and because of the
amount of research done by so many writers interested
in Bergman's life, ideas, and art, the task of writing
about Bergman and his religious quest has been made
easier.

The best specific statement of legitimation for a
literary critiquing of Bergman's films comes from
Birgitta Steene who, obviously, was faced with the
same problem: "One reason for this [literary
approach] may be the recurrence in Bergman's films of
a set of dramatic motifs, the totality of which forms
a personal philosophy or vision and easily lends

itself to thematic analyses that resemble some of the methods used in literary criticism. Another reason could be Bergman's dependence upon a dramatic story...A third and crucial reason for the literary approach to Bergman's films lies in the existence of printed screenplays where Bergman makes no attempt to include technical references to the actual shooting of a film."[6]

As persuasive as Steene's statements and our natural inclination to verbalize all experience are, we are still left with a final paradox. To write about Bergman is really to write about the man. This is true because we are writing, in Bergman's case, about an intensely personal film art, or, as Jorn Donner puts it: "a deeply personal vision...questions put to eternity and to mankind."[7] But this existential critique of life given us by Bergman raises the perennial existential problem--no existentialist, with his intensely personal (indeed, unique!) vision, can have a serious disciple without implying a universal (thus anti-existential) ground for personal truth and its perception. Soren Kierkegaard, the nineteenth century Danish existential theologian, whom in some ways Bergman resembles, tried to avoid this problem by using pseudonyms in his writings. In this fashion he thought that his readers would be forced to encounter the material directly rather than be encouraged to speculate about what he, Kierkegaard, was thinking. Franz Kafka, another nineteenth century existentialist writer whom Bergman admires, tried to solve the problem by using the letter "K" to symbolize the protagonists of his novels.

It is interesting to note that although Bergman
himself does not use this device to avoid the problem
of paradox, Jorn Donner uses it for him in his own
critique of Bergman's work: "The reviewers neither
describe nor analyze the picture. They try to explore
B's real face, his real intentions...What they are
searching for here, in other words, is B's face, his
soul, but they forget to look for the face his film
shows. When he is dead, his films will remain. Only
a few will then care to seek out the private
personality. It is my conviction that B has succeeded
in transforming his private perception into a general
one, understandable to other people. This is his
strength as an artist. It does not then become a
question of seeking the truth about his private
personality, but rather, as much as possible, of
hiding it and not talking about it. Perhaps there is
no consistency in B's private life. The consistency I
have sought is enclosed in his work...This is why
Ingmar Bergman in this book is designated by the
letter B. The person behind the work is a fictitious
figure who undoubtedly resembles the private person
B. Such resemblances do not interest me."[8]

Such resemblances do interest me, and I think,
give legitimation to the critique that follows. I
have not used "B" to designate Bergman because I
believe that Bergman's existential journey gradually
becomes an ontological one, one in which his being,
his self, is understood in terms of and in encounter
with other selves. This is not to imply that he
abandons the existential methodology so much as he
discovers its implication in terms of interpersonal
relation as well as personal choice. Bergman shares
such a journey with the existential ontologist Martin

Heidegger.   Though Bergman does not acknowledge this
fellow pilgrim nor give any indication of having read
his   work,   the   parallels are important to note.
Independent but concurring claims make a powerful
witness.

Both   Bergman and Heidegger believe that our
experience in being human is one of finding ourselves
"thrown"   into   existence,   we   know   not   how or
whence--other than biologically speaking.   Our
self-awareness is that of a stranger in a strange
land, estranged not only from others but even from our
own true being.   We know ourselves, in popular
terminology, to be hypocritical and pretentious, our
actions marked by duplicity and pathetic posturing.
We find that human existence is contoured not by the
classical   Greek   virtues of wisdom,   courage,
temperance,   and   justice but by the existential
preoccupation with death, care, anxiety, and guilt.
The objective world of facts and figures (our popular
standard of measures) is merely the facade we hide
behind as we, often with quiet desperation, try to
work out our salvation.

Both   Bergman and Heidegger believe that we appear
to be of a world from which God is absent. Our search
thus   becomes a religious quest without focus or
center; it is the ethos of T. S. Eliot's "The Hollow
Men:"   "Shape   without   form,   shade   without
color/Paralysed force, gesture without motion."[9] It
is not a position of atheism or theism; in Bergman's
terms: God is silent, and I am unable to make a
judgment about Him one way or another.

Under   these   circumstances,   our   search for
religious   truth   abandons the Classical, rational
arguments or proofs for God's existence and, instead,

with "care," i.e. concern, concentrates on exploring the "fallen" or inauthentic world of human existence itself. "Care" means for Heidegger (and, I believe, for Bergman as well): we accept the "facticity" of our "being-there" in the world; we are aware of our potentiality for the future; and we acknowledge as fundamental to our identity the moods, understanding, and language which communicate our presence.

Moods, for Heidegger, are not something we "have" but are--we are our moods. This is most noticeably true in our anxiety over death, which Heidegger identifies as a "mood." It is our present awareness of the finality of death that governs how we value our life and times; it is death that puts the question of meaning into radical focus. In Bergman, from The Seventh Seal to From the Life of the Marionettes, death plays such a role.

The above term "understanding" for Heidegger does not mean mere comprehension but is an activity involving my openness to the world, a receptivity of the revelation, the ex-pression, of all being whether human or other. Such revelation is the source of truth and is inseparable from being; we must let truth be. Truth, like death, has become a central theme for Bergman as well. It is, as for Heidegger, not something to be dis-covered by reason alone, but something in which I participate by living my life, sensitive to the world.

Again, we must explore the role of man's speech in his comprehension of authentic living. To be human is to speak, and the world presents itself for, in, and through such speaking. "Language," says Heidegger, "is the house of being." Man lives within the structure of language only because language has been structured by man out of a compelling primordial silence. Words are more than just arbitrary sounds; they are ontologically linked to that which calls them forth. When we ignore or belittle this truth, language deteriorates into chitchat and gossip and the quality of our lives deteriorates in like measure. Language--the word--plays a major role in the structure of reality for Bergman, as well. With consummate skill he uses the vocabulary of vision and voice, of sound and silence, to structure his reality, to let the truth be. It is this linguistic understanding of reality which makes it possible for Bergman to establish a significant connection with Judaism and Christianity, both respectively responsive to the word of God, both employing symbol systems expressing the existential search for God.

Bergman (and, again, I suggest Heidegger) sees life not in terms of the classical eternal verities but in terms of a dynamic, timeful presence which may or may not be authentic, which may or may not be responding to the presence of God. These possibilities become the contouring dilemmas of our journey.

Finally, one of the things which makes the study of Bergman so fascinating and instructive is that his religious quest is a spiritual recapitualtion of the history of modern theology. To be specific, Bergman's journey is a microcosm of the development of Christian thought from the Reformation to the present. He begins in The Seventh Seal posing the question of God in its classical Scholastic form. Then, film after film, his quest takes him through the critical theological debates which bring us into the twentieth century. I do not believe that this journey is in any way contrived. Indeed, it would lose much of its value as existential history were that the case. His search is that of a man living in the dynamic present, struggling for meaning, whose formal and cultural religious training had left him stranded in the now quaint debates of the Enlightenment.

A final word about the films themselves needs to be noted. Although the text explores ten of Bergman's films from 1956 to the present, a number of films with religious motifs made during this period have been excluded. This is in no way to imply that these are inferior films (though some listed below are), but that, in my judgment, these films do not advance the theological argument about which I have been writing. Also, in the case of The Virgin Spring, we have a script which is not a Bergman original. The excluded films are as follows: Wild Strawberries (1957), Brink of Life (1958), The Virgin Spring (1960), The Devil's Eye (1960), All These Women (1964), Hour of the Wolf (1968), The Ritual (1969), The Touch (1971), The Serpent's Egg (1977), and From the Life of the Marionette (1980).

Bergman, Man and Artist

"No other art-medium--neither painting nor poetry--can communicate the specific quality of the dream as well as the film can. When the lights go down in the cinema and this white shining point opens up for us, our gaze stops flitting hither and thither, settles and becomes quite steady. We just sit there, letting the images flow out over us. Our will ceases to function. We lose our ability to sort things out and fix them in their proper places. We're drawn into a course of events--we're participants in a dream. And manufacturing dreams, that's a juicy business."

Bergman

THE MAN

If times and events help make the man, July 14, 1918, was a most propitious birthdate for one with the natural abilities, creativity, and responsiveness of Ernst Ingmar Bergman. With the end of the First World War, the end of one era and the beginning of another was ritualized. The world would never be the same again in its sense of optimism, social complacency, and "inevitable" progress. Though Western culture certainly did not admit this at the time, the dramatic theological and philosophical changes, manifested in economic, social, and political upheavals, were evident to numbers of artists who warned us that the very foundations of what we called "reality" were crumbling, and that we had best be aware of what was happening if we didn't want to destroy ourselves. To the prophets of the nineteenth century--Nietzsche, Soren Kierkegaard, Dostoevsky, Marx, Freud--can now be added the descriptive artists of the twentieth, e.g., Pound, Eliot, Stravinski, Picasso, and Chaplin. Into this distinguished line of artists, one can place the name of Ingmar Bergman. To follow his development in theater and cinema, his confrontation with the life and times of twentieth-century Sweden, is to be present to a remarkable culture-chronology of the period. His journey takes us from a confrontation with the moribund classical perceptions of Greek Metaphysics (which had governed our religious and philosophical formulations for two thousand years) to our present urgent attempts to perceive or create the sources of meaning, of authenticity, or to devise ways of worship which will maintain our integrity in an age of questing, uncertainty, and doubt.

As indicated in the "Introduction," Bergman is not a theologian or philosopher, but his personal background itself did, undoubtedly, provide some of the incentive and direction. Bergman's father was a Lutheran pastor in Sweden who became the Court Chaplain to the King. Consequently two of the passions which have dominated his productive life have been nurtured in him from the beginning, religion and ritual-drama. Bergman's biographers have noted that he often accompanied his father on trips to the rural churches of Uppland where he was not only exposed to the doctrines of Swedish Lutheranism and Scripture, but also to the imaginative mural paintings, wood carvings, and religious symbols which characterize the interiors of these churches. No one who has seen The Seventh Seal or Winter Light can doubt the fertile power of this formative period and the contribution it has made to his creative life.

Bergman's childhood, despite the many attempts by Freudians and Jungians to stress parental and sibling conflicts and scars, seems to be that of the normal bourgeois child of the twenties and thirties. From some of the things he has himself said about trips with his father, we can surmise that his family was not without love and affection even though the usual adolescent rebellions were met with some unusual parental restraint. No doubt Bergman did experience the added pressure of growing up as a pastor's son, i.e. under the ever-watchful and judgmental eye of the Church; that in itself is enough to explain some of the intensity of Bergman's religious doubt. "A child who is born and brought up in a vicarage acquires an early familiarity with life and death behind the scenes."[10] Yet, in general, Bergman's youth followed the pattern of cultural normalcy; the

difference which has proved to be so fertile and
stimulating in his creative work seems to have come
from his own sensitivity and keen perceptiveness
rather than any extreme domestic aberrations. "My
father and mother were certainly of vital importance,
not only in themselves but because they created a
world for me to revolt against. In my family there
was an atmosphere of hearty wholesomeness which I, a
sensitive young plant, scorned and rebelled
against."[11]   The scorn is normal to the adolescent
search for individuality and independence; the
rebellion against the "hearty wholesomeness" gives
more early evidence of the existential revolt,
reminiscent of Dostoevsky's claim in Notes From
Underground that he "came home on a dark and rainy St.
Petersburg night with the exquisite feeling that he
had committed some loathesome act again." Bourgeois
conformity for both men implied inauthenticity.

The above claims for normalcy, however, are not
meant to minimize Bergman's reactions to life as he
perceived it as a child. Normalcy is not an automatic
immunization to trauma. In fact, for one as sensitive
as young Bergman, it may have been a conditioning
context for it. "I had very few contacts with reality
or channels to it. I was afraid of my father, my
mother, my elder brother--everything. Playing with
this puppet theater and a projection device I had was
my only form of self-expression."[12]   Such
imaginative and creative play, whatever its motive,
was certainly conducive to the development of those
talents to which we are now responding. It was also
an immediate way of coping with those experiences
which, to a child, pose a great emotional threat. In
the vicarage, "the devil was an early acquaintance,

and in the child's mind there was a need to personify
him. This is where my magic lantern came in. It
consisted of a small metal box with a carbide lamp--I
can still remember the smell of the hot metal--and
colored glass slides: Red Riding Hood and the Wolf,
and all the others. And the Wolf was the Devil,
without horns but with a tail and a gaping red mouth,
strangely real yet incomprehensible, a picture of
wickedness and temptation on the flowered wall of the
nursery."[13]

Not all of Bergman's traumatic, formative
experiences were so imaginative or subjective, of
course. One such experience Bergman relates is that
of being locked up in a dark closet prior to being
beaten by his father. The instance finds expression
in at least two of his films--Hour of the Wolf and
Face to Face--and is apparently significant in his
feelings about parent-figures in general. "This
happened forty or forty-two years ago, and not just
once. It was a ritual. It's amazing I came out of it
with my life."[14] Robin Wood, who gives us this
information, also provides a necessary cautionary
note: "I am not concerned with the factual basis of
this and have no wish to blacken the character of
Bergman's Lutheran Pastor father. What is relevant
here is that the whole nature of Bergman's early work
is dictated by his feelings about
parent-figures..."[15] One should also note that the
father figure, in particular, has also colored his
comprehension of God. More about this will, to be
sure, be given in our analyses of his individual
films.

As fascinating as these particular instances of Bergman's early life may be, particularly to one wishing to do a psychological study of Bergman's films,[16] for the purposes of this study, it will be more helpful to go to Bergman's capsule self-analysis of his childhood experience. He cites reaction to parental authorities as only one instance of a more encompassing universal experience which affects his life, his art, and his faith--humiliation. "Obviously there's a more modern view of art and artists and of the terms on which the artist exists; but the humiliation motif is of the very essence. One of the strongest feelings I remember from my childhood is, precisely, of being humiliated; of being knocked about by words, acts, or situations.

"Isn't it a fact that children are always feeling deeply humiliated in their relations with grown-ups and each other? I have a feeling children spend a good deal of their time humiliating one another. Our whole education is just one long humiliation, and it was even more so when I was a child. One of the wounds I've found it hardest to bear in my adult life has been the fear of humiliation, and the sense of being humiliated...To humiliate and be humiliated, I think, is a crucial element in our whole social structure...Our bureaucracy, for instance. I regard it as in high degree built upon humiliation, one of the nastiest and most dangerous of all poisons. When someone has been humiliated he's sure to try and figure out how the devil he can get his own back...If I've objected strongly to Christianity, it has been because Christianity is deeply branded by a very virulent humiliation motif. One of its main tenets is 'I, a miserable sinner, born in sin, who have sinned all my days, etc.' Our way of living and behaving under this punishment is completely atavistic."17

One of the reasons why humiliation plays such a prominent role in Bergman's theater of personal threats is that it is a part of his existential consciousness, of his awareness of those things which try to prevent him from being himself, from living spontaneously and freely. Nevertheless, such tensions provide the stimulus for his creative activity. To Jonas Sima's question, "How can you keep your aggressions so alive?", Bergman responds: "If I didn't I'd commit suicide. There's always a tension in me between my urge to destroy and my will to live. It's one of my most elementary tensions both in the way I create and in my material existence. Every morning I wake up with a new wrath, a new suspiciousness, a new desire to live."18 The accuracy of Bergman's self-assessment here is reassuring, particularly when we must depend upon his word for our own analysis of his cinematic attempts. Since stating these sentiments, Bergman has been thoroughly "humiliated" by the Swedish government in a scandal over tax matters. Despite the fact that Bergman was exonerated and received special consideration from the Swedish Prime Minister himself, Bergman chose to leave Sweden, "never to return." He has, as expected, returned but only after a lengthy sojourn in Germany. In light of the above discussion of humiliation and "getting his own back," the whole experience rings very true.

This same existential consciousness has freed Bergman, as an adult, from many of the snares and traps of Western, bourgeois, materialistic existence. This is not so much an accomplishment of intellectual assimilation as a conclusion to which he experientially came. Being "freed" for Bergman does not mean that one has given up all material comforts and goods; what it does mean is that one is no longer possessed by such possessions. It frees him _from_ things but _for_ art; it frees him _from_ possessions but _for_ people. These are the two areas of genuine importance for him: "When one has had all the success, all the money, everything one has ever wanted, ever striven for--power--the lot--then one discovers (excuse the expression) its nothingness. The only things that matter are the human limitations one must try to overcome and one's relationships with other people; in the second place--also enormously important, of course--one's ethical attitude toward what one is doing, or not doing. What you say 'yes' to, and what you say 'no' to in your work; and to temptations outside your work. Nothing else matters."19 This insight characterizes the area of our primary concern, the cinematic work of the mature Bergman, so let us look at some of the professional influences which shaped that maturity.

THE ARTIST

"The mind of the West has always been hierarchical: the cosmos has been understood as a great chain of Being, from highest to lowest, which has at the same time operated as a scale of values, from lowest to highest."20 It is the world before Pippa passes through--"God's in His heaven/All's right with the world." But the structure of this reality was also linear as well as vertical. Time and

sequence were orderly, dependable, and reliable
structures. One did not violate the order of past,
present, future without chaos and
incomprehensibility. In reading or creative writing,
one could count on the fact that there would be a
beginning, middle and end; that there would be a
climax, to be followed by a denouement; that the hero
or heroine would always represent the higher as
opposed to the lower values; that the higher values
would by logical necessity overcome the lower ones;
that evil (if it could even be said to exist) was the
result of some temporary and abortive reversal within
this value scale. Shakespeare knew his audience would
properly respond when he has Shylock cry out, "My
daughter, my ducats, my ducats, my daughter." The
classical scale of values would never tolerate such a
reversible equation.

But in the nineteenth century all this began to
change. A philosophical critique questioned whether
one could ever know any super-sensible metaphysical
realities, whether they be Forms of the Good or God.
Even the perception of things in themselves as
discrete entities was doubtful; the line between the
contribution of the knower and the contribution of the
known became hard to draw. Philosophical and
theological thinking began to turn in upon themselves;
psychology, as a recognizable discipline, was about to
be born. In the arts, similar transitions were taking
place. Painting, which since the fourteenth century
had been concerned with dimensional, physical space,
with perspective and balance, now began to flatten
out. It turned away from the sensible world of
material objects to the internal world of the
perceiving subject, the inner world of the human

spirit.   Writing, which had always used the polar
structures of time and eternity as the fixed foci for
all human action and drama, now began to free itself
from these objective chronological constraints. The
tyranny of eternality gave way to the subjective
multi-dimensional significance of past, present, and
future for human comprehension. Presence, as Joyce,
Eliot, and Pound remind us, incorporates all three
dimensions of clock-time.

But the transition is neither easy nor orderly.
To be denied the external points of orientation and
fixity is to find oneself in a strange land where
there are no landmarks, no comforting cairns to lead
you to the next point of vantage. But to be turned in
upon oneself with all the elusive illusions created by
the knower and the known, the self and its persons, the
brain and the psyche, the body and the soul, is to
find oneself in an equally bewildering maze. "When
mankind no longer lives spontaneously turned toward
God or the super-sensible world...the artist too must
stand face to face with a flat and inexplicable
world."[21]   It is in such a flattened world and at
such a point that Bergman stands as he tries to
discover, through the art of cinema, what life is all
about.

The most dramatic development of this transition,
however, is the relativization of the classical
structure of values, e.g. beauty, truth, and
goodness.   For the contemporary artist there is no
fixed scale or hierarchy to which to appeal, no
essentiality of being which can permit him to turn to
something or someone other than himself as the source
of authority.   It is that, so frightening and awesome
to most of us, which Ingmar Bergman explores so

painstakingly, so agonizingly, in his films. When
confronting ourselves in Bergman's films, we are made
to realize that man is a creature that transcends his
own image because he has no fixed nature--and that we
are that man. Nothingness has become an active factor
in our life, and Bergman will not let us forget it nor
the fact that we have to deal with it.

The existential critique of the nineteenth and
twentieth centuries is Bergman's heritage and
home-away-from-home, i.e., one can never be "at home"
in the existentialist's world, but one can find a
community of like-minded friends with whom one can at
least share one's angst. Asked if he, as a film
director, felt lonely and isolated from his crew and
actors, Bergman replied: "I've never known that sort
of loneliness. I've felt lonely in the outside world,
and for that very reason I've taken refuge in a
community of feeling, however illusory."[22] But even
though we are dealing with Bergman the cinema
director, it is necessary to note at this point that
he has a reputation in Swedish theater that rivals his
film making. The theater, he said is "like a loyal
wife, film is the big adventure, the expensive and
demanding mistress--you worship both, each in its own
way."[23] It is through his involvement with theater
that his primary encounter with existentialist ideas
took place. This is understandable because cinema is
a very young and new art form, struggling to discover
its own potential and nature; theater is an ancient,
perhaps the most ancient of art forms, long used to
confront us with our enigmatic selves. Birgitta
Steene informs us that Bergman has staged some
seventy-five productions in his theatrical career
between the years 1938 and 1966, in addition to radio

and television plays. Dramatists whose works he
produced include Moliere, Goethe, Ibsen, Strindberg,
Chekhov, Pirandello, Brecht, Camus, Anouilh, Tennessee
Williams, and Edward Albee--the majority of these are
existential dramatists.24

As might be expected from one reared in the North
Country, two of the above are of particular
importance: Henrik Ibsen, whose life spanned most of
the nineteenth century, and August Strindberg, born in
1849, whose dramas and novels dominated the Swedish
scene at the turn of the century. Bergman's
experience of the somber moods of the doubter, the
brooder--one estranged from his family, his country,
and the dehumanization of Western bourgeois
culture--found a spiritual mentor in Ibsen. Like
Soren Kierkegaard, the Danish religious thinker whose
productive life overlapped that of his own, Ibsen
asserted the strength of radical individualism, a
search for the "Gyntian Self" in a world where "whirl
is king." For Ibsen, true individualism, true
identity, occurs when one succeeds in being oneself
and not in just separating oneself from the mass of
humanity. There is also in Ibsen a sense of the
macabre. In his last play, Ibsen portrays human
beings with beast-faces, a foreshadowing--perhaps--of
Bergman's film, The Hour of the Wolf.

Strindberg is of even greater importance in
Bergman's development. "If you live in a Strindberg
tradition," states Bergman, "you are breathing
Strindberg air. After all, I have been seeing
Strindberg at the theater since I was ten years old,
so it is difficult to say what belongs to him and what
to me."25 So it seems. Both Strindberg and Bergman
seem preoccupied with religion and women in their

professional and private lives. With some
modifications, both men are like Jacob--both have
wrestled with God, but seemingly without subsequent
blessing; both have had many wives but without Jacob's
apparent tranquility.

Strindberg's journey in search of God takes him
into some strange theological countries. First as
pietist: "What do we mean by religious beliefs? Not
one's acceptance of certain teachings, but rather his
transformation into something better--to such an
extent that he is no longer the person he was!"26
Such pietism is understood by Strindberg as the
suppression of all theoretical matters and the freedom
to say anything one would not regret. Under the
influence of Theodore Parker, whom he had been
reading, Strindberg stretched this injunction to
include not regretting anything that he did. Then
followed a period in which the ethical insights of
Kierkegaard's _Either/Or_ dominated Strindberg's
decisions, and he found himself charged in a heresy
trial for suggesting that the Eucharist is an infamous
deception. This was followed by periods of pessimism
and doubt that led to his "Inferno" crisis: "Not
Strindberg, but God was to blame for making such a
damned mess of the world."27 This began a
Manichaean phase in which God seems to be in league
with Satan in devising schemes for and against man.
God and Satan are the personifications of good and
evil; the Eternal One, the Godhead if you like,
remains passive, remote, and silent. However, in
1907, just five years before his death, Strindberg
could write of Christianity: "One should take it
unrefined, stock and block, dogmas and
miracles...uncritically, naively, in a deep gulp; then

it goes down like castor oil in hot coffee. Gape and
shut your eyes. That is the only way."[28] Such
consumption can hardly be a final resting place. In
Strindberg's Talks to the Swedish Nation he states:
"Kierkegaard with his confessionless Christianity has
once again become my banner."[29] Though the
vocabulary is somewhat different, Bergman's religious
journey bears a striking parallel to that of
Strindberg's, as will be apparent in our discussion of
Bergman's films. The questioning, the agony, the
doubt, the silence of God, the cautious new
exploration--all are there. Bergman has the distinct
advantage, however, of having the existential
descriptive categories for his use.

Women, we know, have always intrigued and troubled
Bergman. Many of his most compelling and interesting
protagonists are women. But, there does seem to be a
danger for the critic in being too Freudian about the
whole thing. It is true that Bergman's inheritance
from Strindberg borders on misogyny--"His
[Strindberg's] whole vision seems blood-shot with
it."[30] "In every woman he always hoped to see
something of a mother, a Madonna, a reconciler--until
disappointment took over and provided him with terms
denoting roles diametrically opposed to these."[31]
It is also true that many of Bergman's women
characters are powerful, all are vivid, but Bergman's
creations do not seem to emanate from an obsessive
love-hate relation. Bergman's women are not powerful
or destructive because of some feminine trait or
quality, but because they are human beings possessed
by powerful drives or forces. In this sense Bergman's
women are more in the tradition of Ibsen's Hedda
Gabler, a liberated woman before her time.

More immediate to Bergman is the influence of the Swedish writers in the 1940s, as Birgitta Steene informs us: "Bergman's formative years as an artist coincided with the emergence of a new generation of Swedish writers whose mood was one of existential _Angst_ and religious skepticism. The encounter with this 'school of the forties' may have helped crystallize Bergman's own doubts about God although his pessimism was never as complete as that of the literary group. The Kafka fever that raged in Sweden about the same time may also have shaped Bergman's concept of a distant and silent God, of God as a need but not as fulfillment, and of modern man's rootlessness in a world of outmoded values."[32]

What we have seen is that Bergman has come of age as an artist in a period which has just started to self-consciously acknowledge that an era has ended. Belief in God can no longer be taken for granted and "knowledge" of God is absolutely denied; the same may be said for any so-called metaphysical Absolute--belief seems arbitrary, knowledge impossible. Religion is reduced to "doing good;" philosophy is "playing language games." But what happens to values? What happens to truth? What happens to beauty? What happens to love? Indeed, what happens to anything we once thought meaningful? If ever we were in need of prophets and people of vision, now is that time. With the structures of Western culture being shored up by frantic calls for loyalty, positive thinking, perseverance, and even vanity, we are slowly beginning to acknowledge that the old mythologies no longer, of themselves, have the power to hold us together, to demand our loyalty, to interpret our life's experience. If we are to be

saved from ourselves, from the defensive postures we
are forced to take in order to face the new heathen
hordes, then we must have a new mythology or at least
a new understanding of the old.

But mythologies are strange, because they are the
symbol structure of reality for us; they are the
ground out of which all else meaningful comes,
including the ground of our rationality. This is
perhaps another way of saying that one just does not
sit down and think out a new mythology, nor does one
arbitrarily create one. Mythology is something that
happens to us, that dawns upon us, and understanding
that we intuit; it is that to which we respond with
our total selves rather than critically, skeptically,
half-heartedly, or indifferently.

So when we look to Bergman as one of the artistic
geniuses who is helping us to search for a new
mythology, we must not look to him as one who is going
to create it for us. What he can best do, and what he
has done, is to share his own journey of discovery and
exploration. He has let us as fellow journeymen,
fellow explorers, see his frustrations, his despair,
his dreams, his hopes. He does not pontificate any
more than he expects us to judge. He expects us to
travel and dares us to expose ourselves to the risk of
discovery. It is the excitement of this risk that
drives him, no matter how wittily he puts it: "Making
films has...become a natural necessity, a need similar
to hunger and thirst. For certain people to express
themselves implies writing books, climbing mountains,
beating children, or dancing the samba. I express
myself by making films."[33]   Films for Bergman are
"self-combustion," "self-effusion."

It is not difficult to see that the questions
which obsess both contemporary art and contemporary
theology are intimately related: they both see us
alienated and estranged in our world; they both
reflect the ambiguity, fragility, and contingency of
our existence; they both witness to the central and
overwhelming reality of a life lived without anchorage
in the eternal. It is this identity between religion
and art that provides art with its prophetic purpose
and power.   "Modern art...begins, and sometimes ends,
as a confession of spiritual poverty. That is its
greatness and its triumph, but also the needle it jabs
into the Philistine's sore spot, for the last thing he
wants to be reminded of is his spiritual poverty."[34]

Religion and art so coincide because the quest is
a common quest for reality, for meaning, for an
authentic self-expression of man--in short, for an
effective religious mythology.   That Bergman
understands this is evident from his response to the
accusation that his films often have a disturbing
effect on his audience.   Asked if he does not have
some moral qualms about such disturbance, Bergman
replies: "No!   If I weren't to be quite honest with
you, I could say I've been in a state of moral
conflict.   But if I'm to be quite frank, no, I don't
feel the least bit shaken by bringing out someone's
latent schizophrenia just because someone in one of my
films crawls under her bed--on the contrary. If one
can get ordinary people to shut their mouths for a
minute after the curtain has fallen, or get ordinary
folk to make themselves a sandwich and sit together
and have a chat in the kitchen for five minutes after
seeing a film, or if someone is suddenly happy as he
recalls certain scenes as he walks home afterwards, or

someone suddenly cries, or feels shaken, or laughs, or feels better or worse--if people are influenced the least little bit, the film has done its job."[35]

Of course, to be a self-conscious prophet, one who dares to disturb the universe, places a heavy burden on one's shoulders (not to mention mind and heart)--not to produce the ANSWERS so much as in maintaining one's integrity in asking the right questions. One is exposed to all sorts of pressures to desist probing the human psyche, everything from being called a heretic by the establishment or a bore by the bourgeoisie to the self-imposed restrictions occasioned by one's feeling of responsibility for others. Bergman's words, here, are brave, but to my knowledge he has had no occasion to genuinely regret them, nor has he seemingly betrayed them: "No matter how insecure my material existence may become, never again [a reference here to making the film This Can't Happen Here, 1950] will I let anyone buy me--no one--no matter for what money. Making films is my justification for existing. If I start playing fast and loose with ethics, I'll lose my inherent value as a human being, everything that gives me the feeling I've a right to make films...Starve--I've done that. When one is young it's not so bad. Usually one is pretty sure there's a loaf somewhere just around the corner. But not to be able to support the people you're responsible for, that's hell. Personally, I've almost no needs. Gradually one gets to be that way."[36]

Though we have labelled him a "self-conscious prophet" above, this is not to imply that he can easily be identified with any given form of Lutheran Protestantism or even Christianity-in-general. Like

Martin Heidegger, his religious integrity, his
prophetic voice, is really to be heard in calling our
attention to our human predicament, to our lack of
understanding, to our lack of security, to our
experience of contingency, whether these things lead
to an encounter with Nothingness or with God. This
is, perhaps, another way of saying that Bergman
recognizes the limitations of being a cinematic
prophet; he recognizes that his obligation is to be
himself. Pressed by his friends about the role of the
artist in the political, religious, and artistic life
of the times, Bergman responds: "I think he [the
artist] must reflect a hell of a long time about what
way he can be of use, and possibly whether he can't be
useful simply by taking a positive attitude to himself
and just being an artist."[37] An extreme but telling
instance of this artistic integrity comes in Bergman's
response to an interpretation of the artist's role as
portrayed in his film The Hour of the Wolf. Asked if
the artist was not one who was "sent by God...Who
suffers from a Platonic belief in inspiration,"
Bergman replies: "That's not how I mean it, even if
in this case it may seem so...What Johan Borg wanted
to say was that he is faced with a 'must', an unending
torment, toothache. He can't escape it. There's no
question, that is, of a gift from on high. No other
worldly relationship. It's just there. A disease. A
perversion. A five-legged calf. He takes a very
brutal view of his situation...My view of my work as
an artist is that I make articles for consumption.
If, in addition, a film turns into something more,
that's nice. But I don't work 'sub specie
aeternitatis'--with one eye on immortality."[38]

This raises an interesting point which needs some clarification. The rather diffident way in which Bergman equates films with "articles for consumption" should not be understood as a denial of what has already been argued about the seriousness of art and the artist. "Consumption" refers, in its broadest sense, to human use, only one aspect of which is commercialism. We will only misunderstand Bergman if we do not recognize that for him art is a revelational experience. It is a revelation of both ourselves and of the times in which we live--both at once, as one. As such, it carries with it the power of inevitability. Such a judgment does not imply some form of metaphysical determinism. Rather, it is the force of the judgment: "the truth will out," or more accurately, the force of the Heideggerian injunction: "Let the truth be." Here truth is understood to be the active, dynamic expression of Being itself in all its forms and modes. Another way of stating that, of course, is simply to say that truth, i.e. Being, is revelational. In the following exchange with Jonas Sima, Bergman makes this point for film:

> JS: In my view there ought to be a
>   moral and psychological
>   congruence between form and
>   content.
>
> IB: I suppose it's largely built-in.
>
> JS: It's Godard, isn't it, who has
>   said this about form and ethic?
>
> IB: I thought it was
>   Antonioni--about it being an
>   ethical decision...But it's
>   true. One discovers very
>   quickly that a scene can only be
>   shot in one way.

This "congruence" between form and content, understood as having ethical force, really means that film art has, for Bergmam, this revelational power to express being, and that when film is conceived of as simply a product of electronic technique, it betrays its own integrity. "It is my opinion," states Bergman, "that art lost its basic creative drive the moment it was separated from worship. It severed an umbilical cord and now lives its own sterile life, generating and degenerating itself. In former days the artist remained unknown and his work was to the glory of God."[39] Such a quote may make Bergman sound like a shouting evangelist, but I think his point here is only that film has a "religious" responsibility to revelational truth, that form and content must be left to structure each other. Any arbitrary pre-structuring can only distort the truth. "I never try to tell my ideas what to do--I just let them emerge as they come."[40]

Such an attitude has radically altered his whole approach to producing a film: "Nowadays I don't write dialogue at all, only a suggestion of what it could be. The script is nothing but a collection of motifs which I work over with my actors as the filming proceeds. The final decisions I make in the cutting room, where I cut away all obtrusive elements. What I write nowadays looks much more chaotic than the scripts I used to write. In the old days I stuck to a hard-and-fast line, and when it went badly the results were what they are in Through a Glass Darkly: it became 'gewollt.' But Winter Light is not 'gewollt.' Everything grows of its own accord. The drama has built itself."[41]

Even the word "motifs" used above must be carefully understood, for Bergman does not want to imply by that word any preconceived idea or conviction around which he then structures events and dialogues, both tailored to those motifs. Such an artistic practice would violate the integrity of "letting the truth be," of letting form and content interact in such a way as to mutually structure each other. When Torsten Manns tries to pin Bergman down about four types of "child-motifs" in his pictures, Bergman explodes: "My first reaction to all you're saying is a dreadful feeling of oppression. Not specially aimed at myself, but a feeling of powerlessness. I can't explain it. A feeling that it's all so dull, that it will get duller, and what I've made, suddenly, is all dull and uninteresting too. I can't explain it. I don't know why it is, but as I sit here listening to you I feel furious—don't misunderstand this Torsten. I've nothing against you personally. That's just how it is. When someone pulls out a thread like this and says: 'Yes, well, surely it's this way? Aren't things like this? It's like this and it's like that,' I feel completely paralysed. I can't utter a word. Well it's possible, things may be that way, I don't know. I'm not being cagey. It's simply that with me things don't work that way...I can't discuss any leitmotif running through my films...This search for motifs, this form of analysis is something we've inherited from the study of literature, where it's reached the lunatic stage. They fit any work into its historical context, until in the end every piece of the puzzle fits so perfectly there's nothing to be added for the chap who's actually created the work. Here we have an unbridgeable gulf—at least between me

and the people who write commentaries on my films. I
can't correspond with such people...I think I can
explain it chiefly like this. For me, a film can
never be something theoretical. What I've been trying
to tell you all the time is that behind each
production there has lain a practical, tangible
reality. It has never been 'invented' or 'made-up'.
Sooner or later, whenever I've...'intended something
consciously' I've had to reject it as bad."[42]

Intentionality in this last statement of Bergman's
refers to that which is specific, a detail of action
or plot or dialogue within the conceived whole. In
general, Bergman, of course, does have an intention
which is to "try to tell the truth about the human
condition, the truth as I see it."[43] Though Bergman
has reservations about the success of such
intentionality, he does not seem to shy away from
claiming its validity. Perhaps the reason is
obvious. "Truth as I see it" is a kaleidoscopic
category, not a static one, an ontological assertion,
not a metaphysical absolute. Bergman makes this point
specifically in his interview with Charles Samuels.
Bergman has just rejected Samuels use of the word
Truth as a discrete metaphysical category by
responding, "Some sort of truth." Samuels: "All
right: a truth." Bergman: "No! No! No! No! Excuse
me. I dig for secret expressions and relations that
we hide...Please don't talk about truth, it doesn't
exist! Behind each face there is another and another
and another...."[44]

This whole consideration of preconception,
intentionality, and truth raises the question of
creative origins. If Bergman has reservations about
this classical trinity, what are his sources? As one

might expect, his understanding of the creative act is
a dynamic one: creativity is an expression of Being,
of be-ing.   However, this is not to imply that
creativity is totally subjective.   Being, in this
case, is the total context of my life, both internal
and external: it is my life in community, and, at the
same time, that life acknowledged deep within myself.
It is a reflection of the paradox to which Martin
Buber gives the symbol I-Thou, each person being
defined in terms of the other--a relationship which
itself is creative as well as being the context for
creative self-expression.   Bergman tells us this in
two different interviews, one with Samuels and the
other with Simon.   To Samuels: "My impulse has
nothing to do with intellect or symbolism; it has only
to do with dreams and longing, with hope and desire,
with passion...So when you say that a film of mine is
intellectually complicated, I have the feeling that
you don't talk about one of my pictures."[45]   To
Simon: "My pictures always come out of tensions,
specific situations, changing conditions. It's always
like that.   And why one picture appeals and another
doesn't, I don't know...My creative life is movement.
It's like water.   I don't want to be logical or find
motives."[46]

The word Bergman finally chooses to describe his
creative activity is "intuition." "So my intuition is
my best weapon and my best tool."[47]   Bergman
provides us with the description of this "weapon" at
work: "A film for me begins with something very
vague--a chance remark or a bit of conversation, a
hazy but agreeable event unrelated to any particular
situation.   It can be a few bars of music, a shaft of
light across the street...These are split-second

impressions that disappear as quickly as they come,
yet leave behind a mood like pleasant dreams. It is a
mental state, not an actual story, but one abounding
in fertile associations and images. Most of all, it
is a brightly colored thread sticking out of the dark
sack of unconscious...This primitive nucleus strives
to achieve a definite form, moving in a way that may
be lazy and half asleep at first. Its stirring is
accompanied by vibrations and rhythms, which are very
special and unique to each film. The picture
sequences then assume a pattern in accordance with
these rhythms, obeying laws born out of and
conditioned by my original stimulus."[48]

It is in the development of this latter phase that
Bergman's hard intellectual work takes place. Anyone
studying his films is always impressed with the
consistency of the details, the employment of symbols,
the orchestration of themes and motifs. These are not
contrary to Bergman's intuitive approach, they are the
augmentation of it. "One of my strongest
cards--perhaps my strongest card of all--is that I
never argue with my own intuition. I let it make the
decisions. Sometimes I can say to myself: this is
going to the devil, it's all completely up the spout.
Yet I stick ruthlessly to my intuition. Over the
years I've learned that so long as I'm not emotionally
involved--which always clouds one's ability to decide
matters intuitively--I can follow it with a fair
degree of confidence. But then, after one has decided
something intuitively, it's necessary to follow it up
intellectually. Intuition reaches far out into the
dark. Afterwards, one must try to go on foot to the
spot where intuition's javelin has landed, using one's
common sense."[49]

There are three ways in which one can come to some understanding of this process of creation and implementation. Birgitta Steene sees Bergman's creativity as representative of Siegfried Kracauer's theories, a kind of Jungian response to the collective unconscious: "Siegfried Kracauer's theory of film-making, although dubious as a general thesis, certainly applies to Bergman: 'What films reflect are not so much explicit credos as psychological dispositions--those deep layers of collective mentality which extend more or less below the dimension of consciousness.'"[50] Bergman himself is more inclined to give the process an existential interpretation, which is not so surprising considering the influence the existentialists have had on his work: Film-making is a "game." "What is so peculiarly stimulating about a game is that it must be taken seriously all the time, even though at the same time one is conscious that, even at those moments when one makes one's most searing announcements, it's all just a game. Everything happens by mere chance. That's how it is when one is writing a script. Maybe you're borne up on a wave. Then in comes someone and says the phone's ringing. When you come back, the wave has subsided, and something else has been born instead. It's all just chance. Or a game. I disagree deeply with commentators and critics--though I can only speak for myself, of course. They assume all sorts of conscious lines of thought, intellectual penetrations, carefully laid courses. But for me everything just happens unreflectively, formlessly.

"Afterwards, in manufacturing the artistic product, one does one's utmost--often quite helplessly--to find out what it was one really meant.

The purposeless game which is so serious, but which at the same time is so chancy and indifferent and pointless, is something one becomes more and more conscious of, I think, as the years go by. It would be crazy not to bear this constantly in mind, I think: that it's all just a game; that one is in the privileged position of being allowed to ritualize a lot of tensions and complications within and around oneself."[51] Bergman is no more successful here than other existentialists in resolving the paradox of ultimate gamesmanship: the seriousness with which one is committed to the fact that everything is a game is, in itself, not a game--"The purposeless game which is so serious..."

It would appear to me that Martin Heidegger, more the ontologist than existentialist, offers us the third and more adequate explanation of what is going on here. Creativity is not a matter of chance or random external circumstance: that is too external to the experience or action, too materialistic for the subjectivity involved. Nor is creativity simply a matter of uncovering archetypal forms; that is too structured and does not account for the diversity and individuality that characterize all great art. Creativity is the authentic act of being-in-the-world, of responding-to-the-world, of any self, of conveying one's mood as expressive of a way of being, of "being there." "Moods" for Heidegger, as noted in the "Introduction," are "Affective States" which are expressive of our very selves. They are not merely vague feelings that color our dispositions. We are our moods and creativity involves their authentic expression.

The shifting and moving experience Bergman has described above, instead of pointing to the exegencies of chance, really point to the shifting response to the world about him, revealing in the process who he is and how he understands the nature of that who-ness. The power of such an understanding of selfhood is in its recognition of total-person--an emotional, intellectual, spiritual being-in-the-world. So the creative act we call great art is really the gifted expression of what it means to be in the world in any of our many moods or its many modes; the reason that those of us who are not so gifted can and do respond to such creative acts is that we, too, as creative beings (however marginal) are able to recognize and feel the authenticity of genuine expression.

The critical mood for Heidegger is anxiety, the apprehension of Nothingness which confronts us everywhere, but most inexorably, in death. It is death which drives us to define life, to search out its meaning. Only in the confrontation of death in all its many guises--e.g., emptiness, sorrow, despair, meaninglessness, tragedy, finitude, limitation, time--do we free ourselves for life. It is the contention of this study that it is just this quest, just this confrontation with death that motivates Bergman, whether he is posing the question in metaphysical terms in The Seventh Seal, in psychological terms in Through a Glass Darkly, or in temporal terms in Cries and Whispers. Death poses the question, and it will not let Bergman alone until he comes to some ontologically satisfying resolution. It is a "game, a deadly game, and for this reason it is most appropriate that Bergman has the Knight Borg

playing chess with Death in <u>The</u> <u>Seventh</u> <u>Seal</u>; that
sets the stage; that poses the problem and names the
odds in the struggle.

It is not a matter of chance. It is a matter of
life: of meaning, purpose, care, resolve, and hope.
For Heidegger and for Bergman, these are the new
virtues (ontological virtues), the new rules of the
game, rather than wisdom, temperance, courage, and
justice, the metaphysical virtues and guides. It is
because Bergman seems, intuitively, to "know" this and
because his creative gifts are used in its expression,
that his films reach deep within us, and we find them
disturbing, unnerving, even terrifying. They linger
with us, prod us, catch us unawares; we cannot dismiss
them as simply superb but fanciful craftsmanship. He
holds the mirror so clearly up to our own inner lives
that we recognize ourselves despite the distortions we
see. I believe that it is for this reason that we
often say: "I don't understand his films. What's he
driving at? If he has something to say, I wish he'd
just say it. Maybe he's had too many wives...." But
despite our caustic bravado, we find that we can't get
his films out of our minds. The scenes are vividly
there--those scenes we don't understand and wish to
forget. Bergman has powerfully and successfully
trespassed the defense perimeters of our psyche, and
we resent the fact that he won't leave us alone.

If this thesis is correct, it may also account for
Bergman's attitude toward critics and criticism. "I
believe the reviewers and critics have every right to
interpret my films as they like. I refuse to
interpret my work to others, and I cannot tell the
critic what to think...A film is made to create
reaction."[52] Bergman, here, is very consistent. It

would be impossible, literally, for him to interpret his films in any particular or exhaustive way, because each viewer brings to the film experience his own being, his own self, with that incredibly subtle network of experience, thought, and emotion, which cannot be duplicated or anticipated. This is not only true for Bergman's film audience, it is true for Bergman himself. In speaking of a specific scene from The Hour of the Wolf, Bergman can state: "For me that scene has changed meaning many times..."[53]   This does not mean that Bergman is indecisive, or vague, or inept; what it does mean is that Bergman is symbolizing reality in his film, which cannot be finally rationalized, logicized. It confronts us and him in an ontological way, in being which is natural, continuously moving and flowing.[54]

It is with this understanding that he takes issue with Charles Samuels:

> B.   You must realize...I never ask people to understand what I have made....
>
> S.   ...Films, plays, poems, novels all make propositions or observations, embody ideas or beliefs, and we go to these forms...
>
> B.   But you must understand that you are perverted. You belong to a small minority that tries to understand...
> I make my pictures for use! They are not made sub specie aeternitatis; they are made for now and for use.[55]

Because   Bergman's   approach   is   an
existential-ontological   one,   the   "now"   in   the   above
quotation is important to him. If there be what we
call reality, it is _now_, a time reference which
incorporates   past,   present,   and   future   in   its
orientation   to   the   experience   of   _presence_,   the
relation of _being_ and time. It is this understanding
which makes sense of Bergman's response to Simon about
his   (Bergman's)   august   reputation   in   the   film
industry; "When I start writing a new picture, or
start shooting or cutting it, or when I release it to
the audience, it's always the first time, and always
the last time.   It's an isolated event, and I never
think back or forward."[56]

This   same   existential   approach   also   makes   it
difficult for him to explain clearly the craftsmanship
of his work.   If something is going to be an
existential expression of art, must one not eliminate
the critical function of reason and logic in preparing
the work for an audience?   Must there not be a
spontaneity that criticism would destroy? One might
be led to that conclusion if one had read only
Bergman's response to Frederick Fleisher: "Bergman
once dismissed a 'charge' that he was a writer with
the argument that he worked 'entirely spontaneously.
I vomited forth what I brooded over without bothering
about the aesthetic qualities.   The words stood
absolutely naked.   A dramatist cannot hide himself in
word-magic like a novelist or a poet.'"[57] But this
hyperbole is corrected by two later statements by
Bergman, each expressing his sense of responsibility
yet at the same time maintaining the claim to
spontaneity.   To John Simon he says: "I feel
responsible only for the craftsmanship being good, for

the thing having the moral qualities of my mind and if
possible, for my not telling any lies."[58] To Jonas
Sima he says: "All the time you're producing, you're
continually criticizing what you're doing. Where I've
been successful, maybe, is in never allowing this
criticism to have a devastating effect on my
productivity. They're like two wild beasts. I keep
them away from each other."[59] Perhaps, for such a
religiously sensitive, existentialist director as
Bergman, it is inevitable that we end this point on
criticism with a Lutheran paradox: "sin bravely."

This section on Bergman's craft cannot be
concluded, however, without some mention of Bergman's
relationship to his actors and technicians. Like his
fellow artist Federico Fellini, Bergman has gathered
about him gifted actors like Max von Sydow, Gunnar
Bjornstrand, Bibi Anderson, Ingrid Thulin, Gunnel
Lindblom, Liv Ullmann; a cameraman like Sven Nykvist;
a Production Manager like Lars-Owe Carlberg. Because
these artists are with Bergman in most of his
productions, they are part of the creative effort,
participate in it. Liv Ullmann, in preparing for the
part of Jenny in Face to Face, acknowledges just such
cooperation with Bergman: "The day Ingmar gives me
the manuscript he also gives me the right to feel that
hence-forward I understand the part best. She becomes
my reality as much as she is Ingmar's. With his help,
genius, his sensibility in listening and looking, I
know that my knowledge of her will be captured by the
camera."[60] Liv Ullmann's assurance is born of the
intimacy Bergman achieves by making the human face the
existential focal-point for film--"I concentrate on
the face. The backgrounds are an accompaniment."[61]
It would be next to impossible for him to do that

without the skill and understanding of Sven Nykvist. In talking of his technique, Nykvist says: "In the past, I've put grease on the lens, used all sorts of filters, played tricks in the lab; but after 30 years of work I've come back to simplicity in lighting and framing. Bergman has taught me this: always work to bring out the emotional truth in a scene and take out everything that is there just for effect or beauty."[62]

As one would have to expect, Bergman's existential-ontological approach to life affects his relationships with all his colleagues, but particularly those with his actors: "I realize how exposed actors are. They are the ones, always, who go on to the stage, or before the camera. Who have to strip themselves naked down to their very skeleton. We're protected. We can always make a grimace or resort to some verbal evasion. They can't. They can neither run away, nor explain things away. They just have to stand there with their bodies and their faces. That's why the only respectable and decent thing to do seems to me always, unswervingly, unshakably, to stand up for my actors."[63]

The sensitivity displayed here lets us know that Bergman treats his actors, crew and staff first as human beings then as human beings with a specific function. There could be little better indication of this than Sven Nykvist's account of the starting of a new film: "Two months before shooting is to begin, Bergman and the entire crew (including the men who will move the lights and furniture around) go off to a hotel in the north of Sweden. On the first morning Bergman discusses the new picture at length--what he is trying to say in it, and why each of their

contributions is important.   Then the script girl
begins to read the screenplay aloud from the very
first line, with members of the crew frequently
interrupting to ask questions and challenge individual
points and Bergman, in turn, explaining, analyzing,
persuading.   We do this for two or three days."[64]
Only such personal consideration as this can explain
the loyalty and devotion of Bergman's associates.

Consistent with the approach in this study, this
interrelationship is not simply a matter of courtesy
but of genuine creative technique. Birgitta Steene
gives this interpretation of Bergman's cinematic
characters; "Bergman's strength as an artist--apart
from his unquestionable technical skill--lies in his
ability to create characters who, although they are
carriers of his personal ethics, have the abstract
quality of people in a morality play, and to project
these characters on a scene of great visual clarity
and emotional intensity."[65]   This judgment seems to
be confirmed by Bergman when he responds to John
Simon's question: Is Max von Sydow the
"Bergman-figure" in his films?   "No...I am all of
them, I am inside all of them."[66] But while that is
true, it is only half the truth, for in other places
Bergman acknowledges that the actors themselves play a
much larger role than just the carriers of Bergman's
word.   When talking with Stig Bjorkman, Bergman
reveals that "until I've decided which actor is to
play which part I can't really even begin to write.
But when I have, the role dresses itself up in his
skin, his muscles, his special intonation; above all
his rhythms, his way of being."[67]   From Bergman's
description, one can imagine that on certain minor
parts, the interaction is even more dramatic, the

actor imposing his own particular stamp over that of Bergman's: "Strandmark was an actor with a streak of real genius in him. In The Seventh Seal I remember how he grabbed that actor's role--really it's rather banal, a simple-minded, noisy, one-dimensional type--and turned him into a mediaeval jester, a ferocious, burlesque, bullying, dry, ill-tempered fellow, all quite different from anything I'd imagined. He did what he liked with it."[68]

The above discussion, however, has been only the prelude for the central concern of our study--Bergman's spiritual journey. This does not mean that Bergman's relation to his actors, crew, and associates, his methods of directing, his writing of scripts, etc. have been irrelvant for us. Just the opposite, they have all been illustrative of the central thesis that any profound religious quest will, by definition, effect all aspects of one's life. The more narrowly defined religious speculation about life and death involves a much wider application in the actions and responses which govern all mundane living. We are not dealing with an intellectual exercise but with an existential commitment which, having been made, becomes a formidable challenge to each of us. For this reason one must take issue with the judgment Stanley Kauffmann offered in his review of Bergman's film Virgin Spring; "The hazard, which he has by no means escaped, is that his films have become essentially areas of spiritual wrestling for the author through his characters, rather than disciplined artistic experiences whose prime purpose is emotional involvement of the audience."[69]

Though we do intend to be considering the "more narrowly defined religious speculation" of Bergman, this is not to imply that we will be limiting ourselves to historical sectarian considerations. Bergman is quite adamant about not wanting to be officially associated with Roman Catholicism, Protestantism, or (more particularly germane) his own Swedish Lutheranism--even though it is possible, as we shall see in the analysis of his films, to find the influence or insights of all these expressions of Christianity. When Jonas Sima makes a rather explicit theological interpretation of the plot of Wild Strawberries, Bergman responds: "I've never been much smitten by Catholicism. I've never been committed to any religious dogma of any sort. The film has an underlying religiosity--a basic attitude--of course it has. But it doesn't clash with the general psychological approach...For years the Catholics had me on their blacklist. Then along comes some sharp-witted pater and says, 'Let's take this lad into the business, instead.' And I've been plagued with Catholic interpretations ever since."[70] Asked, then, if under the circumstances he'd thought of converting, Bergman replied: "No, I've never felt any attraction to Catholicism. Catholicism, I think, does have its attractions. But Protestantism is a wretched kettle of fish."[71]

Though Bergman does not give much quarter to sectarianism in any of its forms, he is uneasy about the fact that as historical Christianity has declined in influence in Western culture, nothing seems to have replaced its sense of solidarity or its moral principles. Donner believes that Bergman is aware of this decline and that the experience has been a

formative one for him. Bergman "has not been able to
solve or to ignore the historic social crisis in which
he finds himself. In common with Swedish culture in
general, he has taken over only the Christian
middle-class aspect of the decline of Hegelianism.
The bridges have been destroyed by objective and
materialistic dialectics. This concerns primarily art
and the intellectuals."[72] But surely this is too
Marxist an interpretation of what has been happening
to Sweden and to Bergman. What Bergman is struggling
with is more fundamental than that: it is the
dissolution of classical Western philosophical
presuppositions themselves, i.e., traditional
metaphysics. It is the loss of this solidarity which
the political and social solidarity, per se, cannot
supplant which disturbs Bergman.

When Donner shifts away from the Marxian revolt
against Hegelianism to the existential revolt against
that same idealism, he is much closer to the mark for
Bergman: "While Sweden has proceeded toward more and
more collective solutions, where society's care for
all is regarded as self-evident, its literature has
developed away from this doctrine. Art has become
ever more individualistic. This spirit finds its
extreme expression in the sentence: 'The evil from
which we suffer is metaphysical.' And the term we
means all mankind..Earlier it had been possible to put
the blame for man's lack of happiness on circumstances
outside himself. Now this seemed impossible. For
this reason, therefore, Sartre's philosophy, offering
abstract opportunities of choice, seemed modern and
right. For this reason the lonely Sisyphyus became a
hero of the intellectuals. B's films are not
uninfluenced by this. They are influenced by a

certain   individualistic,   intellectual   tradition,
related   to   Kierkegaard's.[73]   We get support for this
position   from   Birgitta Steene who sees Bergman's work
"...as   an   'allegory' on the progress of the soul--his
own and, by influence, the soul of modern man. Citing
O'Neill,   Bergman   has   stated that any drama is
worthless   which   does not deal with man's relationship
to metaphysical questions."[74]

The   relationship to Soren Kierkegaard is important
here,   for   what existentialism has done for Bergman is
to   free   the   traditional religious question from its
creedal   chains.   Although Donner does not identify it
as   such, he is obviously aware of the universal appeal
that   has   emerged from Bergman's serious struggle with
his   religious   heritage.   Bergman "himself and his
critics   often   stress the fact that he is the son of a
man   of   the   church   and   that his upbringing bore the
stamp   of   the   Protestant religion. Those who are not
Christians   find   it   difficult   to   estimate   this
information   correctly--as well as all the other facts
that   have   been   told   of   B's   life. It is much more
interesting   that   the Last Judgment which the artist B
holds   over   his head and those of his characters has a
general   application.   Of   general   application   are
Knight   Antonius   Block's questions in The Seventh Seal
and   Professor   Isak Borg's dread in Wild Strawberries.
All   this   is   understandable even for the irreligious.
The   questions   in   B's   films   often   deal   with man's
relationship   to   eternity,   but broaden their scope to
include   all   the   painful   experience that plagues the
man   of   our   time.   The dread in B's films relates not
only   to   the   petty   concerns of a materially thriving
society,   but dread about the future of man and of life
on   our   threatened planet."[75]

But such a universalizing does not need to imply a
watering down of Christianity as Donner seems to imply
in the following statement: "In this book I have
tried to show that B's Christianity is so complicated
and at the same time so general and capable of being
regarded from a non-Christian viewpoint that it can be
replaced by any faith."[76]   Christianity's
particularism is evident not in its application but
in the uniqueness of its mythology. There seems to be
no need for concession here. What Bergman may have
discovered is that Christian symbols and human concern
do have, when not rigidly tied to historical
sectarianism, a universal appeal and application.[77]

There is a danger, of course, in any attempt to
universalize a religious tradition or heritage. It
can be that terms get so attenuated or sentimental
that they lose all substance and meaning; except for
sound, they bear no resemblance to the traditional
denotation.   There are critics who believe that
Bergman is constantly in danger of doing just that,
and they cite the word "love" as an example: "It is
my conclusion," writes Jerry Gill, "that Bergman has
tried to paint his view of man without reference to
theological categories, yet his view not only
parallels the Christian view but implies it as well.
Both in his films and in his remarks, Bergman attempts
to substitute <u>love</u> for God...At the very least one
would have to say that Bergman's view is high-minded,
albeit realistic humanism."[78]

Gill is correct if one stops one's analysis at
<u>Through</u> <u>a</u> <u>Glass</u> <u>Darkly</u> in which Bergman does identify
love and God, but this is most caustically rejected by
the next film, the second of his trilogy, <u>Winter</u>
<u>Light</u>.   As we shall see when we examine these films

more closely, Bergman recognizes that salvation cannot
simply be a linguistic moment, a verbal
pronouncement. Nor do I think that Bergman indulges
himself in sentimentality here. Salvation, for
whatever else it means, means a significant life, not
some promise of "pie in the sky." Consequently, he
explores cinematically those things which seemingly
mark life with significance or meaning, affirmation
and/or identity. His method is really that of the
phenomenologist rather than the rationalist; he wants
to reject the preconception, the authority of
tradition, the confinement of definition in order to
be open to the experience itself. Though the
phenomenologist, the existentialist, the ontologist
might see Bergman's search as religious, as a quest
for mythology, i.e., for ultimate reality, popular
Western culture would not see it as religious at all.
So, when Jonas Sima asks Bergman if he ever felt
himself to be some sort of religious preacher or
prophet, Bergman responds in popular kind:

> IB: Certainly not! For me things
> have always been 'on the one
> hand, it's like this--but on the
> other, like that!'

> JS: O'Neill is supposed to have
> said: 'Drama that doesn't deal
> with man's relation to God is
> worthless.'

> IB: Yes, and I've often quoted him;
> and been thoroughly
> misunderstood. Today we say all
> art is political. But I'd say
> all art has to do with ethics.
> Which after all really comes to

the same thing. It's a matter
of   attitudes.   That's   what
O'Neill meant.[79]

Thus,   while   Bergman   rejects   the   titles   of
"preacher" or "prophet" there is little doubt that his
attitudes,   his   "way   of   being,"   is   definitely
religious.   Jorn Donner recognizes this as the
character of all Bergman's films: "In spite of
different disguises, this situation is always the
same,   that   of   the human being who is confronted with
the question: How is it possible to live in this
world?"[80]   It is evident to Donner as it is to this
author that Bergman does not really make any sharp
distinction   between what he terms "ethics" and what he
understands to be "religious."

It is in the early 1950s that Bergman seriously
begins his "religious" quest.   It begins as the
conflict between the traditional world of metaphysical
values   which   must be acknowledged and the existential
world in which one _is_ the value which must be lived
authentically.   This   conflict,   this   dialectic   on
value,   is   evident   in the substance and manner of the
questions Bergman was putting to himself. "At that
time [1950] I was much preoccupied with the fear of
death.   Not of physical death--well, that too....--but
this business of dying spiritually.   That every
action, every choice, either leads to an access of
life or else to one dying a little."[81] At this time
the metaphysical questions, the classical questions of
life and death, good and evil, God and the devil,
judgment and redemption, are intellectual questions
for Bergman--theological puzzles which demand some
logical solution.   In his "Introduction" to Four
Screenplays, published in 1960, Bergman states: "To
me, religious problems are continuously alive.   I

never cease to concern myself with them; it goes on
every hour of every day. Yet this does not take place
on the emotional level, but on an intellectual one.
Religious emotion, religious sentimentality, is
something I got rid of long ago--I hope. The
religious problem is an intellectual one to me: the
relationship of my mind to my intuition. The result
of this conflict is usually some kind of tower of
Babel."[82]   However, on the following page of that
"Introduction," Bergman seems to recognize the
limitations of such a view in terms of the totality of
life.   It is no wonder that the acknowledged
"conflict" in his mind resulted in some kind of tower
of Babel. In terms of the contribution which he hopes
to make to our self-understanding, through cinema, he
writes: "I want to be one of the artists in the
cathedral on the great plain.   I want to make a
dragon's head, an angel, a devil--or perhaps a
saint--out of stone. It does not matter which; it is
the sense of satisfaction that counts. Regardless of
whether I believe or not, whether I am a Christian or
not, I would play my part in the collective building
of the cathedral."[83]

So the stage is set, the screen available, for
Bergman's search for an adequate mythology to begin.
In The Seventh Seal Bergman uses the reality of death
to pose the question of the reality of God, the
inexplicable reality of evil to pose the longing for
the reality of goodness.   Bergman explains his
technique in this regard, when he discusses The
Devil's Wanton, a film made just a short time before
The Seventh Seal: "Now let's get this Devil business
straight, once and for all.   To begin at the
beginning: the notion of God, one might say, has

changed aspect over the years, until it has either
become so vague that it has faded away altogether or
else has turned into something entirely different.
For me, hell has always been a most suggestive sort of
place; but I've never regarded it as being located
anywhere else than on earth. Hell is created by human
beings--on earth!

"What I believed in those days--and believed in
for a long time--was the existence of a virulent evil,
in no way dependent upon environmental or hereditary
factors. Call it original sin or whatever you
like--anyway an active evil, of which human beings, as
opposed to animals, have a monopoly. Our very nature,
qua human beings, is that inside us we always carry
around destructive tendencies, conscious or
unconscious, aimed both at ourselves and at the
outside world.

"As a materialization of this virulent,
indestructible, and--to us--inexplicable and
incomprehensible evil, I manufactured a personage
possessing the diabolical traits of a mediaeval
morality figure. In various contexts I'd make it into
a sort of private game to have a diabolic figure
hanging around. His evil was one of the springs in my
watch-works. And that's all there is to the
devil-figure in my early films."[84]

THE FILMS

"I believe we are all very scared. Someone
said you should pray when you feel such fear.
Even if you don't believe in anything...
      Dear God! You who are in the
      darkness and the wind, help me
      because I am an unimportant and
      scared human being who doesn't
      see anything and doesn't understand
      and doesn't believe..."

                    Jenny
                    in <u>The</u> <u>Day</u> <u>Ends</u> <u>Early</u>

The Seventh Seal (1956)

When the Lamb opened the sixth seal, I
looked, and behold, there was a great
earthquake; and the sun became black as
sackcloth, the full moon became like
blood, and the stars of the sky fell
to the earth as the fig tree sheds its
winter fruit when shaken by a gale; the
sky vanished like a scroll that is
rolled up, and every mountain and
island was removed from its place.
Then the kings of the earth and the
rich and the strong, and every one,
slave and free, hid in the caves and
among the rocks, "Fall on us and hide
us from the face of him who is seated
on the throne, and from the wrath of
the Lamb; for the great day of their
wrath has come, and who can stand
before it?"[85]

*   *   *

When the Lamb opened the seventh seal,
there was silence in heaven for about
half an hour.[86]

Against such an apocalyptic background, Bergman
sets the beginning of his spiritual journey. Within
the allegorical structure of a mediaeval morality

play, Bergman poses the perennial spiritual question
of theodicy: how can there be a good God responsible
for a world so full of evil. It is the question of
Job who laments:

> "Why is light given to a man whose
>   way is hid,
>   whom God has hedged in?
> For my sighing comes as my bread,
>   and my groanings are poured out
>   like water.
> For the thing that I fear comes
>   upon me,
>   and what I dread befalls me.
> I am not at ease, nor am I quiet;
>   I have no rest; but trouble
>   comes.[87]

The plot of the film is simple and
straightforward. Antonius Block, a Crusader Knight of
the Swedish Realm, returns to Sweden after ten years
of futile fighting for the Holy Land. He is
accompanied by his squire Jons. It is the fourteenth
century, and Sweden is being devastated by the Bubonic
Plague. Having arrived on a desolate beach, the
Knight is confronted by the figure of Death who tells
him that his time has come. Caught unprepared, Block
tempts Death into a chess game, Block's life the
stake. The game continues as Block travels home.
Though he is unable finally to save himself from
Death, he does manage, with a trick, to save the lives
of a pair of traveling players, Jof and Mia, and
their son Mikael. Others who have randomly joined
Block and his Squire on their journey find as they
reach the Knight's castle not only the Knight's wife
but also Death waiting for them all. As Death leads

them away, the spared little family of players
continue on their journey.

The allegorical intent of Bergman's characters is
obvious. They voice the hopes and fears of men and
women everywhere in every age: what is the meaning of
life? How can the life of faith be sustained in the
continuous presence of death? Why is God silent?
But, effective as the parallel is to a mediaeval
morality play, any comparison must conclude that there
are some important variations. The doubt which
plagued the mediaeval society was a moral one, not a
metaphysical one. A mediaeval knight might have
raised the question of salvation because of his
sinfulness or his unworthiness, but he would not have
raised the anguished question: Is there a God? He
might have raised the question of theodicy, of God's
purpose in sending suffering and pain to seemingly
innocent people, but he would never have doubted the
ultimate meaningfulness of that suffering. The Squire
Jons, too, differs from the mediaeval prototype. He
is the cynic, the nonbeliever, but he is not the
traditional "evil" character who has substituted lust,
pleasure, or gluttony for God. Jons comes closer to
being a Camus anti-hero with his reverence for life
than a mediaeval villain with his idolatry of self.

Even the figure of Death, one must add, is not
strictly parallel to his mediaeval counterpart.
Bergman's death-figure is no one's servant and
certainly cannot be thought of as part of the "company
of heaven" as he most often is in the morality play.
Nevertheless, the function of death then, and for
Bergman now, is the same--"he" provides the ultimate
and final terror, the inevitable and inexorable
termination of physical life. It is this which

Bergman wishes to convey: "In my film the crusader returns from the Crusades as the soldier returns from war today. In the Middle Ages, men lived in terror of the plague. Today they live in fear of the atomic bomb. The Seventh Seal is an allegory with a theme that is quite simple: man, his eternal search for God, with death as his only certainty."[88]

Peter Cowie has reservations about this parallel: "Of course one can speak readily of the parallel between the fear of the plague in the fourteenth century and the fear of the hydrogen bomb at the present time; but one should never pursue the equation too far because it tends to ignore the historical validity per se of The Seventh Seal. Bergman's characters here are not simply modern men dressed up in mediaeval clothes; at best, they can be taken as allegorical embodiments of Man's aspirations and fears throughout the ages."[89] But I think it is important to suggest that Bergman's acknowledged parallelism between plague and bomb is used to establish a different kind of "historical validity" than the one to which Cowie alludes.

If one accepts Paul Tillich's assertion that there are three great periods in Western culture, governed by the existential anxieties of death (Classical period), condemnation (Middle Ages), and meaninglessness (Contemporary period), respectively, then what Bergman has tried to do is to provide us with a contemporary Morality play. That is, Bergman has kept the allegorical structure but interpreted the specific allegories to fit the times in which we live. That which plagues contemporary man is doubt, not guilt; meaninglessness, not condemnation. It is my judgment that such updating has an historical validity of its own; the allegory functions for us as it would have functioned for one in the Middle Ages--it poses the relevant question. I believe that this is what Donner had in mind when he wrote: "To be sure, the breakthrough in modern art and literature had taken place under the shadow of a disillusionment with the belief in man's chance of a future as a collective creature. Time, however, was not yet ripe for an art which, like The Seventh Seal, was modern in its conception of man, while at the same time posing the central questions about the purpose of life and death. The second World War, nuclear weapons, anxiety about a continued life on earth, and the self-destroying development of technology have made people wonder about the meaning of progress, the meaning of the future. In this situation of crisis, The Seventh Seal appears as a mature philosophic declaration."[90]

Before discussing this film in specific terms, one further statement of background to Bergman's films should be made. The metaphysical quest which motivates Bergman is due to a decline in the acceptance of Christian mythology as well as the cultural shift in basic human anxieties mentioned above. Of course these two things cannot be finally separated because they are reciprocally active, but they can be distinguished. As the age of faith declines, the age of anxiety intensifies, which means that those suffering from the anxiety of meaninglessness make even more urgent and comprehensive demands upon the structures of belief. This is the situation in which Bergman, and most of us, find ourselves. It is the journey we all are taking. Even those whose affirmations are most strong

are unnerved by the dimensions of the threat. William
Barrett deserves to be quoted at length on this point:

> The central fact of modern history in
> the West--by which we mean the long
> period from the end of the Middle Ages
> to the present--is unquestionably the
> decline of religion.
>
> The deepest significance of this change
> does not ever appear principally at the
> purely intellectual level, in loss of
> belief, though this loss due to the
> critical inroads of science has been a
> major historical cause of the decline.
> The waning of religion is a much more
> concrete and complex fact than a mere
> change in conscious outlook; it
> penetrates the deepest strata of man's
> total psychic life...Religion to
> mediaeval man was not so much a
> theological system as a solid
> psychological matrix surrounding the
> individual's life from birth to death,
> sanctifying and enclosing all its
> ordinary and extraordinary occasions in
> sacrament and ritual. The loss of the
> Church was the loss of a whole system
> of symbols, images, dogmas, and rites
> which had the psychological validity of
> immediate experience, and within which
> hitherto the whole psychic life of
> Western man had been safely contained.
> In losing religion, man

lost the concrete connection with a transcendent realm of being; he was set free to deal with this world in all its brute objectivity. But he was bound to feel homeless in such a world, which no longer answered the needs of his spirit. A home is the accepted framework which habitually contains our life. To lose one's psychic container is to be cast adrift, to become a wanderer upon the face of the earth. Henceforth, in seeking his own human completeness man would have to do for himself what he once had done for him, unconsciously, by the Church, through the medium of its sacramental life.[91]

Barrett wrote this at the same time that Bergman was directing The Seventh Seal, 1956. It is as though they had been collaborating which, of course, they had not.

In order to understand the full force of Bergman's search for God, one must distinguish between the contemporary, agnostic, existential critique as his source and the more traditional understanding of man's disobedience and subsequent lostness. It is this latter point of tradition that characterizes Brigitta Steene's approach to The Seventh Seal: "The Crusader's search was also destined to be blasphemous, for as in the archetypal legend of the Fall, a desire for ultimate knowledge is treason against God. Bergman has grasped the paradoxical implications of the old myth: man cannot seek full intellectual cognizance of God without disobeying Him; the more he tries to understand the nature of God the further he removes himself from God. Bergman illustrates this

gradual alienation of man from the divine by depicting
in the crusader a human being at first engaged in a
holy enterprise but in the end willing to sell his
soul to the Devil--could he only find him! For the
Devil, the Knight argues with insane logic, must know
God since he only exists in his opposition to
God."92 Accurate as this may be about the nature
and meaning of the Fall, it is not adequate for what
is happening in Bergman's picture. Here the Knight is
not searching for the nature or purpose of God so much
as for his very existence; not, "What is God like?"
but "Is God?" It is to this latter existential
anguish that contemporary observers have led us and to
which a study of Bergman's film will lead us. But,
such an assertion must be justified, now, by looking
directly at the film.

Death, from the beginning of the film, is present
even though his personification has not appeared on
the screen. The day does not seem to dawn but rather
attenuates the night so that the Knight and his Squire
appear dark against a gray sea and a dark foreboding
sky. "The Knight...falls on his knees. With his eyes
closed and brow furrowed, he says his morning
prayers. His hands are clenched together and his lips
form words silently. His face is sad and bitter. He
opens his eyes and stares directly into the morning
sun which wallows up from the misty sea like some
bloated, dying fish. The sky is gray and immobile, a
dome of lead. A cloud hangs mute and dark over the
western horizon. High up, barely visible, a sea gull
floats on motionless wings. Its cry is weird and
restless."93

For those of us who have read the eighth chapter of "The Revelation to John" from which the title of the film comes, there is little doubt that Bergman is symbolically associating the gull with the Biblical eagle "crying with a loud voice, as it flew in midheaven, 'Woe, woe, woe to those who dwell on the earth...'" The mood is set. The ritualized prayer said by the Knight cannot be heard; in fact, it need not be heard, for we can tell by the Knight's demeanor that it has been totally ineffective--or perhaps negatively effective. The words fly up, but the thoughts remain below, not because of some Claudian guilt but as an enervating doubt.

At this point the Knight is confronted by Death personified and challenges him to a game of chess. Death is the final enemy, the eschatological enemy who must be met and bested if life is to have any ultimate meaning, either spiritually or physically. Any lesser question could not possibly encompass man's existential predicament. The game itself is an important symbol for Bergman: man does not lie down quietly and submissively, waiting for Death to announce the prescribed moment; he must assert himself, risk himself defiantly in order to win a meaningful moment. Bergman's gamesmanship paradox is now evident: the Knight is assuming an existential posture in order to pose a metaphysical question.

But this same paradox is given to us in the contrast between the Knight, Block, and his Squire, Jons. The men are obviously philosophical as well as social foils. The one is high-born, the other low; one elegant, the other gross; one austere and ascetic, the other unreserved and indulgent; one cerebral, the other sensual; one a traditionalist, the other an

existentialist.   But   while   these   contrasts are made
very   evident   to us, Bergman does not go to the extent
of   parody.   Each holds his own as a viable character
in   the   film,   and we, as Bergman desires, agonizingly
associate with them both.

The   contrast   between the men is given us from the
start   of   the   film.   The Squire's awakening is quite
different   than   the   Knight's: "The   Squire Jons is
awakened   by   a kick in the rear. Opening his eyes, he
grunts   like   a pig and yawns broadly. He scrambles to
his   feet,   saddles   his   horse   and picks up the heavy
pack."94   Jons   offers   up   no prayer, but ironically
(since he is not able to see Death) sings this ditty:

> Up above is God Almighty
> So very far away,
> But your brother the Devil
> You will meet on every level

Though   Jons   does   not over step his bounds as squire,
he   treats   the Knight with deferential indulgence; the
Knight,   in   his turn, treats his Squire with a kind of
loyal   indifference--each   making   his claim within the
conditions of their social relation.

The   journal   of these two protagonists takes us to
a   small   chapel   outside   of   which   a monk is reading
admonitions   to   a   girl locked in the stocks--one who,
we   are told, has admitted having carnal relations with
the   Devil.   Again   the   agonizing paradox is sharply
thrust   before   our eyes: the Church, the sanctuary of
God   is,   at the same time, the locus of man's cruelty,
of   torture,   of misunderstanding and magic. Into this
chapel   the   Knight goes to pray, the Squire to talk to
the   local   fresco   painter.   Through each experience,
Bergman has something to tell us.

From the following scene description and dialogue
with Death (whom the Knight again meets within the
chapel), Bergman first introduces us to the
metaphysical doubts and questions of the Knight. They
are the questions that have plagued man since early
Christendom:

> The knight is kneeling before a small
> altar.   It is dark and quiet around
> him.   The air is cool and musty.
> Pictures of saints look down on him
> with stony eyes.   Christ's face is
> turned upward, His mouth open as if in
> a cry of anguish. On the ceiling beam
> there is a representation of a hideous
> devil spying on a miserable human
> being.   The knight hears a sound from
> the confession booth and approaches
> it.   The face of Death appears behind
> the grill for an instant, but the
> knight doesn't see him.

While we watch the Knight mistakenly confessing to
Death, the shadows of the confessional bars crossing
the Knight's face like some subjective prison, this
dialogue takes place:

> Knight: I want to talk to you as
> openly as I can, but my heart
> is empty...The emptiness is a
> mirror turned toward my own
> face.   I see myself in it, and
> I am filled with fear and
> disgust...Through   my
> indifference to my fellow men,
> I have isolated myself from
> their company.   Now I live in

a world of phantoms. I am
imprisoned in my dreams and
fantasies.

Death: And yet you don't want to die.

Knight: Yes, I do.

Death: What are you waiting for?

Knight: I want knowledge.

Death: You want guarantees?

Knight: Call it whatever you like. Is
it so cruelly inconceivable to
grasp God with the senses?
Why should he hide himself in
a mist of half-spoken promises
and unseen miracles?...How can
we have faith in those who
believe when we can't have
faith in ourselves? What is
going to happen to those of us
who want to believe but aren't
able to: And what is to
become of those who neither
want to nor are capable of
believing?

The knight stops and waits for
a reply, but no one speaks or
answers him. There is
complete silence.

Knight: Why can't I kill God within
me? Why does he live on in
this painful and humiliating
way even though I curse Him
and want to tear Him out of my
heart? Why, in spite of
everything, is He a baffling
reality that I can't shake
off? Do you hear me?

Death: Yes, I hear you.

Knight: I want knowledge, not faith,
          not suppositions, but
          knowledge. I want God to
          stretch out his hand toward
          me, reveal Himself and speak
          to me.

Death: But He remains silent.

Knight: I call out to Him in the dark
          but no one seems to be there.

Death: Perhaps no one is there.

Knight: Then life is an outrageous
          horror. No one can live in
          the face of death, knowing
          that all is nothingness.

Death: Most people never reflect
          about either death or the
          futility of life.

Knight: But one day they will have to
          stand at that last moment of
          life and look toward the
          darkness.

Death: When that day comes...

Knight: In our fear, we make an image,
          and that image we call God.

Death: You are worrying...

Knight: Death visited me this
          morning. We are playing chess
          together. This reprieve gives
          me the chance to arrange an
          urgent matter.

Death: What matter is that?

Knight: My   life has been a futile
         pursuit, a wandering, a great
         deal of talk without meaning.
         I feel no bitterness or
         self-reproach because the
         lives of most people are very
         much like this. But I will
         use my reprieve for one
         meaningful deed.
         [after being led to reveal his
         chess strategy, the Knight is
         made aware of the true
         identity of his confessor.
         Vowing to continue the game,
         nevertheless, the Knight then
         says]:
Knight: This is my hand. I can move
         it, feel the blood pulsing
         through it. The sun is still
         high in the sky and I,
         Antonius Block, am playing
         chess with Death.95

Theologically this is a most telling and
fascinating passage to consider. One must not infer
from the following discussion that Bergman constructed
this dialogue with Death from some sophisticated
academic approach to the history of religious
thought.   What seems evident is that Bergman, in this
passage, has lumped together many of the searching
questions he himself has raised or heard others raise
about man's relationship to God. The accuracy is in
the recording, not in any consistent theological
position--for there is none here.   His Lutheran
Protestantism shows a bit here and there, but that is

to be expected, and we shall identify it as we go
along. None of the above remarks should take away the
importance of the passage; it is a masterful summary.

Bergman sets his scene descriptively (above) by
giving us a visual vendetta against common Christian
symbolism. It is not an aesthetic judgment so much as
a social, psychological, and theological criticism.
We are told the chapel is cool and musty, i.e. unused
by the people; it is not a sanctuary of light, filled
with music, radiating acceptance and love. Pictures
of the saints look down, "with stony eyes." Here is,
perhaps, a critical commentary out of Catholic and
Protestant traditions. For many Catholics the
tradition of interceding saints has long been
suspect. Too many prayers seem to go unanswered; too
many lives remain untouched. Under such
circumstances, to maintain that the saints are
there--at work--is tantamount to saying that they are
there in judgment: "Stony eyes"--frozen and
ineffective or judgmental and unforgiving. In either
case, Bergman seems to be opposed. However, there may
be a likelier reason. As one brought up in the
tradition of the Reformation, Bergman may have a
distinct aversion to the personification of saints.
It should be recalled that during the Reformation many
of the beautiful Roman Catholic cathedrals and
churches in Northern Europe had their stone, wood, and
painted images of saints literally defaced,
depersonalized: it is only the Christ who can save
us; it is only the Christ to whom prayer should be
made. For the Reformers, personification of the
saints was tantamount to the displacement of the
Christ, and to think that saints could hear individual
prayers and respond was to grant them Incarnational

authority which belongs alone to Jesus. For Bergman to give them "stony eyes" may be to consign them to the realm of folklore where, to the Reformers, they "belong."

We are next introduced to the most used and most powerful symbol in Bergman's films, the crucifix. In the above chapel description, we are shown the face of the crucified Christ twisted "in a cry of anguish" which has to bring to mind the cry of dereliction in the Gospel of Matthew: "My God, my God, why hast thou forsaken me?" With no hint of the Resurrection, what could be a more powerful symbol of futility than the apparent abandonment of the Son of God by his Father. The savagery of the symbol may reflect Bergman's frustration--the frustration of many of those who did cluster about the foot of the cross--the unfulfilled desire for proof. It may not be exactly the challenge Matthew claims some of the Jews made--"If you are the Son of God, come down from the cross"--but more likely: "If God is your Father, why is your Resurrection not visible to us all?"

Nowhere does Bergman take us beyond the crucifixion in the salvation drama. To make the point even more vivid, above and to the side of this crucifix, is the "representation of a hideous devil spying on a miserable human being." It is hard, here, not to think that Bergman is now reflecting his own Lutheran background. The Devil was all too real to Martin Luther, as the thrown-inkwell episode so vividly illustrates. Luther, in his desire to dramatize how radical evil really is, often comes close to establishing a Manichaean dualism in which the Devil and God are metaphysical rivals for evil and good, a distortion which traditional Christian doctrine since the time of Augustine has tried to avoid by stating that evil is either the absence of Good or created by God to serve His own good purposes. No doubt Bergman is reflecting a popular Lutheranism rather than Luther, which gives the Devil more than his due. In short, life is crucifixion, life is hell. The act of faith which takes the Lutheran beyond this judgment is not yet evident in Bergman's film. Reason for this incompleteness is then reflected in the Knight's conversation with Death in that prison-like confessional. Knowledge, not faith, is the Knight's demand.

All relationships and all questions for the Knight seem to have resolved themselves into one Archimedian question: "How do I know that God exists?" "I want," says the Knight, "knowledge." The argument is classic and classical. Death responds: "You want guarantees?"--the irrefutable assurance of proof, logical or ontological. The knight then puts the question to Death in one of the two great metaphysical stances of historical Christianity: "Call it whatever you like. Is it so cruelly inconceivable to grasp God with the senses? Why should he hide himself in a mist of half-spoken promises [traditions?] and unseen miracles [Gospel stories?]?" To grasp God with the senses is a direct reflection of the Aristotelian-Thomist tradition[96] in Christian theology--one should be able to argue from the beautiful sunset or the order of the universe to the existence of God. But, suggests Bergman, (without a reference to the critical arguments of Descartes, Hume, or Kant), we can't do that. We cannot argue from this world to the next, from effect back to cause, from time to eternity, because in each case we

are limited by the fact that our limitations as human
beings preclude the possibility of such a proof. We
are unable to free ourselves from the limitation of
our own acts of perception. A beautiful sunset is a
beautiful sunset, or, to put it negatively like
Voltaire: How can I possibly know that this is the
best of all possible worlds? What others have I known
with which to compare it?   This rejection of the
classical metaphysical proofs of the existence of God
by the evidence of the senses, Bergman summarizes by
having the Knight answer his own query by asking
another question: "How can we have faith in those who
believe when we can't have faith in ourselves?" If
our evidence is of our own making, then we know we
can't rely upon it as some unquestionable, irrefutable
expression of transcendent truth!

The poignancy of such an awareness comes in the
next lines the Knight speaks--after a telling silence
by Death: "What is going to happen to those of us who
want to believe but aren't able to? And what is to
become of those who neither want to nor are capable of
believing?"   Without metaphysical proof, are we not
left to the wiles of the Devil? Are we not left with
the crucified Jesus, bereft of any hope of assurance
of a resurrected Christ?   On the grounds of the
Aristotelian-Thomist arguments, it would appear so,
but Bergman is not finished with us yet.
Inconsistently, for the Knight but not so for the
broad scope of Christian tradition, Bergman now shifts
his ground to the other great metaphysical system that
has dominated Christendom, Platonic-Augustinian.[97]

To the continuing silence of Death, who, afterall,
can represent only Nothingness, the Knight exclaims:
"Why can't I kill God within me? Why does he live on

in this painful and humiliating way even though I curse Him and want to tear Him out of my heart? Why, in spite of everything, is He a baffling reality that I can't shake off?...I want knowledge, not faith, not suppositions, but knowledge.   I want God to stretch out his hand toward me, reveal Himself and speak to me...I call out to Him in the dark but no one seems to be there." Death responds, "Perhaps no one is there." The Knight replies, "Then life is an outrageous horror.   No one can live in the face of death, knowing all is nothingness...In our fear, we make an image, and that image we call God." In this second great metaphysical system, God is not proved by the evidence of our senses, but is, rather, proved by ontological necessity.   The great "ontological argument" for the existence of God concludes that because God is the greatest, he _must_ exist, because if He didn't, he wouldn't be the greatest, i.e. "existence" adds a factor without which the "greatest" wouldn't truly be the greatest. But as St. Thomas and many others have pointed out, logical necessity cannot be equated with ontological necessity.   There is a tautology here, an unwarranted presupposition about the nature and structure of logic, which provides the ground for the proof. But, of course, that will never do, for the presupposition transcends the scope of the logic, so that any "proof" about that presupposition is already contained in the original premise. What is logically valid is not necessarily true.

It would seem that in The Seventh Seal, Bergman is equating that presupposition with the act of faith (something of which Augustine would not disapprove), but faith for Bergman (as opposed to Augustine) is more like wishful thinking or hope. It certainly cannot be classified as any kind of knowledge. Bergman asks for revelation, but suggests that there is none--except perhaps that of our own making: "In our fear, we make an image, and that image we call God." The internal evidence of logic or psychology is not sufficient for the anxiety of man, his existential encounter with Death. Death says: "Perhaps no one is there."--a doubt-statement that the Knight's faith cannot successfully counter, and he finds himself responding, "Then life is an outrageous horror. No one can live in the face of death, knowing that all is nothingness." This frustration with faith Bergman gives us again in a conversation the Knight has with Mia, the player's wife: "Faith is a torment, did you know that? It is like loving someone who is out there in the darkness but never appears, no matter how loudly you call."

Almost needless to say, Bergman strikes deep here, into the cardinal tenet of the Reformation: justification by faith alone, sola fide, not by works. It is a moot point whether Bergman really understands Luther's comprehension/experience of faith as trust, but the evidence in The Seventh Seal is that he does not. Faith, as shown above, seems to be constituted of hopes and wishes. Another piece of evidence which would seem to support this analysis, is that the Knight concludes his discussion about his lack of knowledge of God with this statement: "My life has been a futile pursuit, a wandering, a great deal of talk without meaning. I feel no bitterness or self-reproach because the lives of most people are very much like this. But I will use my reprieve for one meaningful deed." We seem to be thrown back into works, not faith!

But there is another possibility here. Having
rejected the popular notion of the classical
metaphysics of Augustine and Thomas and the equally
popular notion of Luther's sola fide, Bergman makes
his first overture toward an existential critique.
Bergman gives us two reasons for supporting this
analysis. First, the Knight does get a chance to do
his "one meaningful deed." As a matter of fact, he
accomplishes at least two: he not only engineers Mia
and Jof's escape from death, he also is able to
administer an anesthetizing drug to the girl who is to
be burned at the stake for carnal intercourse with the
Devil. But, neither of these notable and meaningful
acts seems to suffice at the end when death claims
him. He does not cry out: "I've beaten you death; my
life has been meaningful afterall!" Rather, his last
words are: "God, You who are somewhere, who must be
somewhere, have mercy upon us." If anything, one can
say that the Knight seems to lapse into the futile and
uncomforting logic of the second metaphysical position
we discussed.

Second, the "one meaningful deed" may be an
existential claim in itself. For any existentialist
there is a discreteness about each act which does not
need the support of a whole metaphysical system for
its meaning. Again, he ends his
confessional-discussion with Death by making a
statement which would be hard to call anything but
existential: "This is my hand. I can move it, feel
the blood pulsing through it. The sun is still high
in the sky and I, Antonius Block, am playing chess
with Death." This statement of the here-and-now, this
claim of self-awareness, this acknowledged encounter
with the nothingness of Death where the stakes are

life itself, all point to at least a flirtation with
an existentialist posture. It is as though Bergman
were saying, "if classical and historical Christianity
cannot provide the answer to the question of life
posed by Death, then, maybe there's something to be
said for existential defiance."

One is encouraged to speculate along these lines
because of the foil Bergman has given us in the figure
of the Squire, Jons.

> Jons: (to painter after he, Jons,
> paints a small figure to
> represent himself)
> This is squire Jons. He grins
> at Death, mocks the Lord, laughs
> at himself and leers at the
> girls. His world is a
> Jons-world, believable only to
> himself, ridiculous to all
> including himself, meaningless
> to Heaven and of no interest to
> Hell.

"Here we perceive the outline of Camus' modern hero, a
symbol of man's, of the individual's integrity. The
portrait is not fully rounded. Bergman apparently has
not dared to give it the central place it deserves in
modern drama. But the fate of the squire intimates,
in any case, modern man's dramatic relationship to the
world around him. Man's sluggish hopelessness is
contrasted without any religious embellishment with
his courage and dignity. This is more than social
consciousness: this is the most urgent social
message."[98] The reason that the portrait is not
fully drawn is not that Bergman didn't _dare_ to do it;
it is more like Bergman was not yet ready to give it

that much authority. The Seventh Seal represents the breakdown of the traditional mythology with only hints and guesses as to what might follow or take its place. Consequently, Jons plays an interesting but paradoxical role--which may be why he seems to Sorenson more like a Camus' hero than one of Jean Paul Sartre's. Jons scoffs at the pictures of death and the plague which the chapel painter is creating, yet is frightened into asking for a sip of brandy himself. It is Jons who saves a girl from rape, then takes her on as servant only to become subservient himself, at the end of the film. Two of his finest "existential" declarations are followed by indecision and inaction rather than decision and action--the antithesis of existential response. When forced to witness the burning of the young girl accused of consorting with the Devil, Jons says: "For a moment I thought of killing the soldiers, but it would do no good. She's nearly dead already." Jons then addresses the Knight:

> Jons: What does she see? Can you tell me?
>
> Knight: (shakes his head) She feels no more pain.
>
> Jons: You don't answer my question. Who watches over that child? Is it the angels, or God, or the Devil, or only the emptiness? Emptiness, my Lord!
>
> Knight: This cannot be.
>
> Jons: Look at her eyes, my lord. Her poor brain has just made a discovery. Emptiness under the moon.

Knight: No.

Jons: We stand powerless, our arms
         hanging at our sides because
         we see what she sees, and our
         terror and hers are the same.
         (An outburst)   That poor
         little child.   I can't stand
         it, I can't stand it...

His voice sticks in his throat and he suddenly
walks away...But it is not Jons who has helped the
girl with a drug to kill the pain, it is the Knight.
The second time Bergman, through Jons, qualifies the
existential claim is in the final confrontation scene
with death. Jons' existential defiance is reduced to
mere bravado by Karin, the Knight's wife:

Knight: From our darkness, we call out
         to Thee, Lord. Have mercy on
         us because we are small and
         frightened and ignorant.

Jons: (bitterly)   In the darkness
         where You are supposed to be,
         where all of us probably
         are...In the darkness You will
         find no one to listen to Your
         cries or be touched by Your
         sufferings. Wash Your tears
         and mirror Yourself in Your
         indifference.

Knight: God, You who are somewhere,
         who must be somewhere, have
         mercy upon us.

Jons: I could have given you an herb
         to purge you of your worries
         about eternity. Now it seems

<pre>
                    to be too late. but in any
                    case, feel the immense triumph
                    of this last minute when you
                    can still roll your eyes and
                    move your toes.
         Karin: Quiet, quiet.
         Jons: I shall be silent, but under
                    protest.
</pre>

There can be little doubt about the fact that Bergman is intrigued by the vitality, strength, immediateness, courage, and honesty of the existentialist claim, but he is not ready, at this time, to make a commitment to this approach. The traditional claims are still too much with him, still framing the questions which he believes need to be answered.   Perhaps this is best seen in the scene with Tyan, the witch who is about to be burned. As noted above, Jons' protest and sense of outrage are most evidenced.   The Knight seems to be more interested in what, if anything, the girl really knows:

<pre>
         Knight: They say that you have been in
                    league with the Devil.
         Tyan: Why do you ask?
         Knight: Not out of curiosity, but for
                    very personal reasons. I too
                    want to meet him.
         Tyan: Why?
         Knight: I want to ask him about God.
                    He, if anyone, must know.
</pre>

Questioned about the attitude of each, the Knight and the Squire, Bergman responded: "It's two sides of the same thing...To the fanatical believer physical and spiritual suffering is beside the point, compared with salvation.   That is why, to him, everything happening

around him is irrelevant, a mirror-image, a mere
will-o'-the-wisp.   But Jons, he's a man of the
here-and-now.   He feels sympathy, hatred, and scorn;
the other bloke is like the echo department of a large
organ, placed somewhere up in the rafters."[99]

Asked which of these figures appealed to him the
most at the time of the filming, Bergman replied: "I
can't say, really. I've always felt sympathy for the
Jonses...But it's with something more like desperation
I've experienced the Blocks inside myself. I can
really never get shot of them, the fanatics. Whether
they appear as religious fanatics or vegetarian
fanatics makes no odds. They're catastrophic people.
These types whose whole cast of mind as it were looks
beyond mere human beings toward some unknown goal.
The terrible thing is the great power they often wield
over their fellow human beings. Apart from the fact
that I believe they suffer like the very devil, I've
no sympathy for them."[100]

Besides the alternatives of classical Christianity
and existential atheism with which Bergman struggles
in this film, he introduces a third alternative which
plays an increasingly important part in subsequent
films, humanism.   As with existentialism, Bergman's
presentation is powerful but partial; humanism is
effective, but not _finally_ effective. The context for
this alternative is human love. On the journey to his
castle, the Knight spends a part of one evening with
the acrobat-theater family Jof, Mia, and their son
Mikael.   The mutual love and affection which they
share reminds the Knight of his own relationship to
his wife and what that had meant to him: "We were
newly married and we played together. We laughed a
great deal.   I wrote songs to her eyes, to her nose,

to her beautiful little ears. We went hunting
together and at night we danced. The house was full
of life..." This contrasted to his present
circumstances, the cruelty of the times, the desperate
struggle with Death, leads the Knight to say:

> Everything I've said seems meaningless
> and unreal while I sit here with you
> and your husband. How unimportant it
> all becomes suddenly.
> [He takes the bowl of milk in his hand
> and drinks deeply from it several
> times. Then he carefully puts it down
> and looks up smiling.]
> I shall remember this moment. The
> silence, the twilight, the bowls of
> strawberries and milk, your faces in
> the evening light. Mikael sleeping,
> Jof with his lyre. I'll try to
> remember what we have talked about.
> I'll carry this memory between my hands
> as carefully as if it were a bowl
> filled to the brim with fresh
> milk...And it will be an adequate
> sign--it will be enough for me.

As it turns out, as we have already seen, it is
not enough for the Knight. He is still in despair at
the end of the film, and this "adequate sign" turns
out to be inadequate and unrecalled when the final
summons from Death comes. Nevertheless, one must
partially agree with Birgitta Steens about the intent
of this scene: "Strawberries are sometimes associated
with the Virgin in late Northern iconography, but milk
and wild strawberries are also private symbols in
Bergman's world, the Eucharist in a communion between

human beings."[101]   Of course, it is not the
Eucharist, but it would be fair to say that Bergman
wanted the scene to have sacramental intent. It is a
beautiful scene, filmed in soft light, but it is too
detached from the main progression of the plot to
claim more than secondary importance. It is a way
that is yet to be explored.

All three of these ways of struggling with the
human predicament--the rationalist, the
existentialist, and the humanist--are bracketed within
symbolic statements of religious extremes. It is as
though Bergman, as photographer, knew that both
absolute white and absolute black must be present so
that the range of gray tones could achieve their
proper values. For these three attempts to resolve
the problems of life, Bergman gives us both religious
innocence and religious evil as foils. Innocence in
The Seventh Seal is portrayed by Jof, Mia, and Mikael,
who as their names suggest may be symbolic of the Holy
Family. Jof dreams dreams, sees visions (Virgin Mary,
Angel of Death, and, at the end, Death and all his
victims dancing away), and cannot cope with the evil
and malicious world. Mia is goodness, sweetness,
openness, beauty; for her "One day is like
another...The summer, of course, is better than the
winter, because in summer you don't have to be cold.
But spring is best of all." Mikael, the baby, is to
grow up to be a great acrobat--or juggler who can do
the one impossible trick...To make one of the balls
stand absolutely still in the air." Mia claims that
it's impossible, and Jof responds: "Impossible for
us--but not for him." What this family symbolizes is
community, family, and love--all without duplicity,
envy, greed, lust, hate, etc. Donner sees their role

as that of a counter to the philosophical dilemmas of
Block and Jons. "Both the Knight and Jons are, 'by
their philosophical positions, unable to dispatch the
problems presented by death; Mary and Joseph [Mia and
Jof] never commit themselves to this argument and are,
in fact, aloof from it and from the double scourge of
pestilence and a reactionary church. Calm and serene,
they are the only ones who in the end are saved.' If
we place Jof's and Mia's fate in a social connection,
the solution is unsatisfactory. It is just about as
purposeful as to flee to a desert island to escape a
nuclear war. Philosophically, however, the solution
is the right one. The juggler couple ask only the
small questions. Their existence acquires depth from
the power of being together."[102] While one should
quarrel with the idea that the philosophical solution
is the right one because the "couple ask only the
small questions," one cannot quarrel with the
description of the function of this symbol.[103] Jorn
Donner sees in the figures of Jof and Mia the only
truly religious symbolism in the film. However, it is
my judgment that if one accepts Donner's position,
then one is forced to affirm the very thing Bergman is
suggesting is inadequate--the traditional metaphysical
theology just questioned above. Donner states: "The
play of light in The Seventh Seal shows plainly the
contrasts between the contemporary patterns of
action. In the lighting of the Knight's story, the
dark, the black, dominates. Above Jof and Mia there
almost always hovers a brightness of grace, as if the
action took place in another reality...The dream of
paradise and purity in The Seventh Seal cannot become
dramatically (Catholic) correct before B speaks of
evil by its rightful name, which is the sin that lives

in the hearts of men. Accordingly, one should not
seek a religious interpretation of the film outside of
Jof and Mia: their mutual life is God. The Catholic
interpretation presupposes that the paradise of
innocence cannot be found here on earth in the
momentary, but only in God's love, which is the Realm
of the Kingdom."[104]

The other side of our foil-bracket is symbolized
by the evil, the sado-masochistic destructiveness to
be found in Bergman's portrayal of the Church
Militant. To avoid the Black Death, to purge
themselves of sins both known and unknown, real and
imagined, the "faithful" parade about the
countryside: "All of them have steel-edged scourges
in their hands with which they whip themselves and
each other, howling ecstatically. They twist in pain;
their eyes bulge wildly; their lips are gnawed to
shreds and dripping with foam. They have been seized
by madness...."[105] This lemming-like
self-destruction (accompanied by a Gregorian death
chant) is aided and abetted by monks who lead the
procession. One addresses the crowds, "God has
sentenced us to punishment. We shall all perish in
the black death. You standing there like gaping
cattle, you who sit there in your glutted complacency,
do you know that this may be your last hour? Death
stands right behind you. I can see how his crown
gleams in the sun. His scythe flashes as he raises it
above your heads...Do you know, you insensible fools,
that you shall die today or tomorrow, or the next day,
because all of you have been sentenced. Do you hear
what I say? Do you hear the word? You have been
sentenced, sentenced!"

The Church Militant becomes a terrifying symbol. It preaches fear, not love; it promises punishment, not forgiveness; it prophecies death, not the good news. In short, its survival power has been reduced to the manipulation of psychological terror. Its claim to private knowledge (revelation to the Church) identifies all misfortune, after the fact, with the judgment of God and suggests that all ills to come will be the same. Private revelation is as hard to refute as it is to prove, and Bergman has raised the rightness and relevance of it all. For him the private world of goodness and the private world of evil are both unreal and destructive, each in its own way.

With The Seventh Seal our religious journey with Bergman has begun in earnest, and in this initial film his contributions are both negative and positive in form. If religion can be thought of as meaningful and affirmative existence, then we can rid ourselves of the extremes given us in the picture. Religion must not be so sentimental in its understanding of human nature and the world that it cannot cope with or understand evil, human frailty, limitations, or the complexity of inter-personal relationships which leave all of us with guilt, if only by omission--a condition the Gospel acknowledges in terms of the ubiquitous poor. Jof and Mia are projections of sentiment, not reality. Likewise, religion--to be meaningful and affirmative--cannot be neurotic, conducive to self-deprecation and destruction. Sado-masochistic behavior is a sign of the need for grace, not the expression of it. No affirmative life can be nurtured by a religion of fear and induced anxiety. The religious fanatics of this world are sick. They need help, not authority or power.

Bergman also wishes us to see that reason, per se, is inadequate as the ground for religious belief. Life cannot be reduced to an expression of ratiocination, an exercise in logic, nor can life be placed in a test tube in order to yield up its secrets to some form of scientific methodology. Religion cannot be a matter of rational, i.e. public, proof. But, this does not mean that religion must be irrational, some expression of faith where faith is interpreted as "wish" or the "ignorance beyond-known-fact." The mystery of life would seem to require some expression of suprarationalism which would include the rational but not be bound by it. The most suggestive evidence of this which Bergman gives us is in the "feeling of wholeness" generated by the shared strawberries-and-milk; yet this, too, is incomplete, separated from the major human encounters in the film, both intellectual and moral.

Religion, to be effective, must be here-and-now, expressive of the whole man within his total context. It must take seriously man's decisions and his actions, not merely his contemplations.[106] Such actions must bear the stamp of authenticity, characteristic of the identity of the doer, and be marked by courage, dignity, freedom and care. In short, religion must have an existential expression to be genuinely of ultimate concern. But there's the rub, for Bergman. To raise the existential question seems to raise the issues of Death and Nothingness which hold the key to meaning. Jorn Donner understands this to be central: "In order to survive, man must be able to conquer death. It is a matter of escaping both the inner death of feeling and the threat that looms from without. The film lets this

attempt   end   in success and failure, but the important
element   is   the   salute   to human dignity, the longing
for   justice,   for   life in peace, which constitute the
movement of the film."[107]

Out of an existential context the Knight poses the
classical metaphysical question of life to Death, and
Death remains silent; there are no final answers to
such questions.   The quest for the meaning of life
must   take   another direction, must ask different
questions.   Bergman must abandon his rhetorical
approach; he must commit himself to a new creation;
and so he does with another film.

The Magician (1958)

"In our fear, we make an image,
and that image we call God."
<u>The</u> <u>Seventh</u> <u>Seal</u>

Our legacy from <u>The</u> <u>Seventh</u> <u>Seal</u> is fear, a fear born of the doubts which are occasioned by Bergman's search for some ultimate reality, some final truth which, in turn, will give meaning to the rest of our life's experience. Bergman has looked at the traditional, classical metaphysical attempts to prove God's existence and has found them wanting, a futile exercise of the finite mind to comprehend the infinite, of the temporal man to "know" the eternal God. Bergman has also looked at the popularized Protestant claim of <u>sola</u> <u>fide</u> and finds it equally wanting, a product of spiritual imagination, a response of wish-fulfillment--certainly nothing that can be publicly verified. Two other traditional claims are equally unacceptable to Bergman: pristine innocence and sentimental humanism. Innocence in such a world as ours can only be an idealistic dream, a matter of visions; it can never sustain man engulfed by a fallen world. Humanism, on the other hand, seems equally naive and sentimental, unable to justify itself, unable to cope effectively with either death or evil.

The only option which appears to offer Bergman any recourse is that of existentialism. It, at least, confronts both death and nothingness with a radical seriousness and urgency and by so doing enables man to confront life, here and now. Existentialism's claim

upon us is its recognition that death is the one
inevitability that all men share, the one event about
which we can all agree. Yet there is cold comfort
here, for what we are agreed upon in affirmation is
our negation, and Hamlet's assertion haunts us:
"Death doth make cowards of us all." If we cannot be
sure of God but we can be sure of death, fear is our
legacy. Bergman's film The Magician is an exploration
of our predicament.

The film begins, significantly, as The Seventh
Seal: we are on a journey in what appears to be a
dark and strange land. Vernon Young calls it "A world
of sharp shadows...and the shadows are thrown from the
beginning. With frugality of means, the brief
monitory sequence in the forest--at first, silence,
wind-grieved faces, spaced chords from a guitar, a
bird of ill omen, a fox--cast such a spell it is hard
to realize that the rest of the film takes place
inside one house."[108] Albert Emanuel Vogler and his
"magnetic Health Theatre" are on a journey to the
capitol city of Stockholm with some vague hope of
being invited to play before the King.

As they approach the gates of the city, their
troupe consists of the darkly disguised and an
apparently mute Vogler--one who has "developed and
perfected the science of animal magnetism in a
brilliant way"--; Aman, Vogler's boyish disciple and
assistant, who is, in fact, Manda, Vogler's wife
disguised; Tubal,--a rotund "lily of the field" who
certainly toils not--who is the Troupe's front man and
general manager; Granny, a mysterious necromancer
whose witch-like appearance belies her canniness;
Simson, the pleasant and simple-minded coachman; and
Spegel, a debilitated, alcoholic actor whom the Troupe

has just rescued in the forest. As they approach the
city, the ailing Spegel apparently dies and must be
hastily hidden from sight to avoid the endless
investigation that would follow the discovery of a
corpus delicti.

However, because of advanced publicity, the Troupe
is expected in Stockholm and is stopped at the city
gates. The Troupe is literally commandeered and taken
to the home of a city magistrate, Council Abraham
Egerman. They are met here not only by the Consul and
his wife, Ottilia, but also by the Chief of Police,
Frans Starbeck, and the Royal Counselor on Medicine,
Anders Vergerus. This reception has been occasioned
by the rather notorious reputation of the Troupe, a
history of charlatanism, phony miracles, and arrests.
The Troupe is interrogated by the officials, required
to spend the night, and to put on a private show in
the morning, before a permit to practice will be
granted. In the morning show, Vogler is apparently
killed by one of Egerman's servants whom Vogler has
humiliated before the assembled group. Dr. Vergerus,
personally and professionally interested if there is
any physiological reason for Vogler's "magnetic
powers," performs an autopsy on Vogler--but not
Vogler: Spegel. Spegel who had apparently died on
the journey, had really been in a deep coma. He
reappears for a brief moment, then does indeed die.
Vogler, faking death at the hands of Antonsson,
substitutes Spegel, disguised as himself, for the
autopsy. Then, by a series of magic tricks and
sleights of hand, Vogler manages to terrify Vergerus,
an emotion he disavows the moment the tricks are
exposed by Manda.

Publicly disgraced and humiliated by his interrogators for failing to convince them of his magnetic powers (yet exposing them to powers within themselves they could not face), Vogler prepares to leave. His Troupe has been depleted by Granny who has decided to become legitimate and open an apothecary shop (instead of selling magic love potions and rat poisons), and Tubal, who has opted for the warm meals and bed of the Egerman's cook in return for a dubious role in local evangelism. On the other hand, the Troupe has been joined by Sara, an Egerman maid who has taken a fancy to Simson the coachman. But just as the dispirited and desperate Troupe are about to leave, a summons from the King arrives. They leave the Egerman's for the palace with a fanfare of music, and the rain, which had been drenching everyone, suddenly turns to bright sunlight. So the film, with its gothic overtones, ends.

But, Bergman's intentions and his art are rarely simple, and the present film is a case in point. It can be viewed as an interesting study of socio-cultural patterns of nineteenth century Sweden; it may be studied as an expression of the artist's struggle to communicate meaningfully with society and simultaneously to maintain his own integrity and self-respect: it can be seen as an intricate psycho-spiritual struggle of man to resolve the paradoxes of truth and illusion, knowledge and faith, belief and non-belief, life and death; and again, if not finally, the film can be seen as a further attempt by Bergman to explore the mythology of our times. It is primarily these last two levels with which we are concerned, though the first two are not by any means relegated to the bonepile of insignificance. It is a

mark of Bergman's genius that he is able to maintain
some semblance of continuity and theme-integrity on
all of these levels at once.[109] The word "genius"
here would seem to indicate some intellectual
competence, but I intend more than that; it is also a
matter of personal integrity, a recognition that such
discrete levels do, in fact, "exist" only as abstract
categories used for the convenience of analytical
study and discussion. All people live on all of these
levels--more or less fully and authentically--all of
the time. What one distinguishes intellectually one
cannot divide existentially. Therefore, it is more a
mark of "where we are" than "how skillful Bergman has
been" when we make the singular claim that "this is
what the film is about." Anyone who has discussed the
film with friends or critics knows this frustration.

Though there is general interest in the narrative
line, the sociological and aesthetic levels, all of us
as twentieth century seekers and searchers are
interested in the psycho-spiritual level. I believe
that this is why Robin Wood singles it out for his own
comments: "...the spectator finds himself disturbed
less by the films themselves than by his awareness of
the state of mind underlying them. One feels that
Bergman was for a time emotionally and spiritually
paralyzed, and was making films out of his agonized
awareness of the paralysis. Significantly, of all
Bergman's films they are the ones where one senses
least genuine progression, but rather (whatever
happens on plot level) an emotional stalemate."[110]

That Bergman was creating out of an "agonized
awareness" of the state of his own psyche is surely
the case, but to describe that state as "paralysis" is
too confining: "lostness", "indecision", and "fear"

would be much more to the point. While such emotional and spiritual states do seem to preclude movement farther into the space-time world of public relationships, they do not prevent movement further into the psycho-spiritual world of meaning and belief. In the latter the encounters are forceful and dramatic, a necessary part of the Iliadic journey that Bergman is making. Many would say that rather than a paralysis, this is the most significant movement of all: it is the encounter with our own ultimate reality. So Bergman, in The Magician, would have us face up to the spiritual poverty of our own selves, our own indecision, our own fear.

The protagonist of the film is Albert Emanuel Vogler, the leader of the Magnetic Health Theater. It is through him that we find Bergman pushing at the limits of his own spiritual experience. Without metaphysical proof, without faith, without innocence or sentimental humanism, Vogler is depicted as a man cut adrift, lost, unable to establish any point of reference and, consequently, any genuine identity. The result is a Janus-like character who cannot decide which of his personas is the real one. He is, as Dr. Vergerus accuses him of being, on the one hand "the idealistic Doctor Vogler who practices as a physician according to Mesmer's rather doubtful methods. Then we have a somewhat less than idealistic magician who arranges all kinds of hocus-pocus..." We meet Vogler first in the persona of the magician. He is dark-complected; his hair and eyebrows are dyed black; he has a false beard and mustache. The overall effect is to present a man of dark mystery: intense, unknowable, godlike, and, indeed, Christlike. As this mysterious magician, Vogler feigns muteness in his

relation to the outside world. What he has learned is
that the world wants it that way, craves a mystery
that is unfathomable so that each can interpret it in
his own way.

The only one to see through his disguise
immediately is Spegel, the debilitated actor, and,
perhaps, Vogler's alter-ego in the film. When they
first meet, Spegel (whose name resembles the German
word Spiegel meaning "mirror") says, "Are you an
actor, too?" When Vogler simply shakes his head,
Spegel continues: "Why, then, are you disguised,
sir? You are wearing a false beard and your eyebrows
and hair are dyed. Are you a swindler who must hide
his real face?" Vogler laughs, but we have the
feeling that it is an ironic laugh because Spegel is
both right and wrong. He's right in that Vogler is a
charlatan who hides behind his mask; he's wrong
because when Vogler is in disguise, he becomes the
mysterious magician who maintains his silence even
with his colleagues who know....It is apparent that at
one time he believed in his powers to heal. Manda,
his wife, reminds him that there was a "time when we
really believed that we healed people. That there was
some meaning in it." "Then Tubal came," responds
Vogler, "and we earned money." "Then Tubal came,"
replies Manda, "People started to laugh at us. Found
us suspicious. As swindlers we were not very
successful. There were others more skillful."

But this confession comes halfway through the
film, when Vogler is without disguise--blond, fair,
seemingly defenseless, and devoid of illusion. He has
just spoken to Manda his first words in the film: "I
hate them." By "them" he really means his public,
those who demand that he play the role so that they

might respond. What Vogler seems to realize is that
the power to heal has been twisted into the power to
distort or to destroy. What he once thought was a
gift has become his curse. He is the spiritual mirror
in which each man sees what he wants to see of the
world and of himself. For Ottilia Egerman, he is the
Christ, the prophet who can tell her of God, of why
her little girl has died, and even of why she is
frigid except for thoughts of him; for Vergerus, he is
the charlatan whose exposure will prove that science
is right: there is no God; for Antonsson (who tries
to kill him) he is justification for his anxiety, his
hostility toward the unknown that threatens all life,
that enchains all potential.

    Bergman has brilliantly picked up the summation
theme in The Seventh Seal and personified it in
Vogler: "In our fear, we make an image, and that
image we call God." Vogler functions as the
personification of the image, but he is no savior. He
has only the ability to reflect what each person
wishes to think of as the mystery of life, so he is
mute. Vogler (like the German word for fowler), is
the one who catches the elusive bird of the spirit and
turns it into a mocking bird of faith. "I hate them.
I hate their faces, their bodies, their movements,
their voices. But I am also afraid. Then I become
powerless." He can be the savior for all but himself,
and his public will let him be nothing other. I think
there is little doubt that Sartre's point on human
identity is not far from Bergman's mind here. We are
what other people say that we are, whether we like it
or not. So hell is other people. It is this fact
which produces the almost unbearable irony at the end
of the picture. Having failed at the Egerman's,

having been humiliated by his hosts and forsaken by
two of his troupe, his chance to escape to a new life
with Manda might have come.   In the midst of this
apparent failure, apparent success arrives with news
of his command performance before the King. In a
scene reminiscent of the Keystone Kops, the troupe
rides off to the palace, and Vogler once again must
don the mask and become the spiritual charlatan.[111]

In Vogler, Bergman has given us a frightening but
verifiable picture of the spiritual temper of the
times.   As Arthur Gibson points out: "...we should
advert to the revival of necromancy these days under a
thousand guises, from horoscopes to Black Masses, from
the dubious brand of 'parapsychology' to voodoo and
the crowded mental hospitals of our day (for many
mentally ill persons themselves tell harrowing tales
of 'possession' and weird preternatural experiences).
This revival of interest in an apparent experience of
the necromantic should not be too hastily interpreted
as the dark side of a religious phenomenon; it may
simply witness to a mental instability within a
perfectly acceptable atheistic, naturalistic context.
But it does indicate that something quite specific is
wrong within the soul of modern man. It certainly
suggests that there are voices in man's blood that
cannot easily be stilled, and that when miracle is
removed, magic may well strive to take its place. It
suggests that even though there be no God, man still
desires to get possession of him and his power,[112]
or, one might add, to be subservient to Him.

While Vogler seems to dramatize the state of
conscious and unconscious fear to which we have moved,
and to suggest, at the same time, the resolution
through apotheosis, other characters throw light on

the human predicament on the psycho-spiritual level. In fact, Robin Wood believes that Bergman's spiritual "paralysis" is so pervasive in the film that it leads to a dramatic "paralysis" there: "The leading characters seem only to exist as mouthpieces for explicit statements, the subsidiary figures to fill functions intellectually calculated rather than emotionally necessitated."[113] While it is hard to accept this judgment in the case of Vogler, who speaks rarely in the film, there does seem to be some justification for suggesting that Bergman uses some of his minor characters for representing specific positions or viewpoints. Granny is a case in point.

Granny is the symbol of religion become magic, the expression of a faith which has become detached from relationship to God and become fate. She is the worshipper who has become witch, the seer who is now court-prophet, the prophetess who is now the fortune teller, the Eucharist-supplicant now the willful necromancer, the miracle-worker become trickster. Granny is full of incantations: "Wound in the eye, blood in the mouth, fingers gone, neck broken, he calls you down, he calls you forth, beyond the dead, the living, the living dead, beyond the raised hands..." It is she who interprets the weird sounds heard in the forest: "It's a fox! A fox on two wasted legs, bloody, with his head hanging by a few sinews perhaps. A fox without eyes, but with a rotten hole for a mouth..." It is Granny who warns Vogler at the Egerman's by telling him, "It doesn't smell good in here. Today smells sour, but tomorrow smells rotten, and then it's best to withdraw," advice he doesn't accept. It is Granny that hints to Antonsson his own death as a murderer. Though he never becomes

one, he does hang himself believing he is--so that
Granny may be guilty of planting the seeds of a
self-fulfilling prophecy! Granny also makes signs and
symbols to ward off the threatening spirits about, the
inverted sign of the cross--thought to be almost
everything from the sign of the Devil to an act of
exorcism.   Yet Granny, for all her black magic, is one
who is respected for her powers and feared because of
her awareness of the spirit world.

It is Tubal, the Troupe's opportunistic public
relations man, that is directly threatened: "Dear
Jesus, this old woman makes me nervous...Granny's
tricks are passé.   They're no fun any more because
they can't be explained.   Granny, you ought to be
dead."   Tubal was remembering Ostende where, because
of Granny's telekinetic antics, Tubal was jailed,
Vogler fined and Granny herself was flogged in the
market place.   Granny's response to all this is: "It
was wonderful in Ostende." But Granny knows that she
must be careful. It is not easy to confess faith, and
even less easy to confess magic, in an age dedicated
to scientific rationalism.   When asked if she can
perform magic, she replies, "It's happened.   But
nowadays nobody believes in my secrets, so I have to
be careful.   One must not offend the new faith,
because then one might be put in a madhouse."
Exclusivism and ideology always go hand in hand, and
Bergman was perhaps more accurate here than he
knew--knowing what we know of political-deviation and
confinement in mental institutions in our present
ideological world.

But a decaying religious stance is just that, and
it is not devoid of any redeeming features. Bergman's
insight here is superb, and many, including Arthur

Gibson (who considers Granny as God's mouthpiece in The Magician[114] are carried away by the one very affirmative act that Granny does, the only truly "healing" act in the whole movie. When Sanna, Egerman's kitchen maid and the young innocent of the film, is terrified by this strange troupe of people who have come to the house and have, obviously, upset the whole household, Granny sings her to sleep with a ballad about love. The last stanza states: "Love is trust and love is rest,/Love gives strength to the cowardly breast;/Love is one and never two,/Love is for every lover new."

It is true that love is central to the Christian ethic, but that does not mean that all love is Christian. Just prior to singing Sanna to sleep, Granny gives her a present to console her. It is a miniature ear. "And if you whisper your wishes into this ear, you'll get what you ask for. But only one one condition...You can only wish for things that live, are living, or can become alive." Even here, the transcendent has been conditionally eliminated--unless one wants to work very hard to bring in the Incarnation, God "alive" in the Christ. It might be possible, but it would not really be in keeping with Bergman's crucified but unrisen Christ figure to date. It is more likely that Granny is saying, "Be sure your wishes are really wants, not airy-fairy hopes." "Granny," states Vernon Young, "is...a mixture of diabolic superstition, fakery and memories of Christian love, with which she sings the frightened Sanna to sleep..."[115] We live in an age where popular Christianity has become little more than a soporific for the theologically innocent.

Gathered at the Egerman's the night the troupe arrives is a cultural microcosm, a world where law, government, society, and science are contending the authority of magic, credulity, and faith.[116] It is a struggle of the "new" culture against the "old" in which neither one is a final victor for each is crippled by its own parochial vision. Frans Starbeck, the police chief who represents the law, is presented as a petty functionary, a Gilbert-and-Sullivan buffoon, whose only real sensitivity is to the direction of the winds of power. Bergman describes him as a costumed, rather fat, middle-aged man: "From time to time he moves his hand over his wavy hair in a coquettish gesture. His face wears a sarcastic expression which changes occasionally to one of sudden insecurity.[117] So much for the flatulence of the law which has been removed from its metaphysical base of justice. Law without justice is simply the current function of power; might makes right. From Plato's Republic through the grotesqueries of modern warfare the problem has not really changed. Even tradition, Bergman seems to be saying, is in the eyes of the powerful beholder. Because obedience is all he truly knows, Starbeck would as soon obey Pope as potentate.

The Consul, Egerman, is more urbane, almost aloof from it all. He is pictured as one who hopes that there might be something to this "magnetism" and "magnetic healing" not because it would substantiate faith but because it would prove to be rather titillating entertainment for his guests. He places a bet with Vergerus favoring Vogler's powers, a bet he off-handedly admits to losing at the end of the picture. For him, faith and belief are all part of the bread and circuses to be provided for the masses, not expression of spiritual knowledge and power. A superficial man, he is content, along with Starbeck, that might makes right for he, at the moment, is the might. His wife, Otillia, however, is not quite so sophisticated as her husband. She seems to represent those unreflective souls in society who believe that it's important to believe--in what makes little difference.118 When Otillia thinks that she is alone with Vogler, she says, "I understand you!" but instantly after that she takes another step closer to him and says, "Who are you, really?" The ambiguity of soulmate-as-stranger doesn't seem to faze her; she is so desperate to believe in something, someone, that she imposes that function on Vogler (as we have seen earlier): "You will explain why my child died. What God meant. That's why you have come. To soothe my sorrow and lift the burden from my shoulders." The linking of the former function, the salvific one, with the latter, the sexual one, causes her no discomfort or anxiety at all. Otillia has so fixed Vogler in his role, that when she finally sees him without his disguise she denies that she knows him: "I have never seen you before. I don't know you. Get out of here!" So do we, suggests Bergman, dismiss our saviors once their frailty, their finitude has been exposed, even though they may not have claimed the role in the first place. Belief must have an object for its passion; and, skeptically deprived of the Christ, we must move from one claimant to the next, the undertaking of an almost Sysiphean task of recurring apotheosis.

Vogler's antagonist in the film, however, is Dr. Vergerus, the Royal Counselor on Medicine, the symbol of reason which lacks the power of self-justification,

so that every challenge of faith, belief, or even
magic is a threat to be reckoned with:

> Vergerus: It would be a catastrophe if
> scientists were suddenly
> forced to accept the
> inexplicable.
>
> Egerman: Why a catastrophe?
>
> Vergerus: It would lead to the point
> where we would have to take
> into account a...that we
> would be suddenly forced
> to...logically we would have
> to conceive of...
>
> Egerman: A God.
>
> Vergerus: A God, if you like.

When reason has identified itself with logic or
empiricism, everything must eventually yield up its
secret to that process or formulation. Mystery and
mysticism are only helpful euphemisms for the unknown,
not the unknowable. This is why Vergerus, after a
humiliating public examination of Vogler's throat to
see why he is mute and after an unsuccessful attempt
on Vogler's part to mesmerize him, finally says:
"...You think that I hate you, but that's not true.
There is only one thing which interests me. Your
physiology, Mr. Vogler. I would like to make an
autopsy of you. Weigh your brain, open your heart,
explore a little of your nerve circuits, lift out your
eyes." Just as Tubal calls Granny's love potion
"Materialized stimulation," so Vergerus wants to
materialize Vogler's psychic-spiritual powers, to
dispel his mystery.

Yet Vergerus' intensity keeps betraying him. Everyone at the Egerman's house seems to be aware that he doth complain too loudly. Otillia says to Vergerus after his denial of effect during the initial mesmerizing confrontation, "Why do you lie?" Vergerus claims not to understand. Otillia continues: "But we saw that you lied. You experienced something that frightened you terribly, but you don't dare tell us what it was." Vergerus responds: "Pardon me, Mrs. Egerman, but I have nothing to hide, and no prestige to protect. Who knows? Perhaps I regret that I was incapable of experiencing anything." Bergman is at his cinematic best here. We have watched, too, and tend to agree with Otillia, but Vergerus' speech suddenly makes us question whether we, like Otillia, say that it's so just because we want it to be so ourselves....I believe that Bergman really does want us to agree with Otillia here, for he gives us another scene with Vergerus and Manda which seems to suggest that Vergerus really does regret that he is incapable of experiencing the spiritual world, that he really understands the issues at stake:

Vergerus: Your husband has no secret power. No, perhaps not. I remained uninfluenced at his first attempt. I just felt a certain cold excitement. He failed.

Manda: It is meaningless.

Vergerus: So I ought to feel at ease.

Manda: Yes, of course, feel at ease. We can prove our inability as many times as you like.

Vergerus: It seems to me that you
          regret this fact. As if you
          wished for something else.
          But miracles don't happen.
          It's always the apparatus and
          the spiel which have to do
          the work. The clergy have
          the same sad experience. God
          is silent and people chatter.

Manda: If just once...

Vergerus: That's what they all say. If
          just once. For the
          faithless, but above all for
          the faithful. If just once.

                    *   *   *

          Has it always been this way?

Manda: No.

Vergerus: Perhaps you believed once?
          (Manda nods silently)
          Because you felt you were
          useful and your activity had
          meaning.

Despite the advancement in philosophy, the
emergence of science as the New Truth, Vergerus is
really putting the question from The Seventh Seal all
over again: why does God not prove himself? Jorn
Donner's point is well taken here: Vergerus "is
Vogler's adversary. But many characteristics bind
them together. Both intensely wish that they could
believe. Vogler is forced to continue an existence
which he knows is a fraud. Vergerus is forced to act
as is expected of him. His coldness is an obstacle to
experiencing the world. They stand on either side of
a boundary in society. Both are stripped of their

protective qualities. The process produces neither
victor nor vanquished, since both are imprisoned in
anguish. On this basis we may conceive of the leading
characters as spectra in a portrait, as parts of one
single image."[119]

The truth of this shared identity explains, I
believe, why Bergman could tell Charles Samuels in
1972 that in The Magician, Vergerus is his favorite
character: "He, Vogler, used to think of himself as a
priest. Once he was idealistic; now he simply does
the tricks without any feeling. The only completely
integrated man in the film is Vergerus. He's the one
I like, not the magician." When Samuels questions him
on this, Bergman responds: "A good intellectual, in
my opinion, is one who has trouble with his emotions.
He must doubt his intellect, have fantasies, and be
powerfully emotional."[120]

Such intellectual doubt on Bergman's part reflects
his concern with the nature of truth and also points
to the transition to the mythological level in this
film. Aman (Manda) introduces truth as a topic of
discussion at the beginning of the film by reading
from a novel to the travelling troupe: "'Swindling is
so prevalent that those who speak the truth are
usually branded as the worst of liars.'" Spegel
immediately responds, "The author thus assumes that
there is some great general thing called truth
somewhere upstage. This is an illusion...Truth is
made to order; the most skillful liar creates the most
useful truth." Once again, the lesson of The Seventh
Seal is brought home by Bergman. Spegel's speech is
the assertion that we no longer have access to Plato's
metaphysical Forms, specifically Eternal Truth, or
Aristotelian universals. Thus, the respective

metaphysical claims of Augustine and Thomas about our knowledge of God and truth are not only specious, they are meaningless. There is no possible way that our finite minds can comprehend some "great general thing called truth somewhere upstage." That would seem, also, to eliminate the Protestant claim of "knowledge" through faith, where faith in any way becomes public enough to be labeled a "general thing." The logical conclusion for this line of argument is given us later by Manda in a conversation with Vergerus. Manda makes the claim about her husband Vogler: "He doesn't speak." Vergerus queries: "Is that true?" Manda: "Nothing is true." If truth means the comparison of propositions to absolute metaphysical Forms, then Manda is right: nothing is true, for there are no Forms; there is no correspondence theory of truth.

In this banter about truth, the meaning and function of language, which are central to the later films The Silence and Persona, are considered for the first time. Without any attempt at an exhaustive study, Bergman presents us with a paradox: language is descriptive and definitional and therefore important; but without any corresponding transcendent Truth, language becomes relative and arbitrary and therefore unimportant. Aware of this dilemma, Vogler's response is to remain resolutely silent, to neither confirm nor deny, define nor delude. The paradox of language results in the paradox of spirit: Vogler is resolutely irresolute.

But Bergman does not leave us there. If that were the end, and the only end, then his journey would also be at an end. As in The Seventh Seal, a way out of this metaphysical dilemma comes through an existential alternative which is also given us by Spegel. Just before his death, Spegel says to Vogler: "I have prayed just one prayer in my life. Use me. Handle me. But God never understood what a strong and devoted slave I had become. So I had to go unused. (Pause) Incidentally, that is also a lie. (Pause) One walks step by step into the darkness. The motion itself is the only truth." Here, as for Jons in The Seventh Seal, truth is in deeds, not words; actions, not arguments. Bergman, however, good dramatist that he is, lets Spegel's prayer be answered, nevertheless--it is Spegel upon whom Vergerus performs the autopsy, not Vogler, i.e. Bergman is not ready to equate lack of metaphysical Truth or faith as Knowledge with a denial of God. That remains a mystery and continues to be so throughout Bergman's journey.

If truth is to be discovered in motion, in action, a second look at the action of The Magician begins to yield some familiar landmarks. We should have been alerted by the fact that the magicians name is Albert Emanuel Vogler. A second glance at the second name tells the story: Emanuel--"God with us." One must hasten to add that Bergman is not saying that Vogler is God, but he is alerting us to a symbol, in fact a rather elaborate symbol system. Emanuel is a name that is applied to Jesus as the Incarnate Lord, and it is with reference to Jesus that the symbol evolves. Without attempting to be exhaustive, enough details should be given to establish the point. Vogler is, in disguise, similar in appearance to the stereotypical presentation of the historical Jesus. He and his troupe, his disciples, make a less-than-triumphal entry into Stockholm, the capital city. There they are seized and taken before the authorities to answer for their activities. At the inquiry, the questioning of Vogler, who remains silent, is simply a somewhat distorted version of Jesus before Pilate. Vogler is asked such questions as: "Can you heal the sick?"; "Do you possess supernatural powers?" "Do you possess the power to provoke visions?" The insensitivity of the mockers, the misunderstanding of the followers eventually force the enraged but silent Vogler to drive his fingernails through his own hands. He is purported killed (the police chief, Starbeck, uses the word "executed") by Antonsson who then goes out like Judas and hangs himself. Two of his "disciples" leave him despite his apparent resurrection in humility, and finally he is called by the King to his reward. There are other more questionable parallels--Spegel is a Lazarus brought back from the dead; Otillia is Pilate's wife in her defense of Vogler--but without these the evidence is clear enough that it was intentional Bergman symbolism.[121]

I think that on the basis of the above it would be absolutely wrong to suggest that Bergman had in mind making Vogler a Christ-figure. But then, what was his intent? First, I think Bergman wishes us to know that the search for meaning, purpose, truth, and ultimacy is a religious quest which involves a kind of death and resurrection; it cannot be a mere academic exercise, for, as Soren Kierkegaard reminds us, existence is too rich, too risky, and too dense to be merely a concept. Second, Bergman wants to show that any genuine search for truth is bound to disrupt the status quo and to incur the hostility and violence of those for whom power alone is reality. Third, I believe that Bergman wants us to see that in the presence of God's apparent silence, symbolized by

Vogler's silence, we will create our own <u>Imago</u> <u>Dei</u> and project it as reality. Man cannot abandon at will the desire for God. Last, if truth resides in motion, then life must be understood as myth, not logic; drama, not fact; history, not principle.

It is with this preparation that Bergman begins his exploration of man's relationship to God in the trilogy: <u>Through</u> <u>a</u> <u>Glass</u> <u>Darkly</u>, <u>Winter</u> <u>Light</u>, and <u>The</u> <u>Silence</u>.

Through a Glass Darkly (1961)

"People will pay anything for love..."

The Magician

Our spiritual journey with Bergman continues with
<u>Through</u> <u>a</u> <u>Glass</u> <u>Darkly</u>, but we shall notice a definite
shift in both style and content in this film. Up to
this time, Bergman has been attempting to deal with
God as a metaphysical object, as though the
explanation for God and his creation was to be found
by some speculative or demonstrative reasoning which
did not existentially involve the self. Yet in the
progression from <u>The</u> <u>Seventh</u> <u>Seal</u> through <u>The</u> <u>Magician</u>
we have become acutely aware of a human need for
security that lies beyond the realm of objective
metaphysics, an awareness occasioned by a shift from
speculation to decision, from fact to either/or, from
humanity-in-general to us. It is Soren Kierkegaard's
shift from the "aesthetic stage" (life as a spectator
sport) to the "ethical stage" (life as a moral
responsibility for oneself), recognizing that in such
a shift not all of our activity will respond with
comparable insight, maturity and responsibility.

Thus the need for security in a world where we
have discovered ourselves to be strangers starts us on
a journey deep within the self, a quest of heart and
soul rather than a crusade of the mind. It is not
insignificant that this thematic shift is accompanied
and augmented by a new visual technique which Bergman
employs. In this film, and except for one other,[122]
all subsequent films, Bergman has the cameraman Sven
Nykvist working with him. Nykvist's use of natural

lighting, his sensitivity to the movements and
expressions of the human face, and his ability to
incorporate the insightful dimension of
still-photography, all lend themselves to Bergman's
new introspective, subjective development.

Although after the fact, Through a Glass Darkly is
acknowledged to be the first film of a trilogy which
includes Winter Light and The Silence.123   There is
not only a continuity of content and style, but also
of religious development--what Bergman calls a
"reduction:"   "The theme of these three films is a
'reduction'--in the metaphysical sense of that word.
Through a Glass Darkly--certainty achieved.   Winter
Light--certainly unmasked.   The Silence--God's
·silence--the negative impression."124   Bergman is
really describing the spiritual struggle of
contemporary man who, bereft of transcendent
certainty, is threatened by isolation,
meaninglessness, and death.   Besides thinking of these
three films as a trilogy, Bergman also refers to them
as "Chamber Works."   This is a phrase first used by
Strindberg to describe some of his plays, plays which
had a very limited cast, action confined to one
location, a time representation approximating "real"
time (clock-time), and usually an intimate thematic
issue.125   Both Bergman and Strindberg acknowledge
the relationship of these works to musical
composition: "Through a Glass Darkly and Winter Light
and The Silence and Persona I've called chamber
works.   They are chamber music--music in which, with
an extremely limited number of voices and figures, one
explores the essence of a number of motifs.   The
backgrounds are extrapolated, put into a sort of
fog...It was stimulating, too, to let things happen

within a certain short period of time. As far as I can see, all three films in the trilogy have that in common."126

Along with this interior journey, this new subjectivism, the intimacy of the Chamber work, comes a new awareness of the importance of the commonplace--an experience for which many American audiences are really not prepared. For many, it is initially boring--"Where's the action?"--then it is threatening; for they realize it is about them, about their own inner lives, and they have no place to hide in the banality of their own lives. This is part of the secret of Bergman's power over his audience and an expression of his existential awareness. "For the thinker, as for the artist," writes William Barrett, "what counts in life is not the number of rare and exciting adventures...[one]...encounters, but the inner depth in that life, by which something great may be made out of even the paltriest and most banal of occurrences."127

But such intimacy along with such provincialism also make great demands upon Bergman himself, for in order to create effectively he must expose his own hopes, dreams, thoughts, and love to millions of us; the Chamber work is a very autobiographical one. But this fact is just what makes this kind of a study so valuable: Bergman is not leading us down some pseudo-intellectual or trivial entertainment path; he is showing us his soul, his own energy, his own tears. That is the nature of any existential reciprocity between thought and action, or life and artistic creation. "...The people in my films are exactly like myself--creatures of instinct, of rather poor intellectual capacity, who at best only think

while they're talking.   Mostly they're body, with a
little hollow for the soul. My films draw on my own
experience; however inadequately based logically and
intellectually...I come from a world of conservative
Christian thought. I've absorbed Christianity with my
mother's milk.   So it must be obvious that
certain...archetypes, aren't they called--stick in
one's mind, and that certain lines, certain courses of
events, certain ways of behaving become adequate
symbols for what goes on in the Christian system of
ideas."[128]

It is important to keep this last claim of
Bergman's in mind.   In it he is not laying claim to
Christian symbols, events, and stories for any narrow
purpose of apologetics or dogmatic instruction;
rather, he is suggesting that it is a mythology which
does provide for him (despite his own doubts) some of
the descriptive metaphors necessary to communicate the
nature of human experience.[129]   Consequently, in
studying and interpreting Bergman, we must be careful
not to confuse, for example, the claim that life is
anxiety and pain, a crucifixion, with The Crucifixion
of Jesus.   In Bergman's conversation with Jonas Sima,
this distinction is made specifically clear:

> JS: If one sees the trilogy as a
> Passion Story--Gethsemane, the
> sacrificial death and the
> grave--then Persona can be seen as
> the resurrection. The women stand
> for Christ--Karin in Through a
> Glass Darkly, Marta Lundberg in
> Winter Light, Ester in The
> Silence, and Elisabet Vogel in
> Persona.

> IB: No, not at all!
>
> JS: Such an interpretation doesn't interest you a scrap?
>
> IB: Not a scrap--it goes altogether too far.[130]

"Too far" is not a denial from Bergman; just a caution. For the most part, with the exception of Winter Light where he specifically argues the case through the character of Tomas, a Lutheran pastor, Bergman uses Christian symbolism to convey an existential dimension of religious meaning rather than an objective dimension of doctrinal certainty.

The same creative principle holds true for those who would turn his films into exclusive studies of psychology. While he does employ a rather sophisticated understanding of psychology in the development of his characters and plot, Bergman does not do so to demonstrate that he is Jungian or Freudian. To the religious apologists and to the psychologizers Bergman says: "A plague on both your houses."

> JS: Others...have taken exception to your way of turning psychiatric into religious problems. Behind all this, of course, one perceives a sort of dogmatism.
>
> IB: People think there's a solution. If everything is distributed in the proper quarters, put into the right pigeonholes, everything will be fine. But I'm not so sure.
>
> JS: It's a common atheistic notion that religiosity is just a symptom of psychosis.

IB: Quite right! Precisely. And in
religious circles, one might say,
it's the other way round. I find
this sort of criticism hard to
understand. I don't even feel its
relevance. I don't think it has
anything to do with the motifs in
themselves.[131]

Two further points should be briefly made about
Bergman's shift in style and content in the
development of Through a Glass Darkly, both of which
lend emphasis to his existential personalism. Each of
the trilogy is a film about events in the present;
there can be no escape into the past through the
artful context of some period piece--as in The
Magician or The Seventh Seal. The problems and the
world are ours; we have nowhere to run. The second
point is Bergman's shift from the apocalypticism of
"The Revelation to John" to the personal confrontation
supplied by a reference to what is the most widely
known passage in all of St. Paul's letters, the
thirteenth chapter of his "First Letter to the
Corinthians." Now we are not confronted by
intimations of cosmic judgment and disaster but by the
personal admonition to love. The thirteenth chapter
ends with these words from which the title of the film
is taken and by which the context of the film is
described: "When I was a child, I spoke like a child,
I thought like a child, I reasoned like a child; when
I became a man, I gave up childish ways. For now we
see through a glass darkly [in a mirror dimly], but
then face to face. Now I know in part; then I shall
understand fully, even as I have been fully
understood. So faith, hope, love abide, these three;
but the greatest of these is love."[132]

In keeping with the aforementioned insight about the profundity of the mundane, the plot of Through a Glass Darkly is deceptively simple. Four members of a family--David, the father; Minus, the son; Karin, the daughter; and Martin, the son-in-law are spending part of the summer on an island off the coast of Sweden. Each is in a state of isolation, estranged from each of the others, and each is frustrated in his attempt to experience the one thing that would bring meaning and security into life: love. There is no genuine communication among them, and without such communication love is impotent. Consequently, each is desperate and lost, locked (as Minus described it) in his little cube or confined (according to David) within his magic circle of personal defences, condemned to a lonely struggle with his longings for love. Each wants to communicate; each is afraid; none knows how. Karin, with a history of mental illness, flees from such lovelessness to the security of God, but her god turns out to be a spectral spider--not a redeemer but a grotesque destroyer. However, the suffering and final schizophrenic breakdown of Karin proves to be a vicarious suffering for David and Minus and the beginning of the resolution of their estranged relation. God, for them, is redefined in terms of love.

Bergman himself is now dissatisfied with the plot resolution--"Through a Glass Darkly I feel has a serious element of escapism and gross unveracity [sic] about it. A sort of desperate desire for security. An attempt to present a solution. A sort of weariness at always arriving at the question and never getting an answer"[133]--but the "unveracity" he alludes to is not that of intent but that of inadequacy. That is

all the more reason for our study of this film. On
this existential spiritual journey what is rejected or
discarded as inadequate is as important as what is
affirmed, for in any existential equation each factor
is implicit in the other even though the priority
rests with the affirmation. We are as much known by
what we are-not as what we are. What Bergman has
learned by directing Through a Glass Darkly is that
any answer to an inadequate question is really no
answer at all but actually part of the next question.
Asking the right question is the critical issue, but
to find that right question is not a matter of luck or
merely impeccable logic; it is a matter of living
through one's failures, disappointments, frustrations
at the same time that one is recognizing one's
successes, affirmations, and approbations. Should
Bergman ever find The Answer, his spiritual quest
would be over, and so would his films.

As with earlier films, we shall arbitrarily
examine Through a Glass Darkly on relevant levels of
interpretation, keeping in mind Bergman's holistic
intent and the film's total impact. We begin,
therefore, where The Magician left off: man isolated
and estranged searching for some kind of meaningful
communication and relation. The most immediate way of
assessing the effect of isolation and the tensions of
estrangement is to look, in turn, at each of the
characters Bergman has given us.

David, the father, is a writer with some public
recognition if not fame. He has returned to his
family on the island after a trip to Switzerland where
he completed a manuscript for a new novel. But, more
importantly, while in Switzerland he discovered that
his writing had become an escape from life, not an

encounter with it. In an effort to avoid tragedy,
anxiety, and despair he had tried to withdraw from
those situations and contacts which produce them:
"It's like this. One draws a magic circle around
oneself, shutting out everything that hasn't any place
in one's own private little game. Every time life
smashes the circle the game turns into something grey,
tiny, ridiculous. So one draws a new circle, builds
up new barriers." David had spent his life drawing
those circles. He had fled his wife's illness and
death in order to write his first book. He confesses
to Karin that when she became ill, he fled that, too.
"I couldn't bear it, your inheriting Mummy's illness.
So I fell headlong. After all, I had to finish my
book." As a result, he is estranged from all his
family. We are graphically shown this at the very
beginning of the picture. David, on his return to the
island has brought each a small present. Not only is
the gesture woefully inadequate, the gifts themselves
are inappropriate and betray him as the stranger.
Aware of his inadequacy, he retreats within the house
which symbolically encircles him; we see him cruciform
against the window and hear his crying.

David's agony is born of a double dilemma; it is
the need for a love which can adequately communicate
itself, and it is coping with the demands of a love
which does not yet know its own nature or limits. His
children see him only as the father who has sacrificed
them for his art. For their part in his homecoming,
the children stage a morality play, written by Minus,
in which the protagonist, a king/artist, is asked to
sacrifice his life for the love of a princess (fame)
who reigns in the Tomb of Illusions. But, because the
king is one who realizes that his _life_ is his art,

such a sacrifice would be for naught--"Oblivion shall possess me and only death shall love me." He declines the offer. David, whose art is his life, understands the message, but he seems to be at something of a loss about how to respond. So he doesn't. He gathers in fish nets with Minus; treats Karin as a child; talks with Martin about professional matters--all inadequate and patronizing. A similar dilemma confronts him within himself. He writes in his journal about his daughter Karin: "Her illness is hopeless, with occasional improvements. I have long suspected it, but the certainty, even so, is almost unbearable. To my horror, I note my own curiosity. The impulse to register its course, to note concisely her gradual dissolution. To make use of her."

There is no final resolution in the film for David. The conflict of self-love and love for others is not resolved. Cinematically we are shown this in our last glimpse of David--his face shown half in the light, half in shadow. Only when he does, through his own sense of inadequacy, identify with the feelings of inadequacy of the others, does love stand a chance because communication has begun. Only when David recognizes and confesses to Martin his failure as a father does he begin to relate to Martin who has failed as a husband. Only when David perceives that his own "impulses" are not that dissimilar to Karin's two worlds--her spectral "voices", her powerlessness against them--does he sympathize with her, admit his weakness, hold her in his arms. In return for this understanding, Karin opens herself to her father and sees and pities him for the first time--"Poor little Daddy." Only when David can admit to Minus that he cannot control reality does Minus tell him of his own

terror, lostness, and anxiety and a genuine
relationship between father and son is finally
established--"Pappa talked to me."

Martin, too, is isolated, but the restrictions
which alienate him are different than those which
encircled David.   Martin is a physician whose
professionalism always stands in the way of his
professions of love.   His response to Karin is
passionate and kind, but he fails to understand her.
To him she has become a frightened child who must be
protected, not a lover who longs to be accepted and
understood.   Martin knows the medical diagnosis of her
illness, but her child-like fears of nature and her
God-oriented "insanity" are outside of his magic
circle, and he simply denies their existence. He
wants to make love to her, but he fails to comfort her
when she is distraught by the conflicting claims of
her two worlds. So the communications break down, the
impasse ensues:

> Karin: That's the odd thing about
> you.   You always say the right
> words and do exactly the right
> things.   But they're wrong,
> even so. Why's that?
>
> Martin: If I do the wrong thing, it's
> out of love. That's something
> you should know.
>
> Karin: (coldly)   Anyone who really
> loves always does the right
> thing by the person he loves.
>
> Martin: (sadly)   Then you don't love
> me.

It takes the psychological and spiritual crisis of
Karin's epiphany to break through the impasse between
them, but by then it is too late. Karin has made her
"choice" by choosing the fantasy-world she believes to
exist behind the wallpaper. Love now imposes the
responsibility on Martin to see that Karin is cared
for in a mental hospital. We are left not knowing
whether Martin's love any earlier might have made a
difference: we are left with the poignant agony of
love left unfulfilled.

Minus, like the others, suffers the agony of
isolation and estrangement. There are no "friends" on
the island that we know of, and his relationship to
each of the others is colored by agonies of his
post-puberty adjustments. He is jealous of Martin's
relationship to his sister. The text is more explicit
than the film dialogue at this point: "The walls in
the house are so thin, and I can't help hearing when
you and Martin are making love, it drives me mad,
can't you go and do it somewhere else?...You'd better
look out. Keep away from me. And stop kissing and
hugging me all the time. Don't lie there half-naked
when you're sunbathing, it makes me feel sick to see
you." Minus' relationship to his sister is close, to
the point of great emotional confusion and anxiety, as
the above quote indicates. Though there must be some
five years difference in their ages, the two of them
have been driven together by the death of their mother
and the seeming indifference of their father. They
share "secrets" which each makes the other swear not
to tell the others, but the revelations are
inconsequential, shadows of the real "secret" which
would unlock their true identity.

The superficiality of this semblance of love,
which attracts but separates them, is shattered only
when Karin, in desperation, traps him into an
incestuous relation. Then "reality burst," Minus
tells his father, "and I feel out." The "reality" to
which Minus refers is that of his own construction,
his own solipsistic world-view which appears as a cube
rather than David's circle: "I wonder if everyone is
shut up in himself?...Shut in. You in your affairs,
me in mine. Each of us in his own box. All of us."

The terror of tumbling out of that box and David's
sense of guilt by omission prove to be strong enough
catalysts to give some understanding to the
relationships among Minus, Karin, and David and to
unite Minus and his father. Up to this time, Minus'
relationship to his father had been that of the
natural antagonism of any son breaking free from
parental control, heightened by the added antagonism
engendered by a father who simply ignored his son.
David was indifferent to, in fact unaware of, Minus'
puberty problems. David's concern was whether or not
Minus learned his Latin, not whether or not he was
becoming a man; he expressed a socio-cultural
responsibility rather than love. The futility of
their mutual, excluding antagonisms becomes evident in
the crisis of Karin's illness when each has to share
his poverty rather than flex his strength. Their
mutual acceptance becomes the generic precurser to
love.

Karin, who has recently been hospitalized for
schizophrenia, seems to be in a period of remission.
Shock treatments at the hospital have left her with an
acute sense of hearing and sensitivity to light.
Consequently, she is hyper-aware of the natural noises

of animals, birds, sea, and wind, all of which play upon her imagination. Because of her illness she has been relegated to the status of child by her husband:

>   Martin: Rely on me. Karin. Dear
>   little Kajsa.
>   Karin: Dear little Kajsa. You always
>   say that. Little Kajsa. Am I
>   so little or is it my illness
>   has turned me into a child?
>   Do you mean there's something
>   odd about me?

Even after such a plea for understanding, Martin turns around and addresses her as "Darling little Kajsa." That "Kajsa" may be a term of endearment is not even considered by Karin; only condescension is conveyed. Her relationship to her father is much the same. He, too, addresses her as "Kajsa." Just as in his relationship to Minus, David has never let her grow up in his own mind. This mishandling of the normal Electra complex culminates, as we have seen, in the revelation that David is taking notes on her illness so that he might use them sometime in his writing. Only his confession that he is a broken man who is now being "forced to live in reality," enables them to start a new relationship in trust.

Karin's feelings of alienation and sensitivity of perception drive her to seek relief from the hostility of men and the world in the realm of spirits, the secret world of her own mind. It is there that she seeks solace and release by awaiting the coming of God. But, when "God" does appear, he appears as a grotesque spider who tries to rape her. It was the ultimate betrayal. Bergman, on this level, treats the

experience as the culmination of Karin's breakdown,
the precipitating event for her recommitment to the
mental hospital. The helicopter ambulance arrives and
lifts her out of the chaos of "normalcy" into the
sanctuary of the hospital.

The theological implications of what Bergman has
given us are important both in terms of the inner-life
of each of the characters as well as their
interrelations.   All of them find themselves in the
theological world bequeathed us by Bergman's
Magician.   It is a world metaphysically conceived but
not perceived. It is a world where God is supposed to
be _out_ _there_, somewhere, but cannot be heard, seen, or
found.   For David, as we learn in a conversation with
Martin, God has become the _deus ex machina_, a literary
device:

> Martin: You've got a god you flirt
> with in your novels, but I can
> tell you, both your faith and
> your doubt are equally
> unconvincing.   What strikes
> one most is your monstrous
> inventiveness.
>
> David: Don't you think I know?
>
> Martin: Well, then.   Why go on? Why
> don't you do something
> respectable for a living?
>
> David: What could I do?
>
> Martin: Have you ever written so much
> as a true word in any of your
> books? Reply if you can.
>
> David: I don't know.

> Martin: There!   But the worst of it is
>   your lies are so refined they
>   resemble truth.
> David: I do my best.
> Martin: Maybe. But you never succeed.
> David: I know.
> Martin: You're empty and clever and
>   now you think you'll fill your
>   emptiness   with   Karin's
>   extinction.   The only thing I
>   don't understand is how you
>   fancy you can mix God up in
>   all this.   He must be more
>   inscrutable than ever.

In this conversation about God, Bergman has also
shown us his continuing struggle with the nature and
meaning of language and its implication for Truth.
Karin   learns   of   her   father's   ambivalent
loving-clinical relationship to her by reading his
diary.   Words, in this instance, seem to convey more
than mere information; they convey Truth. Yet in the
conversation quoted above, Martin accuses David of
using words to obscure the Truth: "...your lies are
so refined they resemble truth" (an echo of Manda's
statement in The Magician).   It is evident from even
these diverse instances that Bergman imagines Truth to
exist somewhere and that language functions merely as
its conveyor.   Yet Bergman is uneasy with this
traditional claim for two reasons. First, words seem
to have more power than might be credited to an
indifferent, inert medium of communication. As Martin
notes, words seem to have the power to create
something that resembles the Truth, yet isn't.
Second, in a prior statement of Martin's to David,

Bergman gives us the impression that words are simply
inadequate to Truth, i.e. that Truth is not a
propositional thing at all but an existential
phenomenon: "At every moment you have the right
word. There's only one phenomenon you haven't an
inkling of: life itself." The paradox of
necessary-but-inadequate still haunts Bergman; it is a
widening chink in the armor of traditional metaphysics
and any correspondence theory of truth.

Martin is the descendent of Vergerus in The
Magician. For him the world is a rationally ordered
context the metaphysical implications of which are not
only imponderable but meaningless. To him, Karin's
sensitivity to the strange sounds of the night, to her
voices, to her longing for spiritual fulfillment and
divine love are all manifestations of her illness,
aberrations of reason--not truth. The hypodermic
needle, not the Holy Spirit is to be called upon to
meet her anxiety.

For Minus the concept of God is mysterious and the
experience of His presence is, at best, secondhand.
It is part of his cultural inheritance that has never
become existential. So, when confronted by the crisis
in his life precipitated by his relationship to his
sister, Minus falls to his knees and cries out
"God..." but his voice carries all the fears, doubts,
hopes with which desperation has invested his naive
attempt to understand what's happening to him. The
explanation is not forthcoming, and God's presence
goes unperceived. The practical needs of the moment
reassert themselves, and Minus returns to be with his
sister until help can arrive--in the form of David and
Martin. At that moment, God the Miracle-Worker, God
the metaphysical Truth has become extraneous for

Minus; but God, as the absence of love, as the need
for understanding is very much present. It is the
existential experience of despair for which thought is
inadequate.

Bergman places each of his men in a theological
crisis by confronting them with existential situations
which their conventional beliefs cannot handle, but it
is in Karin that Bergman makes sure that we get the
full impact of his spiritual agony. In Karin the
search for God becomes direct and explicit and
wilfull, this despite her apparent mental illness.
But it is important to enter a critical note about
Bergman at this point--one which Robin Wood makes, and
I would fully endorse: "Bergman's great error in
Through a Glass Darkly (an error amply compensated for
later) was to make Karin insane. Her vision of
reality embodied in a 'Spider-God' is (stripped of
pseudo-religious terminology) essentially the vision
of The Silence, or what Elizabeth Vogler sees and
communicates to Alma in Persona, or the world of
inescapable horrors and cruelty of Shame. In Through
a Glass Darkly Bergman is clearly half afraid of her,
though she is an essential part of himself that had
been struggling for recognition through the whole
series of preceding films."[134] In short, Karin is
the emotional and theological heart of this film and
to dismiss her because of her "illness" would be to
miss the power of Bergman's argument.

Beyond the acuteness of hearing, which seems to
have been the result of the shock treatments, Karin is
by far the most sensitive and responsive character of
the film. It is she who sees and understands that her
relationship to her husband has become that of
clinical patient rather than loving wife; it is she

who understands her father's futile quest for fame,
his abandonment of family, his "use" of her as an
object for a study in disintegration; it is she who
understands Minus' sexual and emotional problems, even
though she exploits these in desperation later on.
But it is not just other human beings to whom Karin is
sensitive. She is sensitive to nature--it is she who
knows that it is going to rain, long before anyone
else; it is she who "understands" the message of the
owls and wolves. She is also aware of the realm of
the spirit, the religious dimension of life that gives
meaning to all the rest. So in Karin the clash
between conventional religious expectation and her
existential religious experience is brought into sharp
focus.

We all know (from teachings eviscerated by
sentimentality) that God--that all-powerful Being,
that Friend Upstairs--is loving and kind, One who
knows our needs before we know them ourselves, One who
will make sure that all things will work together for
good for those of us who love Him--we all know these
things because the Church and convention have told us
so. Consequently, it is not at all strange for one,
sensitive to the needs of the spirit, to seek out this
God when people and things of this world have let one
down. Should we not turn to Him in love who first
loved us, if love is what we seek? So Karin, bereft
of love and driven by the voices of the spirit, seeks
out God when she finds herself isolated from those who
should give her life meaning. But there is a kind of
futility, even absurdity, in turning to God out of
desperation rather than in desperation. This is to
treat God as the deus ex machina, the Problem-solver,
the Eternal Bellhop, or the-boiling-point-of-water.

So Karin seeks God conventionally, driven by her existential need. Bergman conveys this by a flood of traditional religious images, each impressionistic enough to convey the meaning but askew enough to deny any final validity or identity. A quick rundown should confirm this observation. The film has its genesis with the four protagonists emerging from the sea, a holy water font, into a world of isolation and anxiety. The suffering is foreshadowed when David is seen, shortly thereafter, silhouetted cruciform against a window. This is followed by a "last supper," where, as in Scripture, the meal ends in sadness with the hint of personal betrayal and loss--David is off to Yugoslavia in the near future, for who knows how long. In the play that follows this last supper, the symbolized betrayal of life by David is signalled by the crowing of a cock. Then Karin, while her husband sleeps, as did the disciples, goes to the Upper Room of the house to await the coming of God. Lest we have missed the New Testament symbols or because Bergman believes that our primitive religious ignorance places us near the beginning of spiritual response, he now adds to the Passion story the familiar images from Israel's bondage in Egypt. The room into which Karin goes is bleak and bare, covered with an old, leaf-patterned wallpaper. As the dawn comes, the sun's rays reflect off the sea through the window. The effect of the flickering light is to cover the wall with flames, creating the "bush that is not consumed." So, like Moses, Karin awaits the presence of God; she, like Moses, has taken off her shoes, for the floor on which she stands is "holy ground." Slowly she sinks to her knees, waiting...

After Karin has failed to make Minus comprehend her Other Life or to be aware of the Other People, she flees to an old abandoned ship which, besides the evident psychological images of womb and waste, may be the symbol of the decaying Church. There, during a furious rain storm, her incestuous relation with her brother marks the beginning of her crucifixion. As the two of them huddle in the hold of the broken ship, the sun emerges, spot lighting cross-shaped beams; and Karin murmers: "I'm thirsty"--one of the seven last words from the Cross. From the ship she is led back to the cottage. As she climbs the hill to the cottage itself, she refuses the offered help of her husband, stumbles, rises, and completes the journey.

The upper room to which she then goes becomes the scene of her crucifixion. The coming of God and the arrival of the helicopter hospital taxi coincide. The thundering vibrations of the helicopter blades jar open the closet door through which God is to appear. With an agonizing cry, Karin experiences God as a brutalizing spider--an imagined form not unlike the helicopter itself, seen through the window descending slowly....In the hysteria which follows, Karin rushes from the room, but is caught by the three men on the stairs where she is subdued with a hypodermic shot. The scene which Bergman gives us of the ensuing calm is the famous pictorial account of Christ's descent from the Cross. The crucifixion is complete. Karin puts on her dark glasses, her final withdrawal, and is taken by the helicopter to the hospital. We last see the helicopter disappearing into the sunset, a most devastating image of the non-resurrection if Bergman ever conceived of one.

With this devastating and ironic Passion story, Bergman's critique is complete. For all four of the protagonists the conventional understanding of God has failed: For David, spiritually; for Martin, intellectually; for Minus, emotionally; for Karin, redemptively. If that were all, however, the film would end on a devastating note of negation and there would be nowhere for Bergman to go; he would have said it all. But that is not the case, for even though the theological level of the film ends on such a negative note, the religious impact of the film does not. Each of the characters takes us to a new level of exploration and understanding which demand that the search go on. Bergman is by no means through with what he has to show us.

Each of the characters in Through a Glass Darkly is brought to a crisis in which he must existentially make a choice, and in each case such a decision is both liberating and terrifying; it demands a creative response for which there are no ecclesiastical rubrics, no historically charted course which indicates the shoals. Bergman gives us no clear picture here--indeed he could not! But what he does do is illustrate the insight of Kierkegaard: the gravity of the either/or choice in life, the "ethical stage," is finally inseparable from the terror of the "religious stage" in which one becomes aware that subjectivity is truth. One does not have the truth, employ the truth, possess the truth; one is the truth, lives the truth. The relational implications of such an insight soon become apparent.

David, Bergman tells us, tried to commit suicide in Switzerland. His attempt "miraculously" failed. His car was left teetering on the brink of a

precipice, and David decides to live rather than die:
"Out of my emptiness something was born which I hardly
dare touch or give a name to. A love. For Karin and
Minus. And you." But in David, Bergman is not quite
willing to look at that "emptiness" directly, even
though he seems to intuit its importance for the
authentic living of one's life. The result is to have
David give a rather conventional Lutheran explanation
to the whole thing:

> David: The main thing is to believe in
> one's own good intentions.
> Then everything solves itself,
> as if by magic. Provided you
> go through the correct
> motions. Activity stimulates
> self-confidence and hinders
> reflection.
>
> Martin: Are you speaking of me?
>
> David: Shouldn't dare. I'm talking in
> general principles. I assure
> you my irony is mostly directed
> against myself.
>
> Martin: But you can find consolation in
> our religion.
>
> David Yes.
>
> Martin: And inscrutable grace.
>
> David: Yes.
>
> Martin: It is inscrutable?

The confession of irony is important here, for it lets
us know that Bergman is not satisfied with such a
salvation by semantics. Martin's final question is
the crucial one; semantics must become alive, must
become scrutable if reality is to be claimed. David
attempts this by taking the one authentic moment he

has had and blowing it up into a universal principle:
God is love and love is God. The film ends with David
struggling with this assertion:

> Minus: Give me some proof of God...You
> can't.
>
> David: Yes, I can. But you must
> listen carefully to what I'm
> saying, Minus.
>
> Minus: That's just what I need, to
> listen.
>
> David: It's written: God is love.
>
> Minus: For me that's just words and
> nonsense.
>
> David: Wait a moment and don't
> interrupt. I only want to give
> you an indication of where my
> own hopes lie.
>
> Minus: And that's in God's love?
>
> David: In the knowledge that love
> exists as something real in the
> world of men.
>
> Minus: Of course it's a special sort
> of love you're referring to.
>
> David: Every sort of love, Minus! The
> highest and the lowest, the
> poorest and the richest, the
> most ridiculous and the most
> sublime. The obsessive and the
> banal. All sorts of love.
>
> Minus: Longing for love.
>
> David: Longing and denial.
> Disbelieving and being
> consoled.
>
> Minus: So love is the proof?

> David: We can't know whether love
> proves God's existence or
> whether love is itself God.
> After all, it doesn't make very
> much difference.
>
> Minus: For you God and love are one
> and the same phenomenon.
>
> David: I let my emptiness, my dirty
> hopelessness, rest in that
> thought, yes...Suddenly the
> emptiness turns into wealth,
> and hopelessness into life.
> It's like a pardon, Minus.
> From sentence of death.
>
> *   *   *
>
> Minus: Daddy spoke to me!

The logic is peccable; the claim for love is so
universal as to become meaningless! But, it seems to
me, that all that is redeemed by Minus' response:
"Daddy spoke to me!" What was being gorged to death
with words was being confirmed by the _fact_ of
feeding. Communication, authentic relation, was
established, finally, between them. Bergman hints at
this paradox himself with one of Minus' last
speeches: "Your words are terribly unreal, Daddy, but
I see you mean what you say..."

For Minus the existential moment was his
incestuous encounter with his sister in the old ship,
when "Reality burst and I fell out. It's like a
dream, though real. Anything can happen--_anything_.
Daddy!...I'm so terrified I could scream." Minus's
redemption, as we have seen above, is to accept his
father's affirmation of love. He does this, not on
intellectual grounds, but because he knows, apparently

for the first time, that he is himself loved despite his incestuous act. Life could have been destroyed for Minus at this point (a reflection of the vulnerability of innocence--particularly youth--which continues to haunt Bergman), but his decision for trust, through love, is redemptive for him.

Martin is brought to this existential crossroads because of his devotion to Karin, an emotional response which makes him aware that there is a choice in life, for which one's logic or scientific reasoning is insufficient. When Karin is in the upper room waiting for God, she is on her knees in an attitude of prayer or supplication. She begs Martin to join her, even though he doesn't believe. In defiance of all that he "knows" as a doctor, as an educated scientist, with excruciating agony written over his face, he kneels down next to Karin. Love for Karin has forced him to acknowledge forces, even in his own life, which he cannot rationally control or comprehend. For once Martin has done the "wrong" thing and it was right. If David's inadequate response was due to over-definition, universalizing, Martin's inadequate response is due to meaningless (reasonless) particularity. In each case, but from opposite ends of the spectrum, Bergman is saying in effect, "Where do we go from here?" Love is affirmed, but it remains an unqualified and unquantified mystery.

In Karin, however, the pandora's box of metaphysical speculation is really opened up. Because she is the emotional and spiritual center of the film,[135] it will be helpful to see what some of Bergman's critics have to say about her. Vernon Young, taking Karin's schizophrenia seriously, is inclined to discount her experience: "Through a Glass

Darkly is subheaded in the published scripts as
Certainty Achieved. Which certainty you may have to
decide to your taste, since God, in the final vision
of Karin, is a spider; the image is immediately
preceded by that of the helicopter which will take her
to the hospital. Bergman describes it in the script
as looking like a monstrous insect. However, since
Karin is clearly divided between herself and her fair
judgment, there is no reason for accepting as a
finality her view of things that nothing will come
from the sky but a gift, sinister in form, of
technology."[136] This view has merit if one is
dealing with the film on its narrative level, but
since Bergman's films are intentionally multi-leveled,
other views must be considered.

Three other critics would understand Karin's
vision of God to be a projection of her own
imaginative, heat-oppressed brain. For these critics,
her "madness" is more symptomatic that causative, the
second and third critics implying that divine judgment
is clearly exercised in that vision. Gene Phillips
states: "At the climax of the film, Karin experiences
an hallucination in which she sees God as a huge
spider trying to ravish her. Since Karin identified
human love with sexual love, which for her seemed a
selfish and devouring experience, her distorted image
of divine love is a magnified version of this."[137]

Jerry Gill is more inclined to see the vision in
terms of hubris than hallucination: "To demand
objective experience of God, whether in the form of
answers (as for Antonius Block) or in the form of
direct confrontation (as for Karin) is to ask for too
much. The only honest way to respond to human
existence is by means of practical, genuine love and

action, tempered by a realistic awareness of the present limitations of our vision. This, in my view, is the alternative that Bergman suggests in the face of precarious human existence."[138] Jerry Gill seems to be suggesting the insight of "Liberal" Protestant thought for which judgment is an imaginative exercise in futility; but the danger, as always, is that in preserving the practical one delimits the divine.

The third critical view, and to my mind the most revealing, is that of Arthur Gibson; here, too, the sin of pride is paramount: "Karin is the quintessence of desperate but still cowardly men, pounding on the walls that separate him from what he fondly imagines will be his heart's desire, his comfort, and his peace; screaming for palpable contact with a God tailored to answer his deepest needs and thus already defamed and demeaned to the status, precisely, of a narcissistic dildo. Karin is screaming to be possessed, to be filled, but without giving anything in return; she and her fellow watchers are passively expecting the great ingress of the deity. Well, she gets her wish with a vengeance, and the nightmare of the ingressing spider is but the brackish aftertaste of the awful intercourse in the hull of the rotting boat, where God teaches demanding man the ultimate lesson that an answer by God to man's selfish prayer for a shamanistic divine counterpart can produce only sterile tragedy."[139]

It is my belief that the vindictive violence of Gibson's statement establishes the very thing which he wishes to destroy--the Spider-God. In Through a Glass Darkly, Karin is presented to us as a pathetic, lost creature--hardly one who craves the aggressive, thrusting, insensitive "narcissistic dildo" that

Gibson asserts. When describing her expectations to
Minus, Karin says: "...I believe God is going to
reveal himself to us. And he'll come in to us through
that door. (Pause) Everyone's so calm--and so
gentle. And they're waiting. And their
love...LOVE..." If Gibson's description of God's
response is correct, then Karin is right: God is a
rapist, a rapist of the fragile soul of man who longs
for love. All three of these views, I believe, are
inadequate because each presupposes as the basis of
its criticism the very classical metaphysical scheme
which Bergman is questioning. If God is simply the
God-up-there, then, indeed, He is letting us wallow in
the futility of our own grotesque imaginings--a
vengeful Spider-God. But, Bergman wants to take us
further than that; otherwise he would not have
included, inadequate though it may be in his
presentation, love as an alternate God-image.

Two further views must yet be considered, both of
which bring us closer to what I believe Bergman was
trying to convey in this film. These critics, Jorn
Donner and Birgitta Steene, see Karin's encounter with
"God" not so much as a metaphysical description of the
nature of God but as an existential description of the
religious predicament of one's own life. Donner sees
Karin's trauma as leading to a crucial decision in her
life: "'This world'is that of adult, active, normal
people, indirectly, indirectly the world of nuclear
weapons and unhappiness, mass destruction and
cruelty. The other world can't be worse, even if God
were to appear as a frightening spider. Karin longs
for peace, freedom, and escape. She belongs among the
characters of B's for whom death is a dreadful and
tempting possibility. The crisis she goes through

concerns them all, the inability to love unselfishly and thereby the inability to surround man with a cordon of protection and care. It is therefore a matter of course for her to choose the reality that is closer to death. This is not possible until she has sunk down in filth and degradation, robbed of all protective armor. There is in the interpretation a frightful torture, a physical force that makes Karin the picture's central figure. Her face is defenseless, ageless, but with great experience."140 I think that one must be careful in suggesting that any choice of such magnitude can be simply a "matter of course." Any alternative that is merely on course cannot really be thought of as posing the existential choice of radical, exclusive possibilities, but surely Donner is right in not talking of Karin's choice in terms of insanity. As a matter of fact, the "madness" she assumes in her new world is perhaps less "mad" than the so-called normal world she is losing.

Birgitta Steene believes that Karin's encounter with God is really an encounter with a form of death: "After her attack, which is also her experiencing of God, Karin is carried away in a helicopter that descends outside the window like a veritable deus ex machina in the very moment when Karin sees the spider god come out of the closet. In the script Bergman makes a special point of describing the silhouette of the machine: it resembles a gigantic insect. It is not, of course, a question of whether Karin has actually seen God or has merely had a hallucination. She has experienced God in that world into which she has been driven by biological and psychological circumstances. But for the spectator it is necessary

to have recourse to a non-mystical explanation of
Karin's vision.   The helicopter with its dark sound
and fluttering, bug-like body provides the spectator
with an opportunity to accept Karin's experience on
purely rational grounds. But for Karin the spider god
is real, in much the same way as death is real for the
dying but unreal for everyone else. And it is into a
realm of death that Karin goes, into total
isolation."[141]   Steene's judgment, that Karin's
encounter is one with a form of death, is in keeping
with what has concerned Bergman in The Seventh Seal
and The Magician.   However, I believe that Donner's
assertion that it represents a metaphysical choice
rather than Steene's reliance upon biological and
psychological circumstances[142] is also the case.
Between the two we begin to get some idea of the
dilemma Bergman is posing for us.

While David, Martin, and Minus have all been
brought by their respective existential crises to the
sentimental conclusion that only communication--that
is, love--can save them, only Karin has had the
courage to look into the heart of things, the creative
center of life (that we have logically and arbitrarily
defined as God), to search for the source of love
itself.   What she finds, looking through her
conventional, metaphysical dark glasses, is not God,
but Nothingness--No-Thingness, as some existentialists
would put it.   She encounters the power of the Void.
It is not a matter of the absence of everything, a
kind of total oblivion; it is rather the active
destructiveness of death, the annihilation of
life-as-love which Bergman symbolizes for us as the
spider-god.

Symbolically, just outside the door of the room where God appears to Karin, Bergman has placed a love seat which is covered and unusable. Bergman is not yet at the point of saying, with Jean Paul Sartre, that all love is sado-masochistic, but the threat of that is there in Karin's vision. Bergman seems to be saying that if one is looking for love as the metaphysical principle which resides at the heart of reality, one is going to find, instead, only death at the end of _that_ rainbow promise. If there be metaphysical consistency in this world of ours, it is the constancy of death--_that_ we can all count on. It is the point H. Richard Niebuhr makes so powerfully in _The Responsible Self_: "The natural mind is enmity to God; or to our natural mind the One intention in all intentions is animosity. We live and move and have our being in a realm that is not nothingness but that is ruled by destructive power, which brings us and all we love to nothing. The maker is the slayer; the affirmer is the denier; the creator is the destroyer; the lifegiver is the death-dealer."[143]

Bergman has brought us along some distance since _The Seventh Seal_. We are now at the place where we must recognize that what we are up against, when we are up-against-it, is death itself. It is no longer just some metaphysical principle; it is an active existential power which threatens us now and always. As a counter to such a threat, Bergman, in _Through a Glass Darkly_, has, for the first time in an extended way,[144] offered us the solution of love. At present it is ill-defined by being over-defined, a value without value's discrimination. Without such discrimination, love lacks the power to confront the power of death, which is what we saw in the case of

Karin.   Nevertheless, an important move has occurred
for us.   We recognize that the threat to our life is
existential and the response, if there be one, must be
of like kind.   Instead of isolating, it must be
uniting; instead of destructive, it must be creative;
instead of negative, it must be affirmative. Love
would seem to be the solution, but the multiplicity of
claims on love itself, keeps the picture confused; we
do indeed see through a glass darkly. "Well we're
grasping for two things at once," writes Bergman about
this film.   "Partly for communion with others--that's
the deepest instinct in us. And partly, we're seeking
security.   By constant communion with others we hope
we shall be able to accept the horrible fact of our
total solitude.   We're always reaching out for new
projects, new structures, new systems in order to
abolish--partly or wholly--our insight into our own
loneliness.   If it weren't so, religious systems would
never arise."[145]

It is now possible to appreciate Bergman's choice
of the Corinthian quotation. In this film Bergman has
put away childish things--though he has by no means
put away children and the innocence they
represent--and turned to look at the world, at life
itself, honestly with all of its complexity and
paradoxes.   There can be no certainty now. "When I
wrote Through a Glass Darkly," states Bergman, "I
thought I had found a real proof of God's existence;
God is love...and I let the whole thing emanate in
that proof; it came to form the coda in the last
movement.   But it only seemed right until I started
shooting the film...For that reason I smash that proof
of God in the new film Winter Light."[146]

Because we now see through a glass darkly, because we do not yet see face to face, Bergman, like Paul, finds that faith, hope and love abide. But Bergman, unlike Paul, finds them as sustaining us for the encounter with Death, not God. Death has become, for both, the final enemy, but for the present, Bergman cannot see beyond that encounter. We reside in the now; the then must wait.

Winter Light (1962)

"Reality burst and I fell out."
<u>Through</u> <u>a</u> <u>Glass</u> <u>Darkly</u>

"I think I have made just one picture that I really like, and that is <u>Winter</u> <u>Light</u> (<u>The</u> <u>Communicants</u>).[147] That is my only picture about which I feel that I have started here and ended there and that everything along the way has obeyed me. Everything is exactly as I wanted to have it, in every second of this picture. I couldn't make this picture today; it's impossible; but I saw it a few weeks ago together with a friend and I was very satisfied."[148] Bergman makes this statement to John Simon in an interview at a time, apparently,[149] before the filming of <u>Cries</u> <u>and</u> <u>Whispers</u>, <u>Scenes</u> <u>from</u> <u>a</u> <u>Marriage</u>, and <u>Face</u> <u>to</u> <u>Face</u>. However, I little doubt that Bergman will have changed his mind in the meantime.

There is something selective about such a judgment. Shown to any off-the-street audience of Western culture, I doubt that you would get such an unqualified accolade. While they might, the more cinematically · perceptive of them, agree to the technical excellence of the film, the acting, lighting, camera work, tightness and spareness of plot, etc., they would hardly get excited about the theological-spiritual thrust of the film. This is true, not because what Bergman is exploring and exposing is unreal or inaccurate, but because Western culture has passed that theological point a generation ago, perhaps longer. Bergman reports that he showed the film to his wife, and she said: "'Yes, Ingmar, it's a masterpiece; but it's a dreary masterpiece.'"150

Spiritually, Bergman's contemporary audience is what his congregation is in the film--moribund. Bergman does not "catch up" to our present lostness and disillusionment until his next film, the third of the trilogy, The Silence. But for those of us who are taking this self-conscious, self-revealing spiritual journey with Bergman, Winter Light is not only crucial, it is every bit as great as Bergman thinks it is. For any member of the clergy or lay orders of the Church, the film is an excruciating experience of self-examination and identification in terms of one's own spiritual agonies of faith and doubt; it is a film which no seminarian should be permitted to miss before his graduation. There is no doubt that Winter Light gets much of its power and validity from Bergman's own struggle with faith and doubt as the son of a Lutheran pastor. Understood in this light, the film is fundamentally a Protestant one as opposed to the earlier films in this journey, which have been marketplace Catholicism. It is not to oppose these two religious persuasions that this is true, rather one should see this as an evolutionary move, a fact that Roman Catholics, post-Vatican II, will readily see and understand.

The movement Bergman dramatizes in his film, the theological shift indicated in the above paragraph, has been so accurately and independently well stated by William Barrett, that I will quote him at length on this point. "Faith is an abyss that engulfs the rational nature of man. The Protestant doctrine of Original Sin is in all its severity a kind of compensatory recognition of those depths below the

level of consciousness where the earnest soul demands
to interrogate itself--except that those depths are
cast into the outer darkness of depravity. So long as
faith retained its intensity, however, the irrational
elements of human nature were accorded recognition and
a central place in the total human economy. But as
the modern world moves onward, it becomes more and
more secularized in every department of life, faith
consequently becomes attenuated, and Protestant man
begins to look more and more like a giant skeleton, a
sculpture by Giacometti. A secular civilization
leaves him more starkly naked than the iconoclasm of
the Reformation had ever dreamed. The more severely
he struggles to hold on to the primal face to face
relation with God, the more tenuous this becomes,
until in the end the relation to God Himself threatens
to become a relation to Nothingness."[151]

In The Seventh Seal we discover the futility of
the classical proofs for the existence of God; in The
Magician we find that truth in life is revealed in
movement not facticity, that death and resurrection
seem to be an integral part of the religious
experience; in Through a Glass Darkly, Bergman
suggests that our death and resurrection is reflected
in our death to an egotistic self and our subsequent
resurrection through communication with others in
love. God, as the ground of such love, can then be
identified with it. But here, Bergman leaves us with
an antinomy: for David, God is love; for Karin, God
is a spider. Our experience in living is both love
and hate, life and death--all powers which struggle
within us, around us. God is the compassionate Father
who respects the broken and contrite heart and saves
us by His love; God is the vengeful and revengeful

spider--god who is totally indifferent to the broken heart and sucks our spirits dry. Bergman can no longer avoid facing these questions squarely (an existential version of the theodicy with which we began this journey), whether he arrives at a definitive answer or not. In _Winter Light_ the confrontation takes place.

The protagonist of _Winter Light_ is a Lutheran pastor, Tomas Ericsson. The film covers three Sunday hours of his life, from noon to 3:00 p.m. during which he conducts a morning Service at Mittsunda and an afternoon Service at Frostnas--"A Sunday in the vale of tears." The reason for the Swedish title _The Communicants_ now becomes evident. Each of the Services is a celebration of the Eucharist, the sacrament of the Lord's Supper, Communion. It is hard to imagine how Bergman could have greater concentrated the issues, symbols, and action of his journey than with this context. All Tomas Ericsson's thoughts and actions must be understood within the context of his ordained ministry, its sacred oaths and responsibilities. Tomas was ordained to the ministry of Jesus Christ by the laying on of hands by his Bishop, an act which places him in the Apostolic succession within the Church, an historical relation to St. Peter himself. At the time of ordination he affirms his "calling" to this ministry and swears his faithfulness to Christ's Church. By the gift of grace he may then preach the Word and dutifully administer the sacraments.

The Sacrament of the Lord's Supper which Tomas serves to the pathetic remnant in his Church is the mark of Real Presence of the Christ _here_ and _now_. I think it matters little in terms of what Bergman is doing whether one thinks of this in Roman Catholic terms, i.e. transubstantiation in which the essence of the bread and wine miraculously become the body and blood of Jesus Christ sacrificed and given again to us, or in Lutheran terms in which the Risen Christ is there as the Real Presence in the faithful act of the Communion itself. Either way the claim of the Church is that here, in this service, God is present as the Christ in a unique and special way. If ever we are to deal with God, His presence, His silence, even His existence, then this is the time and this is the place.

Of course, there may be the purist among us, to keep us honest, who will want to point out that Bergman is not the Church and therefore certainly cannot sanction such a Service, nor is Gunnar Bjornstrand, who plays the part of Tomas, an ordained Lutheran pastor. On these grounds along the film becomes presumptuous and invalid--de jure there can be no Real Presence. It is my judgment that Bergman, with his intimate knowledge of the Church knows this, but is offering us this film experience as a sign which can point to the symbol validity or invalidity of our own experience or that of our friends.

Because this is another of Bergman's "Chamber Films," the musical analogy applies. He divides the film into three movements: 1) the smashing of the coda "God is love" from Through a Glass Darkly; 2) the emptiness after the smashing; and 3) the awakening of a new faith.[152] The narrative plot, which covers a period of three hours of a Sunday in the life of Pastor Tomas Ericsson, likewise follows this three-movement pattern. The action begins with the celebration of Holy Communion at the Mittsunda church

where Tomas is the officiant. Nine people have come
to this morning service but only five of these have
come forward for the sacrament itself: a devout old
woman; Algot Frovik, the hunchbacked sexton at Tomas'
second church, Frostnas; Jonas Persson, a fisherman,
and his pregnant wife Karin; and Tomas' agnostic
mistress Marta, a school teacher.

Following the service, Jonas Persson and his wife
come to Tomas for help. Jonas is worried about the
Chinese possession of the atomic bomb and what it
means for world peace. After a brief exchange, Jonas
takes his wife home and reluctantly returns for
another talk with Tomas. Tomas, reversing the roles,
tells Jonas of his disbelief, his spiritual suffering,
his spider-god. Distraught and getting no help, Jonas
leaves and, subsequently, takes his own life. Between
Jonas' visits, Tomas speaks to Marta and reads a long
letter from her. In each case, she is pleading for a
deeper relationship to Tomas, a relationship which he
is resisting. This first movement of the film all
takes place in the cold, medieval Mittsunda church,
and it ends when the devout old woman returns to
announce Jonas' suicide.

The second movement of _Winter Light_ follows Tomas
as he goes to the location of the suicide; travels to
Marta's schoolhouse home where a most brutal encounter
between them takes place; and drives, with Marta to
the Persson's home to tell, most ineptly, Karin of her
husband's death. The second movement ends with Marta
and Tomas driving on to the Frostnas church for
Vespers, Tomas confessing to Marta on the way that the
only reason for his entering the ministry was to
please his parents.

The third and final movement of the narrative takes place within the Frostnas church. Here, in an insightful talk with Frovik, Tomas sees possible parallels between his suffering and doubt and those of both Peter and Jesus, enough that he is able to officiate at the Vesper Eucharist with only Marta, the agnostic, in his congregation.

The power of the film and its theological importance for this study come from the interpersonal relations and self-searching occasioned by Tomas' encounters with Marta, the Perssons, and Frovik. Each communicant experiences or relates a personal and spiritual crisis during the three hours represented by the film, each crisis important and instructive for Bergman's continuing journey.

The film opens with Tomas intoning: "Holy, holy, holy, Lord God Almighty. Heaven and earth are full of Thy glory," but the scene in the cold, empty church is powerful visual denial of the words as they are spoken. The atmosphere within the church seems more like death than life. The altar of the church, Bergman tells us, is a famous piece of Flemish carving from the sixteenth century, a triptych with the Holy Trinity in the center, Christ on the cross between the knees of God. It is from here, from this God's-eye view that we get the next (and most revealing) camera shot of Tomas. As Tomas turns to the altar, we get a close-up of his pained and distressed but obviously controlled face, and the effect as he recites the words of consecration--"Our Lord Jesus Christ, in the same night he was betrayed..." is devastating. What we see, through God's eye, is the continuing betrayal of the world. We are haunted, here, by the words which have come to us from both The Magician and

Through a Glass Darkly: "Your lies are so refined they resemble truth."

In a masterful way Bergman gives us the whole spiritual heritage in Pastor Tomas: he shares the doubts of the Knight, Block, in The Seventh Seal; the agony of Vogler, in The Magician, who must carry on a charade despite his doubts; and the confused horror of Karin, in Through a Glass Darkly, who finds that reality reveals a spider-god. All of this is brought to conscious focus, when Tomas is obliged to confront Jonas Persson and his inordinate fear of an atomic holocaust.   Tomas says to Jonas "We must trust in God."   But Jonas looks back contemptuously at him, and Tomas is unable to meet his eyes. After a few more banalities, Tomas says: "I understand your fear, God, how I understand it!   But we must go on living." Jonas, almost pityingly, then says: "Why must we go on living?" And Tomas has no answer. He feebly says, "Because we must.   We have a responsibility," but he obviously cannot state what or why it is so.   Jonas leaves with his wife, promising to return.

Left alone, Tomas goes into the Church and stands before the altar.   He looks, almost absent-mindedly, at the triptych with its small crucifix tucked between the great knees of God.   As he gazes at this, he says aloud to himself "Absurd!" and one is given the impression that, for the first time, Tomas is looking objectively at this symbol of his belief and rejecting its claim.   Tomas' "Absurd!" is not that of the devout, third-century Tertullian who is reported to have said, "I believe because it is absurd." For Tertullian it was the witness to the Divine mystery, logically incomprehensible, and therefore, a matter of belief; for Tomas it is the declaration of disbelief,

an unwillingness to worship One who would sacrifice
His only Son, rejecting the life that was lived
perfectly in accordance with His will. Bergman seems
to be saying here that we have reached the point where
we must accept the fact that we cannot argue to God's
existence, either by ratiocination or from the
traditional symbols of God's activity in creation. If
we are to believe, it must be because God has revealed
Himself to us, to me--an existential encounter.

This judgment is reinforced, I think, by the fact
that Marta now arrives on the scene and accompanies
Tomas back into the Vestry:

Marta: What is it, Tomas?
Tomas: To you, nothing.
Marta: Tell me, even so.
Tomas: God's silence.
Marta: God's silence?
Tomas: Yes.   (Long Pause)   God's
       silence.

This three-fold denial of any revelatory
experience does not, at least at this point, reflect
St. Peter's denial of the Christ, "I know not the
man!" The latter is a betrayal; Tomas' agony is that
of lostness, of not knowing, which he confesses to
Marta: "I talked a lot of drivel [referring to his
conversation with Jonas]. Cut off from God. Yet I
had a feeling every word I said was--decisive." The
distinction that Tomas is making here is the same that
Tillich uses talking of art: the style, the form may
be existential even when the content is not (as in Van
Gogh's paintings)--Tomas' urgency, feeling of
lostness, experience of dread was existential even
though what he was saying, e.g. exhortations to trust,
was not. It was "decisive" because his anxiety

reinforces Jonas' anxiety and, perhaps persuades Jonas to, rather than dissuades him from, suicide. It is decisive for Tomas himself, because he now acknowledges his unbelief as a problem which he must directly confront.

Marta is ostensibly of little help to Tomas at this point. When Tomas asks her why she took communion, her flippant reply is: "It's supposed to be a love-feast, isn't it?" Tomas remains distant and agonized and is further irritated by Marta's suggestion that they marry. Finally Marta says: "Sometimes I think you're the limit! God's silence, God doesn't speak. God hasn't ever spoken, because he doesn't exist. It's all so horribly simple...You must learn to love." Tomas replies sarcastically, "And I suppose it's you who're going to teach me?" "It's beyond me," says Marta, "I haven't the strength." So Bergman begins to smash his "coda" from Through a Glass Darkly: "God is love, love is God." Whatever love is, Bergman believes, at this point, that it is not something that can be equated on a one-to-one basis with a transcendent God, nor is love some miraculous cure-all. Marta leaves.

Left alone in the Vestry, Tomas is seen sitting below a huge crucifix that dominates the room. In the screenplay text Bergman gives this description: "It is a crude, roughly carved image of the suffering Christ, ineptly made. The mouth opens in a scream, the arms are grotesquely twisted, the hands convulsively clutch the nails, the brow is bloody beneath the thorns, and the body arches outwards, as if trying to tear itself away from the wood. The images smell of fungus, moldy timber. Its paint is flaking off in long strips." This double crucifixion,

Christ and His agony, Tomas and his, is brilliantly
achieved by Bergman.

We know that Tomas is waiting for Jonas' return
but we likewise know that he is experiencing a
spiritual crisis occasioned by God's silence. The
first words we hear him speak seem to be directed
toward thoughts of Jonas: "He must come!", yet they
apply equally well to his anxiety about God, an echo
of the Knight's (Block) anxiety when confronted by
death. Whether or not Tomas' exclamatory prayer is
answered here, depends upon how one interprets Marta's
letter which Tomas now reads. It was a letter written
to him sometime earlier, which he could not bring
himself to open and read. Now he does. In it she
traces their tenuous and, at times, stormy
relationship, pleading her cause of love for him. But
in it we also get an insight into Tomas' life of
faith, and further development of the paradox
mentioned earlier, that of style and content--of
faithful unbelief. It will be helpful to consider a
goodly portion of that letter which Marta (Ingrid
Thulin) so skillfully recites to us on screen:

> Do you remember last summer? I had
> eczema on both hands and everything was
> so wretched. One evening we were in
> the church together, arranging flowers
> on the altar. There was to be a
> confirmation. Do you remember what a
> particularly difficult time I was going
> through, just then, with both hands
> bandaged and unable to sleep at night
> from the irritation--my skin had flaked
> off and my palms were like open sores.
> There we stood, busy with marguerites

and cornflowers..and I felt terribly
irritable.   Suddenly, feeling angry
with you, I asked you, out of sheer
malice, about the efficacy of prayer,
and   whether   you   believed   in   it.
Naturally,   you   replied   you   did.
Maliciously, again, I asked whether you
had prayed for my hands and you said
no, it was a thing you hadn't thought
of.   I   became very melodramatic.
Suggested you should pray for me there
and then.   Oddly enough, you agreed.
This   compliance   made me even more
angry, I tore off the bandage--well,
you remember.   The open sores affected
you unpleasantly.   You couldn't pray,
the whole situation simply disgusted
you.   Now,   after   the   event, I
understand   you;   but   you   never
understood me.   After all, we'd been
living together quite a while, almost
two   years.   One would think this
represented a certain little capital in
our   poverty,   in   tenderness exchanged,
and   in   our   clumsy attempts to get
around   the   lovelessness   of   our
relationship.   And then, when the
eczema broke out on my forehead and
around my   scalp, it wasn't long before
I   noticed you were avoiding me. You
found me distasteful even though you
were considerate about it and didn't
want to hurt my feelings.   Then the
disease   flamed up on my hands and
feet.   And our relationship ended...

I have never believed in your faith.
Chiefly, of course, because I've never
been tormented by religious
temptation. I grew up in a
non-Christian family, full of warmth
and kindness and loyalty--and joy. God
and Christ didn't exist, except as
vague notions. And when I came into
contact with your faith, it seemed to
me obscure and neurotic, in some way
cruelly overcharged with emotion,
primitive. One thing in particular I
couldn't understand, your peculiar
indifference to Jesus Christ.
And now, anyway, I must tell you a
strange case of prayer being heard. If
you're in the mood, it'll give you a
good laugh. Personally, of course, I
don't believe there was the remotest
connection, life is problematic enough
as it is, I mean without supernatural
factors. Our so-called commonsense has
quite enough on its plate with the
psychological and biological nonsense.
Well, you recall how you were going to
pray for my eczema but--though
afterwards you denied it--were struck
dumb by distaste. Half out of my wits,
I wanted still further to exasperate
you--I saw your terrified face close to
me. Remember how I said: Quiet!
Since you can't pray for me, I'll pray
for myself.

God, I said to myself, why have you
created me so eternally dissatisfied,
so frightened, so bitter? Why must I
understand how wretched I am, why have
I got to suffer as in the hell of my
own indifference?   If there is a
purpose in my suffering, then tell me
what it is!   And I'll bear my pain
without complaining.   I'm strong.
You've made me so terribly strong, both
in body and soul, but you give me
nothing to do with my strength. Give me
a meaning to my life, and I'll be your
obedient slave!   More or less, that's
what I prayed....
This autumn I've realized my prayer has
been heard.   And here's your cue to
laugh.   I prayed for clarity of mind,
and I got it.   I've realized I love
you.   I prayed for a task to apply my
strength to and got it, too.   It's
you....Whether   it's   God   or   my
biological functions which have brought
about my love for you, anyway I'm
burning with gratitude....
What I lack entirely is the capacity to
show you my love.   I haven't the
remotest idea how to go about it. I've
been so miserable I've even thought of
praying another prayer.   But I still
have a little self-respect left, in
spite of all, some feelings of decency.

> Dearest Tomas--this has turned out to
> be a long letter. But now I've written
> what I don't dare to say even when
> you're in my arms: I love you and I
> live for you. Take me and use me.
> Beneath all my false pride and
> independent airs I've only one wish; to
> be allowed to live for someone else.
> It will be terribly difficult.

I suppose the most startling thing about this letter is that it shows the reversal of roles, a religious phenomenon that has puzzled Bergman all along. The so-called agnostic turns out to be the one who is most religiously sensitive, and the professionally religious person is really a crypto-agnostic. It is Marta who chides Tomas about the power of prayer--who seems to realize what the claim has to be even though she doesn't acknowledge any belief in it at present; it is Tomas who is struck dumb. It is Marta who is sensitive to the nature and person of Jesus Christ, who chides Tomas for his indifference to Him. For Bergman there may be a reflection here of Camus' Jean-Baptiste Clemance in The Fall, who calls himself a shabby prophet for empty times yet calls Jesus "my friend".

In any event, it is Marta who ends up offering the real prayer, not for a cure to her eczema but for "clarity of mind" and "for a task" equal to her strength--both of which are answered! How?--she refuses to explore it. Bergman is content to leave it a mystery. He could have used either biology or psychology as a way out, an explanation; but he didn't rise to that bait, which I think is important. (In subsequent films he really disposes of these disciplines as insufficient explanatory myths--biology in The Silence, psychology in Scenes from a Marriage and Face to Face.) Bergman is wise enough to let prayer remain a mystery. Another clue to Bergman's thought here has to be the stigmata-nature of Marta's eczema. He has given us crucifixion symbols, now, for both Tomas and Marta, a point to which we shall return later in the chapter.

For the present, the above letter has truly prepared us for Tomas' second talk with Jonas when, no longer able to dissemble, he confesses his lack of faith and tentatively speculates about materialistic naturalism as a possible substitute. During this dialogue which in fact becomes a soliloquy for Tomas, Jonas sits by, his confusion and anxiety continuously growing. (The following is quoted from the complete text rather than the somewhat shortened film version.)

> Jonas, listen to me a moment. I'll speak openly to you, without reservations. You know my wife died four years ago. I loved her. My life was at an end, I'm not frightened of death, there isn't the least reason for me to go living....I was left behind. Not for my own sake, but to be of some use...Believe me, I had great dreams once. I was going to make my mark in the world. Well, you know the sort of ideas you get when you're young. My mother protected me from everything evil, everything ugly, everything dangerous. Of cruelty or evil I knew absolutely nothing. When I was ordained I was an innocent as a

babe in arms. Then everything happened
at once.   For a while I was a seaman's
pastor in Lisbon.   It was during the
Spanish Civil War. We had a front seat
in the stalls.   But I refused to see,
or understand.   I refused to accept
reality.   I and my God lived in one
world, a specially arranged world,
where everything made sense. All round
were the agonies of real life. But I
didn't see them.   I turned my gaze
toward my God.
Forgive me for talking about myself.
Please don't misunderstand me. All I
mean is, we, you and I, in our
different ways have shut ourselves in
and locked the door behind us. You
with your fear and I--
Please, you _must_ understand.   I'm no
good as a clergyman.   I chose my
calling because my mother and father
were religious, pious, in a deep and
natural way.   Maybe I didn't really
love them, but I wanted to please
them.   So I became a clergyman and
believed in God.   (short laugh) An
improbable, entirely private, fatherly
god.   Who loved mankind, of course, but
most of all me.
A   god   who   guaranteed   me every
imaginable security.   Against fear of
death.   Against fear of life. A god
I'd suggested myself into believing in,
a god I'd borrowed from various
quarters, fabricated with my own
hands.

D'you understand, Jonas? What a
monstrous mistake I'd made? Can you
realize what a bad priest must come of
such a spoiled, shut-in, anxious wretch
as me?
Can you imagine my prayers? To an
echo-god. Who gave benign answers and
reassuring blessings?....Every time I
confronted God with the reality I saw,
he became ugly, revolting, a
spider-god--a monster. That's why I
hid him away from the light, from
life. In my darkness and loneliness I
hugged him to myself--the only person I
showed him to was my wife. She backed
me up, encouraged me, helped me,
plugged up all the holes. Our
dreams...My indifference to the gospel
message, my jealous hatred of Jesus....

                *   *   *

Well, and what if God doesn't exist?
What difference does it make?....Life
becomes something we can understand.
What a relief! And death--extinction,
dissolution of a body and soul.
People's cruelty, their loneliness,
their fear--everything becomes
self-evident--transparent. Suffering
is incomprehensible, so it needn't be
explained. The stars out in space,
worlds, heavens, all have given birth
to themselves and to each other. There
isn't any creator, no one who holds it
all together, no

immeasurable thought to make one's head
spin.
We're alone, you and I. We've betrayed
the only condition under which men can
live: to live together. And that's
why we're so poverty-stricken, joyless
and full of fear. All this stinks of
an antique godliness! All this
super-natural helplessness, this
humiliating sense of sin!

The above speech, delivered in such a masterful
way by Gunnar Bjornstrand, is one of the most
important speeches for Bergman in the entire series of
films that we are considering. It is a watershed
moment in our journey. Up to this time we had been
laboring up the sterile slopes of classical
metaphysical tradition, demanding some logical proof
or some public, mystical experience of God's
existence; we had been seeking some sort of verifiable
justification for our faith. But all attempts have
failed; a Sysiphean task. Nothing has granted us the
satisfaction demanded by the question. So, at this
point, Bergman accepts the verdict Immanuel Kant had
rendered long before: there is no possible way for
pure reason to prove the existence of God; in fact, to
even talk of God's "existence" is a mistake, for
existence is not a predicate. Later existentialists
would not necessarily accept Kant's argument about the
nature of existence itself, but they would have no
quarrel with his or Bergman's rejection of the
classical metaphysical arguments. While Bergman has
nothing, at the moment, to put in their place, he has
at least freed himself from the fatal error of asking
the wrong question, pursuing a specious end.

In speaking with critic Jonas Sima, Bergman puts it this way: "As the religious aspect of my existence was wiped out, life became much easier to live. Sartre has said how inhibited he used to be as an artist and author, how he suffered because what he was doing wasn't good enough. By a slow intellectual process he came to realize that his anxieties about not making anything of value were an atavistic relic from the religious notion that something exists which can be called the Supreme Good, or that anything is perfect. When he'd dug up this secret idea, this relic, had seen through it and amputated it, he lost his artistic inhibitions too. I've been through something very similar. When my top-heavy religious superstructure collapsed, I also lost my inhibitions as a writer. Above all, my fear of not keeping up with the times. In _Winter Light_ I swept my house clean. Since then things have been quiet on that front."[153] Bergman confirms this point in his interview with Charles Samuels. Samuels asks: "Isn't it true that whereas you are frequently concerned with the impossibility of attaining corroboration for one's faith, in _Winter Light_ you show that the search for corroboration is itself the cause of harm?" Bergman responds, "All the time that I treated the questions of God and ultimate faith, I felt very unhappy. When I left them behind, and also abandoned my enormous desire to make the best film in the world...I became unneurotic."[154]

For Bergman to say that he had "wiped out" the religious aspect of his life is something of a hyperbole; his longing for God remains. It is that now he has admitted to himself that one must take a different tack, that one must seek a new mythology to

talk about that which is central to one's life--its
meaning.   Meaning and significance are not qualities
one can manufacture or create for oneself by fiat, yet
that is just what we have done, corporately if not
individually; we have created God in our own image.
We have taken a philosophical concept of perfection
and turned it into our notion of God, endowed it with
our wisdom and our ways, and personified Him in our
image.   Everything fits, except reality.   Tomas had
led a sheltered life, protected by circumstances,
professional insularism, mother and wife.   Tomas and
his God lived in a sequestered world, self-constructed
and "specially arranged," so that neither fear of life
nor death could penetrate.   It was an "echo-god"
ventriloquized by Tomas.   But, just as for Minus in
Through a Glass Darkly, reality burst, and Tomas
tumbled out. When this happened, Tomas found that his
world and his perfectionist God could not be held
together.   The omnipotent, omniscient, omnipresent God
would have to be the author of evil, the sustainer of
suffering, the perpetrator of death.   We faced not a
loving God but a "revolting spider god--a monster,"
whom his wife helped him to avoid. Without her, Tomas
was exposed to the world, unable to hide, forced to
admit his "indifference to the gospel message" and his
"jealous hatred of Jesus."   Tomas is the doubting
Thomas of John's gospel, indeed, with only the holes
of the crucified Jesus to look at, not those of the
resurrected Christ with which to reassure himself.

At this stage Bergman has intensified his
questioning doubt.   What if God--that omnipotent,
omniscient, omnipresent God--doesn't exist?   What a
difference that would make!   There would be no
impossible metaphysical explanations one would have to

make.   One would not have to "turn off one's mind" in
order to "understand" life or death.   Life is whatever
we   make it to be; death is simply extinction.   But
Bergman is not simply being philosophically foolish
here.   He gives Tomas' words a kind of grandiloquence
which make them fall of their own weight: "People's
cruelty,   their   loneliness,   their   fear--everything
becomes self-evident--transparent.   The stars out in
space,   worlds,   heavens,   all have given birth to
themselves and to each other.   There isn't any
creator...."   Needless to say, there is nothing
self-evident or transparent in that.   The words are
still more those of defiance than doctrine, more
freedom from than freedom to.

Bergman's declaration of freedom includes his own
Lutheran   heritage   as well as the   metaphysics of
traditional Catholicism.   He is not only free of "all
this   supernatural   helplessness"   but   also   "this
humiliating sense of sin."   For the Lutheran, life
lived in this fallen world can only be done at the
cost of sin.   The choices which the world provides me
give me no alternative but to sin.   Luther's own
famous dictum at this point is: "Sin bravely."   But
Luther is quick to add the qualifying other half of
the paradox: "...but love God more bravely yet!"
Bergman's crucified-but-not-resurrected Jesus cannot
provide such a paradox of sin and grace--judgment
exercised with forgiveness and love.   For Bergman the
sin and guilt remain.   The yardstick which measures
that sin is not Jesus' exemplary life but God's
perfection,   so that if one can get rid of the
perfectionist-god,   "this   stink   of   an   antique
godliness" as Tomas puts it, one gets rid of sin--a la
Sartre.[155]

At this point Bergman gives us the following description in script instructions: "He [Tomas] lays his arms on the table and supports his forehead on his hands. Shaken by feverish chills, he moans faintly, the sweat breaks out on his forehead and temples and on his hands. Gradually the attack subsides. He becomes quieter. When he looks up, Jonas has vanished. No footsteps, no sound of a door closing. No wind in cracks and crevices. Complete silence. He drags himself over the window. No car, no trace. Not a sound. The snow falls softly and steadily. God's silence, Christ's twisted face, the blood on the brow and hands, the soundless shriek behind the bared teeth. God's silence." Tomas then moans out Jesus' words from the cross: "God, my God, why have you abandoned me?" With that touch of genius, Bergman has made the paradox complete. We do not know, nor does Tomas, whether we are witnessing Tomas' crucifixion, for which the cry of dereliction is a necessary stage before the commitment in faith--"Father, into Thy hands....."--or whether it is a final, pathetic plea to his echo-god.

Tomas steps into chancel of the church where he slumps down to the floor, obviously feeling weak and feverish. At that moment, he is flooded by sunlight through the window, and the bars of the window, which once appeared to us as a sort of prison, disappear in the brilliance of the light. "I'm free now. At last, free." Tomas and, I believe, Bergman here have at last declared their freedom from the "metaphysical god" which had exerted such a tyrannical force over his life. At present Tomas has nothing to put in its place, and, in the film, his relationship to Marta at this point becomes critical.

Bergman himself, however, has exposed us to a more sophisticated possibility. The light that floods over him in his moment of release--his moment of truth, really--carries with it the symbol power of revelation. Of course the revelation could simply be that of self-revelation, personal integrity or authenticity, but the impression given in the film is more. It is almost as though we are present for the awareness of what the theologian Paul Tillich calls "the God above God." This is the God who appears when the metaphysical god disappears; it is the God who appears when we have stopped creating God in our own image and ceased demanding that He appear to us in some prescribed or preconceived way. I seriously doubt if Bergman has consciously worked out the theology of this, but one has the feeling that, cognizant of the mystery with which he is dealing, he will keep his options open. I am encouraged to make this claim because of the way Bergman ends the film and because of his own comments about that ending (to be quoted shortly).[156]

This ambiguity is even more evident in the text than it is in the edited film footage. In the film, Marta, who had been faithfully waiting for Tomas in the sanctuary and had witnessed his declaration of freedom, runs to him, clumsily taking his head in her hands, smothering him with kisses. She recognizes intuitively the importance of his declaration. In the text, however, the ambiguity is given specific expression. Jonas has disappeared without Tomas seeing him go. The question is now raised as to whether he has even been there a second time--maybe the encounter took place in Tomas' head--for Marta, who claims to have been there a while, also claims not

to have seen Jonas leave. With this as background, we
are not sure whether the following conversation is
about Jonas or about God. The ambiguity is obviously
intentional.

> Thomas: You haven't seen Jonas Persson?
>
> Marta: (shakes her head)
>
> Tomas: Then he won't be coming.
>
> Marta: Are you expecting him?
>
> Tomas: (his head sinking behind his
> arms--almost prayerful) I had
> just a faint--a faint hope he'd
> come--in spite of everything.
> That everything wouldn't turn
> out to be illusions, dreams,
> lies.

It would seem that the last speech would not make much
sense unless the possibility of God were intended. At
this point, the old woman arrives to announce Jonas'
death.

Tomas leaves to go to the location of the
suicide. Marta follows. After Tomas' perfunctory
actions of helpfulness to the attending civil
official--more like those of a volunteer fireman than
those of a concerned priest--all seen but not heard
against the roar of the rapids, Tomas and Marta leave
to tell Karin, the widow. On the way they stop at
Marta's home and school for some aspirin for Tomas'
flu. Here takes place that brutal encounter mentioned
in the plot summary. Robin Wood's description is as
good as there is: "The schoolroom scene is, in its
sense of human beings totally exposed to each other,
raw-nerved and vulnerable, among the most painful and
ugly in all Bergman (which is to say, in all cinema).
The analogy that comes to mind is of poisonous

secretion at last erupting from a long-covered wound. Tomas turns on Marta to destroy her because she isn't his wife, because he needs a scapegoat on whom to take out his bitter fury at the wasteful cheat of his existence, because he associates her with the breaking down of his insulating Christianity. At the same time we see the justice--justice untempered by mercy or charity--of all Tomas says."[157]

While there is some justice here, it is a rather superficial kind of justice. There is no doubt that Marta is a frumpish sort of woman, but there is a strength evident there which Bergman has let us see and on which Tomas has learned to depend. Tomas' diatribe can also be seen as bravado occasioned by anger, for when the anger has been spent, Tomas turns and asks Marta to accompany him to the vespers at Frostnas, which she agrees to do. Robin Wood believes that no motive is given for this change of heart on Tomas' part, but the motive, I think, is obvious. Though Tomas has freed himself from his echo-god, he has nothing left to take its place. Only Marta can hold his world together. I believe that this is in agreement with Bergman's own assessment of Marta: "Marta is something of the stuff saints are made of, i.e. hysterical, power-greedy, but also possessed of an inner vision...For me, Marta is something furious, alive, intractable, pig-headed, troublesome. A great and--for a dying figure like the clergyman--overwhelming person...I believe Marta constitutes the clergyman's only hope of any sort of life. For me she's a monstrosity, a primitive natural force. But the poor clergyman's on the way out."[158]

There is a theological point in all this, even though it is not the primary function of the scene. Bergman reiterates a theme here from The Magician: when man is deprived of God, he will fashion one of his own. When Tomas is deprived of his echo-god (which indeed he had fashioned), he must then fashion another if God remains silent--thus the apotheosis of Marta. When they leave the schoolhouse, Tomas gives Marta the keys to the car, and she drives the rest of the journey to Frostnas.

The stop at the Perssons' to tell Karin of Jonas' suicide is a pathetic vignette of the sterility and awkwardness of Tomas' godless ministry. By this time in the afternoon the Swedish winter light has all but faded, and we are shown Persson's house, lights shining through Bergmanian cruciform windows. Tomas, with no preparation or any real show of sympathy, tells Karin the news, but he is more intent on telling her he had done what he could than consoling her. Her response is simply: "So I'm alone then." The overtones are personal and theological, for her children are in the kitchen eating and she is pregnant with her fourth child. Tomas offers to say a prayer; Karin refuses. Her response is so immediate, followed a moment later by an apologetic smile, that we surmise her rejection is of prayer itself, not Tomas. What good is prayer? Tomas leaves, offering to be of help, but we know the two will not meet again until the funeral service itself.

Marta and Tomas resume their journey to Frostnas, Marta still driving. Forced to wait at a railroad crossing for a train to pass (whose boxcars are shaped like coffins), Tomas tells Marta that he became a parson because his father and mother wanted him to,

but he tells of this not with great anger but simply
as part of the exorcism of the echo-god which began in
the Vestry at Mittsunda. When they arrive at
Frostnas, Tomas gets out of the car but cannot bring
himself to walk into the church. Finally, Marta leads
the way, Tomas following docilely behind. Inside is
the sexton Frovik, monitoring the ringing of the
electric bells and waiting for a promised talk with
Tomas. No one is in the church. Frovik seizes on
this opportunity to ask Tomas his question, but begins
by giving us an interesting, if pathetic, insight into
Tomas' pastoral counseling:

> Frovik: Once, when I complained about
> my pains keeping me awake at
> night, you suggested I should
> read something to distract my
> thoughts.
>
> Tomas: I remember.
>
> Frovik: I began with the gospels. Real
> sleeping tablets, they were, if
> I may say so!...Now I've got as
> far as the story of Christ's
> passion. And that's given me
> something to think about. So I
> thought, I'd better have a word
> about this with Rev. Ericsson.
> Christ's passion, Vicar. It's
> incorrect to think of it as
> Christ's passion, isn't that
> so?
>
> Tomas: What do you mean?
>
> Frovik: We think too much about the
> actual torture, so to speak.
> But that can't have been so

bad. Well excue me, it sounds
a bit presumptuous, of course,
but physically, if I may say so
without being too assuming, I
must have suffered, so to
speak, at least as much as ever
Christ did. Besides which, his
torments were rather brief.
About four hours or so?

Tomas: (looks at Algot)

Frovik: I thought I saw a much greater
suffering behind the physical
one...Maybe I've got it all
wrong in some way. But think
of Gethsemane, Vicar. All his
disciples asleep. They hadn't
understood a thing, not the
last supper, nothing. And then
when the servants of the law
arrived, off they ran. And
then, Peter, who denied him.
For three years Christ had been
talking to these disciples,
Vicar, day in day out they'd
lived together. And they'd
quite simply not grasped what
he meant. Not a word. They
abandoned him the whole lot of
them. And he was left alone.
(passionately) Vicar, that
must have been a terrible
suffering! To understand that
no one has understood you. To
be abandoned when one really

                needs someone to rely on. A
                terrible suffering.

Tomas: (after   a   pause):   Yes,
                obviously.

Frovik: Well.   But   that   wasn't   the
                worst   thing,   even   so!   When
                Christ   had   been   nailed   up on
                the   cross and hung there in his
                torments, he cried out: "God,
                my God, why hast thou forsaken
                me."   He   cried out as loud as
                he possibly could. He thought
                his   Father   in   Heaven   had
                abandoned   him.   He believed
                everything he'd been preaching
                was   a   lie. The moments before
                he died, Christ was seized with
                a great doubt.   Surely that
                must   have   been   his   most
                monstrous suffering of all? I
                mean God's silence. Isn't that
                true, Vicar?

Tomas: Yes, yes.   (Nods, averting his
                face).

The dialogue is worth quoting in full, for in it
Bergman has given one possible explanation and summary
of the whole film to that point. Frovik's speech
gives Tomas the opportunity of believing that he, like
Peter, has betrayed Christ, has not understood what
Jesus was teaching or doing; and, by fleeing, is
actually participating in the crucifixion agony of
Jesus.   Tomas is guilty himself of the very thing of
which he accuses God--"To be abandoned when one really
needs someone to rely on.   A terrible suffering."

Bergman could hardly have brought a more powerful
orthodox argument against himself than this one, and
by doing so, raises the whole drama to another level
of possible interpretation. It suggests the
possibility that Tomas, like Peter, may return, may
"take up his cross and follow" rather than run away.

But Frovik's speech does not end with that; it
offers still another possibility. Because of the cry
of dereliction which Tomas made earlier we are able to
associate Tomas with Jesus himself, both having
experienced seeming abandonment by God: "Surely that
must have been his most monstrous suffering of all? I
mean God's silence. Isn't that true, Vicar?" What
can the meaning of God's ministry be in the presence
of crucifixion, of dereliction, with no hint of
resurrection? This seems to be the final question
which Bergman puts to us, but he gives no hint of
solution. He gives us only a paradox of possible
responses which will be discussed presently.

In the meantime Blom the organist has arrived and
is hovering about Marta, like some evil spirit,
caustically joking about her relationship to Tomas.
He urges her to leave while she still can, that Tomas
is washed up, a pathetic remnant of his wife's wiles:
"Listen, Marta. That's how it was with that love.
'God is love, and love is God. Love is the proof of
God's existence. Love exists as something real in the
world of men and women.' I know the jargon, as you
can hear. I've been an attentive listener to the
vicar's outpourings--'Bye--(laughs) you old
turtledove.'" Again the brilliant paradox from
Bergman. Here the coda from Through a Glass Darkly is
quoted directly and smashed to smithereens by the
unctuous presence and evil intent of Blom; yet, just

because it _is_ from Blom, the effectiveness and authenticity of the "smashing" are brought in question.

The service bell has begun to toll, but still no one has come for the service. Marta bows her head (Bergman giving her a naturally-lighted, madonna-like profile) and prayerfully says, "If only we were sure...If only we believed..." But, by the time Marta has uttered the second of these two phrases, the camera has shifted to Tomas in the vestry (Bergman giving him an artificially front-lighted profile) also in the physical attitude of prayer but with his fist clenched. Again the paradox: the communion of mind and desire but the separation of selves. At this point Frovik enters the vestry and asks if the service will be held. Tomas replies, "Yes." Frovik throws on the light switches, the organist with disgust begins his prelude. We see Tomas in close-up, his face drained of emotion, his eyes fixed on the nowhere of middle-distance, begin the service with the same words we first heard at Mittsunda: "Holy, holy, holy is the Lord God Almighty.." And as the camera withdraws from the interior of the sanctuary so that we get the Frostnas church itself in the middle-distance of a cold, dark Swedish winter twilight, we hear the words: "Heaven and earth are full of thy glory."

With such an enigmatic ending, filled with paradoxes, there are many interpretations of the film that have been suggested. John Simon, whose study of _Winter_ _Light_ is without doubt the most detailed and complete, finds that there are essentially three ways of interpreting the film: Christian, nihilist, and existentialist.[159] While I am in agreement with much of Simon's critical judgment and believe that he

is faithful to Bergman's intent, I find it necessary
to modify his categories. Existentialism, as noted
earlier, is not a philosophical system in itself; it
is a _way_ of thinking, a way of _doing_ philosophy or
theology. Consequently I would say that there are
four, not three, ways of classifying the response to
Winter Light: existential orthodoxy (Arthur Gibson),
existential nihilism (Raymond Lefevre, Stanley
Kauffmann), existential humanism (Robin Wood), and
existential agnosticism (John Simon--though not so
self-designated--and myself). We shall examine each
of these in turn.

John Simon states: "The Christian view would be
that Pastor Ericsson, having gone through a series of
trying experiences, finally realizes that even Christ
had to endure his doubts and despondency; fortified by
Christ's example, he regains confidence and true
faith, and proclaims God's glory and
omnipresence."[160] This might be part of a
generalized orthodox position (were there such a
thing), but it would only be the response part. In an
orthodox view, Tomas' actions would be his response,
with penitence and joy, to some prior act of grace in
which God had revealed Himself to Tomas. But we know
that such is not the case. Orthodoxy, in fact, would
be repelled by Bergman's ending, pitying Tomas, not
praising him. But Gibson's view, which Simon has
classified as Christian, is really existential
orthodoxy. Gibson is quite harsh with the traditional
orthodoxy: "The silence of God hangs heavy over
Winter Light....The lesson of Calvary is not
unidimensional. To the truth that free rebellious man
must ultimately crucify his God, there answers, as
deep to deep, the God-truth that a free God, a

freedom-loving God, can show his free human creature
how to find salvation only by Himself going the whole
way with that creature. Algot's evocation of Christ's
agony is a startling revelation of an insight more
traditional theists would grasp if only they would
leave off their cramped pusillanimous Monophysitic
geometricization in their mistaken apologetic for
God: the free incarnate God must show man the road to
salvation by himself tasting of man's worst and most
horrifying doubt, atheism."161

What God shows us, says Gibson, is the
crucifixion--a "staggering truth" to those who have
the eyes to see. "This truth is that the
multi-dimensional silence of God can close not only
over man but over the incarnate God himself; and that
in light of his dereliction man is no longer alone,
for his most intimate fear has been taken up and
transformed and transfigured by openhearted love into
boundless trust. Here is the ultimate answer to the
silence of God, the only answer that is redemptive and
adequate to God's challenge. For that silence, in the
mystery of freedom, impenetrable to mortal eyes, is
itself a supreme act of willing trust in freedom, in
free creatures; and those creatures must rise to
justify the magnanimity of their Creator. As they
abandoned him in pride, so they must find him in
humility with their freedom intact and their spurs won
by pain."162

For Gibson the climax of the film comes at the
very end when Tomas, identifying with Christ, begins
the Eucharist again: "'Christ's twisted face, the
blood on the brow and hands, the soundless shriek
behind the bared teeth.' The challenge is clear: it
is not the simple challenge of mere passive acceptance

of this suffering Savior; not even the mere demand for
penance and reparation.   Man, epitomized by Tomas,
must become as that Christ. Shouldering the burden of
created freedom and responding to the call of the
transforming God, man must mount the cross and himself
proclaim that God is holy in all his ways....Tomas,
who cannot yet say yes to Marta, whom he has seen,
seems for a trembling instant able and ready to say
yes to God, whom he has not seen."[163]

Though a possible interpretation of the film, it
appears to me more like one imposed upon the film
rather than emerging from the film itself or the
sequence of films of which this is an integral part.
Simon's criticism of Gibson's position is right on the
mark, and I see no reason for not quoting him with
approbation: "Nowhere in Winter Light are silence and
love, or silence and freedom, equated; there is no
sense of trust or love coming from anything but
communication.   When Marta and Tomas fight, words,
even wounding words, seem to bring them close
together.   It is by telling him something that Frovik
reaches Tomas and becomes, in Bergman's word, an
angel.   A self-made wall of silence dooms Jonas. And
I cannot see how Tomas's preaching in an empty church,
or the expression on his face in the last frame, could
possibly suggest anything so joyous as fully renewed
faith.   Furthermore, there is Bergman's subsequent
output to consider..."[164]

Existential nihilism is the second possible
interpretation.   Raymond Lefevre, whom Simon cites as
an example here, believes that by the end of the film
Tomas "'plays his role with application. Like an
artist who no longer believes in his art. Like a
lover who caresses the woman he no longer

loves.'"[165]   Stanley   Kauffmann is quoted, supporting
a similar position: "'The crisis is all the worse
because it is a continuing one; nothing changes.
[Tomas'] confession of spiritual vacuity does not
alter his priesthood; he continues. Bergman seems to
be saying that life was once lived in expectation of
answers, now it is lived in continuity of questions.
Crisis no longer leads to resolution.'"[166] Simon
remarks that a cynical nihilist might decide to
continue his role as priest, but "he would surely not
feel compelled to continue to the extent of conducting
services to empty churches, or for the benefit of his
unbelieving mistress. And, again, the expression and
intonation with which that consummate actor Gunnar
Bjornstrand delivers Tomas's last words are not those
of a man to whom everything has become indifferent.
It seems to me that Bergman himself is Tomas, and that
in this work the filmmaker is dramatizing the moment
of his own loss of faith, without having as yet
evolved the anti-God attitude of a later film like
Shame, or the completely God-less world of A Passion.
Hence the aphoria with which the film ends: an open
ending, meant to raise further questioning and doubt
rather than provide hard answers."[167]

    Existential humanism is the third interpretation
which has been offered by critics. They have rightly
discerned that Tomas has freed himself from his
echo-god while at the same time retaining his
relationship to Marta.   In such a case the Christian
myth may provide the signs of communication used, but
the signs are no longer symbols. Robin Wood seems to
favor this interpretation: Winter Light has "an
ending of uncompromising honesty, its complex impulses
and uncertainties evolving inevitably out of what has

gone before. Tomas, for all his 'flu and misery,' has
an awakening if very tentative sense of fresh
potentialities: whether they are Christian or atheist
it is impossible to say. Certainly they are bound up
with Marta and all that has passed between them. He
holds the service at the end for her, and for himself;
the irony is very beautiful and touching, the
disillusioned priest celebrating Vespers for the
confirmed atheist, as a sort of inexplicit communion
between them, using the traditional forms, which are
all he knows, to express something not necessarily
related to any orthodox Christianity."168

John Simon may fall into this category of
interpretation as well, yet he includes enough
religious insight to lead into the last
classification: existential agnosticism. Simon
labels his interpretation as simply "existential."
"We have seen how, in their various ways, Marta,
Jonas, Algot (perhaps even Karin, by her patient
endurance) become Christ figures, as does, in his
sense of abandonment, Tomas himself. In Algot's
sermon to the vicar--for it is hardly counseling that
Algot seeks; at the utmost, confirmation--Christ is
revealed as yet another suffering human being. And,
indeed, for all their Christlike features, Marta,
Jonas, Karin, and Algot are much more secular than
religious figures: Marta is a nonbeliever, Jonas a
suicide, Karin refuses all religious help, and Algot
has the presumption to set his physical sufferings
above Christ's and to reinterpret Christ's passion.
And if we are all Christs, Christ is a symbol for
something in us, just as God's silence is really a
metaphor for the winter light that prevails around and
inside us."169 Much of what Simon writes I can

agree with, and I believe that Bergman would, too.
But, I think he moves too quickly into the humanist
interpretation, both in terms of his understanding of
the symbols that are used and the development of the
plot itself. I think that Bergman does intend for us
to come to the conclusion that we are all like Jesus
in our suffering, our crucifixion. To say with Simon
that we are all "Christs" implies a messianic claim
that is not intended here (there is surely no
incarnation or resurrection implied by Bergman).
Likewise, I do not see why Algot's understanding of
the Passion constitutes a reinterpretation of the
gospel. The feeling of abandonment, the cry of
dereliction, is at the very heart of the Christian
doctrine of the Incarnation, the creedal affirmation
that "Very God of very God...was made man: and was
crucified...." Orthodoxy's claim is that an absolute
paradox is symbolized by the title "Jesus the Christ;"
he is all man and all God, simultaneously and
unconfusedly. That stands as an affirmation of faith
not a rational determination. It may be true that
this affirmation has become meaningless to Tomas at
the moment, but that does not mean that he has
abandoned its possible validity; at present he simply
does not know.

One must likewise be careful not to be trapped by
Simon's logic about our identification with Christ,
which reduces Christ to some innate, human quality or
essence. Simon states, above, that "if we are all
Christs, Christ is a symbol for something in us."
That, of course, is not necessarily the case.
Orthodoxy's claim has always been that we live in a
fallen world, that the condition is universal, and
that Christ has come to be identified with us. Thus,

what we share with Him is not His essential nature but
His experience of this mundane world, this finite
existence that ends in death. For the present, it
seems to me that this is as far as Tomas can go.
Tomas sees the suffering and death; he does not see
the resurrection and life. But, he has not reached
the point where he is willing to make an absolute
denial of the traditional claims. He is waiting,
waiting for the initiative of God which alone can
confirm the claim of faith.

It is for this reason that I have termed the last
of Winter Light's interpretations as "existential
agnosticism." Tomas, at this point simply doesn't
know. He has rejected the philosophical proofs of
God's existence; he does not know himself as one of
the elect; he is unable to say with Luther "sola
fide"--by faith alone. So Tomas waits. I believe
that this is what Bergman had in mind when he said to
John Simon: "You know, I was still convinced that God
was somewhere inside the human being, that he had some
answer to give us, and the end of the picture was
exactly that. You have to continue; if God is silent
you still have to go on with your work, the service,
without believing anything. Suddenly, one day, God
answers, but it's your duty to go on."[170] We are
given further insight on this through a response of
Bergman's to a question by Jonas Sima: "In some way I
feel the end of the play was influenced by my father's
intervention[171]--that at all costs one must do what
it is one's duty to do, particularly in spiritual
contexts. Even if it can seem meaningless."[172]

Bergman, in good Lutheran style, presents this
understanding of Tomas' position of waiting as a
paradox. As Tomas begins the vesper ritual, we are

aware that he is surrounded by artificial light and minimal candlelight. As opposed to Mittsunda which we saw in natural light and candlelight, the harshness of electric lights at Frostnas reminds us of the artificial, cold, and controlled context we are now in. But in contrast to that, the crucifix between the knees of God is not a part of the triptych of Frostnas. Here the center panel portrays the Virgin and child, the symbol of birth and rebirth, of renewal and grace, of acceptance and love; the side panels seem to portray the saints and members of the early Church who are gazing out at us, their expressions saying: "What think ye of this?" At this point Bergman seems to be saying, "I just don't know."

If we can accept this interpretation, it goes a long way in answering Jorn Donner's criticism of Winter Light. Donner states: "Of its kind, Winter Light is the most impressive film B has created. One may also, however, view it from a critical perspective, with respect to both the style and the perceived meaning. The movement of the film, the individual compositions, the essence of its cinematography are the result of great and loving care. But in its narrative style there is a touch of calculation, which prevents the spectator from being surprised. One often meets exactly the images and the attitudes one has been expecting. The spontaneous movement is gone, and has been replaced by a masterly asceticism, which also can become academic. Winter Light may appear too evenly gray in its character."[173]

What better way than "evenly gray" could Bergman present the spiritual dilemma he now finds himself in. The frustration of not-knowing, not-deciding, not-loving is all there in the gray winter light. This impression is heightened by the Protestant cast that Bergman has given the film. The Early Church, in the Donatist Controversy, averred that the state or belief of the priest can in no way affect the efficacy of the sacrament at which he officiates. Man cannot interfere with or disrupt the act of God. There is a tendency in Protestantism to connect the efficacy of the sacrament with the character of the administering clergy. In Frostnas the church is empty, as the organist Blom tells us, because Tomas has nothing to give. Donner makes a similar observation about Bergman's statements on love. "Exactly the same words which the father uses to his son in Through a Glass Darkly, Pastor Ericsson is said to have used in his sermons: 'God is love, and love is God. Love is the proof of God's existence. Love is found as something real in man's world.' These words, applied to the father-pastor, achieve a strangely ironic meaning, since neither of these persons seems to live up to his gospel. The doctrine is helpless and crippled, because the proclaimers of the doctrines are themselves weak."[174]

At the end of this second film of Bergman's trilogy, we are in a position best described by Martin Heidegger's philosophy. It is "neither atheism or theism, but a description of the world from which God is absent. It is now the night of the world...the god has withdrawn himself, and the sun sets below the horizon. And meanwhile the thinker can only redeem the time by seeking to understand what is at once nearest and farthest from man: his own being and Being itself."[175]

The Silence (1963)

"To be abandoned when one really needs
someone to rely on. A terrible suffering."

Winter Light

One of life's experiences for which existentialism
gives us a new vocabulary (and a new insight) is that
often described in terms of loss, abandonment, the
ambiguity of limitation, or even fate. Existentialism
reminds us--warns us--that there is a cost to every
genuinely new and creative venture. When we choose to
govern our lives by that personal freedom which marks
and *is* our authentic being, we necessarily sacrifice
the security and comfort of our previous understanding
or position. At the same time, we create new tensions
and fears for ourselves. It is at this point that we
find ourselves in Bergman's spiritual journey.

With Winter Light the traditional and comfortable
universe governed by a wise and good God has
disappeared.   The classical metaphysical supports
which enabled us to connect each event with every
other event, which enabled us to see "eternity in a
grain of sand," have collapsed. The leap of faith,
predicated on the misunderstood promise that "all
things work together for good with those who love
God," has proved to be a sentimental journey into the
labyrinthine halls of our own mind, leading to only an
echo-god.   We are left with Nothing, deprived of God,
and sealed off from others by the encirclement of our
own egos.   God is silent, and Tomas, alone and lost,
waits.

In his study of the film Winter Light, John Simon
states that at one point, in Private Screenings, he
quoted the Swedish poet Gunnar Ekelof to characterize
the film's ending: "'It is its meaninglessness that
gives life its meaning.'"[176] Simon could have been
quoting the theologian Paul Tillich's The Courage to
Be. No matter; Simon now believes that that is too
bleak a view. Yet before dismissing it, I think it
deserves a second look. Most critics have rejected
this aphorism in its theological set because it is a
crypto-use of the classical ontological proof of the
existence of God, posing as an existential or
phenomenological insight. The rejection applies if we
are simply claiming, by using this argument, that we
can't even understand the term "meaninglessness"
except from the vantage point of meaning; or, as
Tillich would argue, meaning is always logically prior
to meaninglessness or Being logically prior to
Non-Being. Here one has really employed a traditional
Idealist argument; proof of God is but a step or two
away. However, to use the term "meaninglessness" in
such a way is to deprive it of its existential
orientation, its phenomenological descriptive power.
For Idealism it is a game for the brain rather than
the gut-experience of angst.

But if the term "meaninglessness" is used in an
existential way, then Ekelof's aphorism holds pretty
true, for this existential angst is not a totally
negative experience. "Nothingness" or "void" is my
terror, but it is also my opportunity. The experience
is a paradox--the same paradox reflected in Sartre's
famous dictum: we are "condemned to be free,"
"condemned," here, does not refer to an act of divine
intervention but simply an existential condition. The

meaninglessness of my existence is the facilitating
condition of my ability to create, to choose. That is
the hope we are given at the end of Winter Light,
meager as it may seem. Though one cannot say that
Tomas has consciously recognized such a hope by the
end of the film, it is obvious that Bergman has by the
beginning of his next film, The Silence. The film is
not entitled "God's Silence" but The Silence; God is,
as Robin Wood observes, "not so much silent as
completely absent."[177]   At this point in Bergman's
journey the "waiting" of Winter Light seems to be
over, or it has at least been abandoned as a useless
ploy. In the face of The silence, nothing is left for
one to do but to begin to make one's own noise.

Much more cryptically, Bergman has said the same
thing about The Silence: "At the film's bottommost
layer lay the collapse of an ideology and a way of
life. I remember writing down something I was
tremendously pleased with, though of course it's
nothing remarkable in itself. I wrote that life only
has as much meaning and importance as one attributes
to it oneself. There's nothing remarkable about
that. But for me it was like a mining concession,
full of potential wealth."[178] .But his film is less
sanguine than his interview. In The Silence the
terror of Nothingness, of Death, is never very far
away both physically and psychically; spiritually such
terror has arrived, i.e. what is "religious" in this
stage for Bergman is the self-conscious awareness of
the inevitability of choice without external
guidelines or values. Choices are matters of ultimate
concern. Bergman never lets us forget that we are not
in some sylvan idyll picking beautiful bouquets of
fragrant flowers; man's existence is absurd in the

midst of a cosmos where he is a stranger. The only
meaning that man can have is that which he gives
himself, that which he creates for himself out of his
nothingness and under the sentence of death.

To say that Bergman's concerns are "religious" at
this point is not to say that they are Christian. For
the moment that is in abeyance. Bergman is convinced
at this point that Christianity, at least as it is
popularly understood, raises more problems than it
solves. Therefore, because it is a source of neurosis
rather than a cure, the sooner we abandon its premises
the better--as this exchange with Jonas Sima confirms:

> JS: May I ask, was it after The
> Silence you became agnostic?
>
> IB: What do you mean by agnostic?
>
> JS: Well, an agnostic, I suppose, is
> someone who, after struggling with
> a group of problems, just drops
> them. Since he has found no
> answer to them, he simply drops
> them.
>
> IB: One might say the problem
> dissolves. Anyway the crux of the
> matter is--the problem doesn't
> exist any more. Nothing,
> absolutely nothing at all has
> emerged out of all these ideas of
> faith and scepticism, all these
> convulsions, these puffings and
> blowings. For many of my fellow
> human beings on the other hand,
> I'm aware that these problems
> still exist--and exist as a
> terrible reality. I hope this

> generation will be the last to
> live   under   the   scourge   of
> religious anxiety.[179]

It is my judgment that Bergman is using the phrase "religious anxiety" as one synonymous with "Christian anxiety." But "anxiety," as used in the existential analysis of this study, has a religious origin, i.e. it is that which is characterized by ultimate concern. Jorn Donner, I believe, is aware of this distinction: "Swedish critics have also...tried to interpret The Silence as a Christian film--because, forsooth! it deals with the absence of God. But nowhere does one seem to discover among the persons in the film motives of action which have anything to do with Christian questions. B goes back once more to the struggle for authority which is so central to his films. Now he has finally given up the use of Christian symbolism....[180]

Donner's statement concerning authority is too simplistic, and his dismissal of Christian symbolism is a bit premature; Christian symbols do keep recurring in Bergman's films, and even in The Silence a few symbols of negative intent do occur. But, one has to approve of the general sense of Donner's observations: the symbols are incidental. The power of the film comes from its starkness, its authenticity in angst, its graphic portrayal of the human predicament.

Before taking a critical look at the film itself, a warning of Robin Wood's, substantiating the above, is very much in order: "The Silence is one of the most difficult films to feel one's way to the heart of; to do so requires an act of courage that testifies to the extraordinary courage of the man who made it. One watches the film almost emotionlessly, as if

paralyzed, and comes out feeling that one has
experienced very little. Then hours, or even days,
later, one comes to realize how deep and disturbing
the experience has been; or one finds ways of
insulating oneself--it's a 'sick' film, its piling on
of miseries and perversions is ridiculous, one was
really laughing at it all the time; or, alternatively,
it's too obscure to be accessible, it doesn't
'communicate'. And in the latter case one goes on to
talk of symbols....There is nothing in The Silence
that cannot be explained 'naturalistically', in the
generally accepted dramatic-cinematic use of the word,
and the film is not particularly obscure. I am not
sure that attempts to allegorize The Silence are not
also rooted in a subconscious desire to distance and
perhaps reduce it--to resist the idea that the
characters on the screen are direct reflections of
ourselves."[181]   Two of Wood's points--Bergman's
courage and an interviewer's insulation--are apparent
in an exchange Charles Samuels has with a gracious
Bergman: Bergman: "The Silence? I think it is about
the complete breakdown of illusions...It's very
difficult to tell you....It's about my private
life...It's an extremely personal picture." Samuels:
"Which is why it doesn't communicate." Bergman: "I
think that's true. It is a sort of personal
purgation: a rendering of hell on earth--my hell.
The picture is so....It is so strange to me that I do
not know what it means."[182] Risking presumption in
the face of that demur, we must now consider the film
itself.

For purposes of analysis, a plot summary is
necessary, but, in this case it does raise some
interesting critical problems. A simple narrative

account of the action may actually be misleading,
because what one is describing is not so much an
action as a mood. Carol Brightman, in her discussion
of the film, is adamant on this point: "The Silence
makes sense not according to what happens, but to how
it happens.   The plot synopsis is irrelevant because
the film is not "about" a plot, but about certain
emotions, about character.   Events serve to provoke
characters to certain quintessential routines through
which we see their existences circumscribed."[183]

Nevertheless, for clarity if not for profundity,
the storyline must be related.   Two homeward bound
sisters, Ester and Anna, along with Anna's
ten-year-old son, Johan, are traveling by train
"somewhere" in Europe.   Because of Ester's serious
illness, the journey is broken in a garrison city,
Timoka, whose occupants speak a language neither
sister knows. While Ester rests at the deserted, once
opulent hotel with her nephew, Anna goes to a local
bar, picks up a waiter with whom she has sex, and
arranges for an assignation that evening at the
hotel.   Upon Anna's furtive return, the first liaison
is begrudgingly related to a prying, jealous Ester.
The second meeting is observed by Johan who tells
Ester.   Ester tries to intervene, but Anna uses the
occasion to humiliate her, to spite her obvious
lesbian attraction to Anna. Anna and Johan leave the
hotel and continue their journey home; Ester, too sick
to travel, remains behind, alone, perhaps to die.

With this information, one can now appreciate
Carol Brightman's summary in mood: "Should the film
begin anywhere else but in the clammy heat of the
train compartment, where again it ends, the whole
would collapse.   We would lose the thematic unity

which seals the three lives in an inescapable vise at each end: from their emergence out of a mutually debilitating past into a foreign city, to the return of the two back to the same past, without future, by the same route, while the third surrenders to an actual death, locked in the middling labyrinth of the strange hotel."[184] Though I think one has to quarrel with the complete pessimism of this summary, its mood of isolation, disease, despair, and death is correct enough.

The Silence is, like the first two films of the trilogy, a "chamber play." The time represented is just over one full day, and we are concerned with three character's forced interaction, each tormented by the claustrophobic nature of his own existence, each pathetically dependent upon the approval and acceptance of another, which never seems forthcoming. In setting, plot, and mood, The Silence is very like Sartre's No Exit, and, knowing Bergman's admiration for Sartre, it may well have been a suggestive model. In No Exit, three people are consigned to a "Second Empire" drawing room in hell. Each finds it impossible to "live" without the approval or appropriate response of another, but that is just what each is denied. Their relationship is a vicious circle from which there is no exit. "Hell," states Sartre, "is other people." So it would seem, too, in The Silence; Bergman has brought us a distance from the facile formula: "Love is God; God is love" of Through a Glass Darkly.

The Bergman-Nykvist images of Anna and Ester are so artfully done, so superbly particular, that most of us can identify with one or the other, or both, of these women, even though Bergman seems to have

developed them as polar images. Keeping Robin Wood's
admonition about protective distancing in mind, it
will be helpful to note some of these polarities.
Ester's manner is tight, Anna's is easy; Ester's dress
and grooming is fastidious, Anna's is casual and
provocative; Ester is sophisticated, Anna provincial;
Ester is intellectual, Anna is sensuous; Ester is
dutiful, Anna rebellious; Ester is fair, Anna dark,
Ester is cool, Anna sultry; Ester is a lesbian, Anna a
nymphomaniac. There may well be endless other
polarities not mentioned, but the portraits do become
clear and distinct.

However, we must avoid transforming each woman
into a mere symbol as Vernon Young has done: "The
sisters are respectively Mind and Body."[185] Ester's
concern about her own sexuality, Anna's concern that
she achieve respect in the eyes of her sister, their
common affection for Johan, and their mutual love/hate
relation belie such caricature designations. The
women, as individual people, are believable; each, as
a character, can stand alone--neither is simply the
personification of a symbol. However, Bergman wants
us to see that neither is a fulfilled human being.
Each needs the sympathy and understanding of the
other; each needs the approval of the other.

The one thing which can provide a basis for the
communication of these needs is the one thing that is
now missing--or may be impossible--love. If we are
following Sartre's insights here, that kind of love
implied above, agape love--the compassionate love of
the New Testament--does not exist. For Sartre, love,
particularly sexual love, is a powerful confrontation
of sado-masochistic dimensions. Each of us wishes to
possess the beloved, yet because each can never

possess that freedom of self-expression which is the
other, we turn that other into an object in order to
possess it.   Consequently, love is condemned to the
continuous tension occasioned by sadism and masochism,
their expression and interaction. As a sadist, I try
to reduce the other's life to an expression of my
desire or whim; as a masochist, I offer myself to
another in order to entrap him or her. Such is the
dilemma of Bergman's characters in The Silence.

With the I-Thou relationship--the compassionate
love of agape--denied, Bergman explores the
possibility of sex itself as the ground for
communication or relationship, but this, too, proves
to be inadequate.   Bergman seems to be saying that
there is nothing wrong with sex, per se, but that the
personal context is as important as the physical
experience.   In talking with Samuels about The
Silence, Bergman said: "This is hell--perversion of
sex.   When sex is completely totally isolated from
other parts of life and all the emotions, it produces
an enormous loneliness. That is what the film is all
about: The degradation of sex."[186]   When The
Silence appeared, Bergman was accused by some critics
of being anti-sex, but this he denies: "My ceaseless
fascination with the whole race of women is one of my
main-springs.   Obviously, such an obsession implies
ambivalence; it has something compulsive about it.
But that I've any anti-sexual traits--that's a label I
find it very hard to accept."[187]   Those who have
seen Bergman's prior and subsequent films would have
to agree with him; something more is going on in
Bergman's films than the sheer rejection of sex.

I think a parallel can be drawn, here, with Bergman's attitude toward religion, Christianity in particular: one can no more experience love and its meaningful relationship by going through the physical ritual of love than one can have a genuine religious experience by participating in the public and physical rituals of the Church. Ester, whose rejection by Anna, leads her self-indulgently to masturbate for sexual release, finds herself humiliated by it all. It has all become a matter of "erectal tissue and secretions...I think semen smells nasty. You see, I've a sensitive nose. I found I stank like a rotten fish after being fertilized...Well, it's optional." Of course, what we know and what we have seen is that it is not optional unless it is functioning on the superficial level of Kierkegaard's aesthetic stage, i.e. as an instance of auto-eroticism rather than an existential claim of personal authenticity.

Anna's heterosexual predicament is no better. On the first occasion that she leaves the hotel, she stops in a local theater where she witnesses a couple copulating in the darkened balcony where she has been seated. On stage for "entertainment" dwarfs are going through acts usually associated with trained dogs. The animalistic, primitive relations are gross but engrossing, repulsive but powerful. Robin Wood's description is excellent: "The lovers and the dwarfs are both presented as grotesque spectacles, with an effect of degradation; but the differences are at least as important as the resemblances. The dwarfs are performing for money; society has reduced them to prostituting themselves and exploiting their own deformities. The lovers, on the other hand, are performing not _for_ an audience but despite it; they

look up briefly at Anna, as she is shown to her seat,
as an intruder, and then lose all awareness of her.
The dwarfs on the stage are reduced to the status of a
mechanical toy; what Bergman emphasizes in the lovers
is their total abandonment, so that they are aware of
their environment only as a set of minor incidental
obstacles insignificant in relation to the
overwhelming force of their immediate need. What is
important in the scene is not that we are shown
copulation, but how it is presented. Leaving aside
depictions of rape, has any director shown sheerly
physical desire and ecstasy so powerfully on the
screen?...The awkwardness of the bodies on the seats,
the force and brutality of the movements with which
the couple handle each other; beside this, almost all
other cinematic love-making tends to look too
aesthetically beautiful. By reducing human
love-making to its basis in brute desire among such
surroundings, Bergman isn't expressing disgust but
insisting on man's divided nature: on the continuing
and unassimilated power of basic drives after
centuries of civilization...If it evokes horror in the
spectator, through his civilized sense of love-making
becoming a public display in squalid surroundings, it
equally evokes a powerful erotic response...The
presence of the dwarfs in the scene brings closer to
explicitness the sense of the messy and accidental
nature of man's evolution, the radically un-Christian
sense of human existence as a weird anomaly, that
underlies the whole film."[188]

It is this scene where sheer physical passion has
been substituted for tenderness and compassion, where
the couple is genitally coupled but facially, i.e.
personally, distant. It excites Anna sexually and

prepares us for the brutalities of her relationship
with the waiter she subsequently picks up. After
their first sexual indulgence at the hotel (which we
are spared) we see Anna stroking the waiter's bare
back, her fingers tracing what appear to be long
scratch marks: "How nice," she states. "How nice it
is we don't understand each other." Sex, rather than
being the medium of relation, has become the
indifferent means of emotional self-gratification.

The polar self-indulgences of Ester and Anna are
the most powerful and explicit examples of the abuse
of sex and the absence of love the film portrays; but
in order that the mood is not compromised and the
power of the message muted, the perversion of sex
exploited is evident in the other relationships
present or implied in the film. The relationship
between Ester and her father was apparently
incestuous, as are the overtones of Anna's
relationship to her son, Johan,--to the extent that he
finds it difficult to relate physically to Ester
without a sense of betrayal of his mother. Because
Anna exploits this power over Johan to control his
behavior, he becomes the ready victim of betrayal and
jealousy when he sees his mother and the waiter kiss
passionately in the hall before they disappear into
the hotel room together. Johan's relationship to the
dwarfs, who happen to live in the same hotel, is
potentially violent and destructive. Johan is lured
into the dwarfs' apartment for the ostensible reason
of fun and games; but, as adults watching the film, we
strongly feel the overtones of potential rape as the
dwarfs dress Johan as a girl. Johan's relationship
with the old porter of the hotel is also a potentially
homosexual one, the old man luring the boy to his room

with a candy bar (after Bergman has shown us the porter symbolically "castrating" a wiener wrapped in a lettuce leaf, a pantomimic act to amuse the boy). The art displayed in the hotel also relates sex and violence. A great lighted painting in the hotel hall, after the style of the seventeenth century painter Rubens, depicts a corpulent, nude woman about to be abducted and raped by a satyr. Even outside the hotel, the violent sexual symbols persist. In a city seemingly populated only by men, we are given shots of an army tank pushing its way through narrow streets, its cannon protruding like a great phallus, while inside the hotel we have just seen Anna keep her liaison with the waiter. In each and every case, sex is perverted or exploited, the unleashing of destructive forces within us that we seemingly can't control.

This becomes an important insight for Bergman. It is not sex that is bad, it is the great, primitive, natural forces that seem to be at work within and without us, ravaging us, exploiting our potentially positive relationships with others by turning them into grotesque acts of self-gratification. After Ester has confessed to the uncomprehending porter her disgust at heterosexuality, she then says: "We try them out, one attitude after another, and find them all meaningless. The powers are too strong for us, I mean the monstrous powers. You have to take care, moving among ghosts and memories. Let me tell you!....I'm babbling. Anyway, it's something to die." Carol Brightman sees these forces as identified with the body: "From the intellectual pride (a pride, as well, in the appurtenances of intellect) which we observe manifested so coolly before the typewriter, we can deduce a long history of such 'attitudes' desperately assumed--but none the less authentic for that--to withstand the invasion of irrational forces which will fracture not only the attitudes but the human will-to-assume itself. The 'forces'--incestuous attraction for father, then sister, finally for self--achieve their proper magnitude as the shriek of flesh, once repressed, or exiled by disjunctive demands of intellect, becomes intolerably mean and animalistic. The forces of the body, finally, its 'secretions and excretions,' prove too strong for the assumptions of the will."[189]

Bergman's intent, I believe, is larger than Carol Brightman's interpretation. It is not that physical passion is not sometimes stronger than rational intention; it is that Bergman, through Ester, ties these "monstrous forces" finally to death and destruction. These seem to be the "inevitables" we face in the living out of our lives--what we cannot ever escape. Consequently, they take on the characteristics of ultimacy which brings us very close to our definition of "the religious" in life. Though Bergman does not make that specific identification, he most definitely understands the "forces" in those terms: "If you have a faith, if you've some deep conviction, whether you're a Nazi or a Communist or what the hell else you are--then you can sacrifice both yourself and others to your faith. But the moment you've no faith--from that moment you live in a deep inner confusion--from then on you're exposed to what Strindberg calls "the powers.'"[190]

This transcendent reference to the "powers" is made in the film by the symbol of the spider, the mark of the echo-god, the grotesque and the monstrous,

which has been present in each of the trilogy films.
For Bergman it has become the mark of death, and it
appears in this and every subsequent film. In The
Silence its symbol forms the front of the fan, turning
as an ever-vigilant monster presiding over the
death-throes of Ester.   Without God, without faith,
without love, the "monstrous powers" prey on us with
fear, and we suffer the suffocation of isolation:
"No, no, no!" whispers Ester, "I don't want to die
like that, no, no! I don't want to stifle. Oh, it
was horrible!   I'm frightened now. It frightened me
that time.   It mustn't come back. No, no! After all
I can't..."

Anna's fate is little different--psychic rather
than physical.   Her defiance of her sister and her
sexual self-indulgence have alienated both Ester and
Johan.   Our last view of Anna is in a train
compartment with Johan.   To relieve the oppressive
heat, she opens the train window to let the rain
strike her face, but when she withdraws her head, it
is obvious to us that the rain has been of no physical
or sacramental help. She finally knows herself to be
alone; Johan views her with contempt. The "powers"
have claimed another victim.

This ability of the "monstrous forces" to destroy
human relationships is one of the things that disturbs
Bergman the most.   What they breed is hatred, not
love.   When Ester discovers Anna and her waiter in
another room of the hotel, this exchange takes place:

    Ester: Why've you got to revenge
            yourself all the time?
    Anna: (silent)
    Ester: When Father was alive...

Anna: When Father was alive he decided things. And we obeyed him. Because we had to. When Father died you thought you could carry on in the same way. And went on about your principles, how meaningful everything was, how important! But it was just a lot of poppycock. D'you know why? I'll tell you why. It was all in aid of your self-importance. You can't live without your sense of your own importance. And that's the truth of it. You can't bear it if everything isn't a "matter of life and death" and "significant" and "meaningful" and I don't know what else.

Ester: How do you want us to live, then? After all, we own everything in common.

Anna: I always thought you were right. And tried to be like you. And I admired you. I didn't realize you disliked me.

Ester: It's not true.

Anna: You dislike me. And always have. Though it's only now I've realized it.

Ester: No.

Anna: Yes! In some way I can't understand, you're scared of me.

Ester: I'm not scared, Anna. I love
       you.

Anna: (scorn) You're always talking
       about love.

Ester: You mustn't say...

Anna: What mustn't I say? That Ester
       hates. That's just a silly
       invention of silly Anna. You
       hate me, just like you hate
       yourself. And me. And
       everything that's mine. You're
       full of hate.

Ester: You've got it all wrong.

Anna: You who're so intelligent,
       who've taken so many exams and
       translated so many books, can
       you answer me just one thing?
       When Father died you said: "Now
       I don't want to live any
       longer." Well, why do you live
       then?

Ester: (doesn't reply)

Anna: For my sake? For Johan? For
       your work, perhaps? Or for
       nothing in particular?

       A long silence.

This is a very remarkable passage for a number of
reasons. First of all, it gives further evidence of
Bergman's break with the traditional (classical)
metaphysical past which by definition gave superiority
to mind over body. Plato's image of the charioteer
(mind or soul) holding the reigns of his spirited
horses (the passions and appetites) is no longer
acceptable--not because passions and appetites have

won   the day but because we can no longer accept such a
definition   of   humankind.   Contemporary psychology
simply   dismisses any such primitive bifurcation of our
nature,   as   does existentialism. It is interesting to
observe   an   audience   seeing   this scene for the first
time.   Despite other and prior reactions to Anna, not
all   laudatory,   this exchange gets full approval. The
impression   is: here's someone who is "telling it like
it   is."   My   emotions,   my feelings, my loves and my
hates,   are as much "who I am" as my intellect. Enough
viewers   remain   caught   in   the   classical   tradition,
however,   to   change that spontaneous reaction once the
response   is   explained;   they suddenly feel threatened
and   are not yet ready to risk losing the known for the
unknown,   the   new.   But,   by   this time, Bergman has
already made his point.

        According   to   Vernon   Young,   there   is   another
insight   to   be   gleaned   from   this   exchange.   If we
understand   "Father" as the historic euphemism for God,
then   Bergman   is again announcing the death of God and
with   it   the   cessation   of   transcendent   order   and
authority.   Our inheritance from this "death" is that
we   now   "own   everything in common." Any significance
or   meaning   associated with our lives is that which we
ourselves   create.   Justification   for Vernon's claim
has   to   be   contextual,   but   one   has   to concede its
probability.

        A   third and related accomplishment of Bergman's in
this   scene   is   the   presentation of Ester's cinematic
lineage.   In   Anna's   first long speech above, we see
Ester   in   a direct line from The Knight, Vogler, David
and   Tomas. God, the Father, who was silent, now seems
to   be   dead.   Such silence, such death, destroys all
metaphysical   landmarks.   Tradition   for   tradition's

sake may be quaint but it's not quintessential to the
understanding or living of our lives. "Principles,"
"significance," and "meaningfulness" without God,
without some Archimedian point, are simply relative
terms.   A thousand policemen directing traffic, T. S.
Eliot reminds us, cannot tell us where we have been or
where we are going. This is the insight at which we
have arrived in Bergman's journey.   The Knight
demanded proof; Vogler carried on, but with growing
anxiety and suffering; David was confronted by the
spider-god and sought the imposition of love; Tomas,
who acknowledged the spider-god to be his own, could
only wait for someone or something to fill the void;
and now Ester, who sees the void for what it is--death
and destruction--acknowledges her sickness unto
death.   This Kierkegaardian insight is carried to its
existential conclusion in this dialogue between the
two sisters. It ends with neither sister convinced by
the other, but each so shaken in her own assumptions,
that certainty remains.   "In some way I can't
understand, you're scared of me," says Anna; "I'm <u>sure</u>
you're wrong," says Ester.

    It is at this point that one must take issue with
the conclusions which Arthur Gibson has drawn from
this film.   Gibson would have us believe that what
Bergman is dramatizing is not the death of God and the
subsequent encounter with Nothingness but rather the
dark night of the soul--the purgative emptiness which
precedes the profound insight of divine love and human
freedom:

>   I submit that this secret message can
>   be   articulated   with   retrospective
>   glance at <u>Through</u> <u>a</u> <u>Glass</u> <u>Darkly</u> and
>   <u>Winter</u> <u>Light</u>, in these eminently

theological terms: I [God] have a love
to offer you, a healing, serene,
creative, and re-creative love. It is
neither the fierce destructive love of
helpless adolescence nor the
self-interested love of romantic
adulthood. Yet this love must destroy
something in you, your skittish radical
independence--you must not shy away
from me so when I try to touch you!
And this love does of course have its
ultimate fulcrum in myself, for I am
the only one who can translate into
your language the strange and vital
words of the book in the
incomprehensible tongue.
The silence of God creates a negative
impression in this film because the
entire action is a savage explication
of God's ultimate respect for human
freedom. He will not, in a very real
sense he cannot, force that freedom;
yet not for one moment does he abate
his claim! And as the film progresses,
it becomes painfully clear that what
Ester expects and demands and needs,
for her creative and redemptive action
on Anna and Johan alike, is not
comforting and spontaneous affection,
but the total submission to a free
agent by a free agent, the willingness
to admit radical inferiority and accept
the sort of gift that can come only
from one side of the partnership. Anna
refuses utterly to make any such
admission. But at film's end little
Johan is studying, with open heart and

knitted brow, the secret message.

Johan, the child is still trying. So
there is still hope.

In The Silence we witness God's weakest
hour, as he battles the one virtually
impregnable barrier that can block him,
the drastic centrifugal thrust of the
free human will in rebellion.[191]

Gibson's point is that made (more effectively) by
Dostoevski's Grand Inquisitor in The Brothers
Karamazov. The Grand Inquisitor admonishes the
returning Christ that He cannot add anything to His
original revelation lest He impair the Church's
rightful authority and man's freedom to respond. But,
in order to make this point for Bergman, Gibson has to
turn Ester into the God-figure of the film: "As the
palpable silence of God takes shape before us, it is
the brooding elder sister with the enormous
eyes."[192] I can find no specific or contextual
justification in The Silence either for this or the
ultimate affirmation of God. The latter demands a
metaphysical confirmation which is contrary to
everything else Bergman has been telling us. One has
to believe that Gibson's logic is imposed from
without, not implied from within. His argument from
negation (the silence of God) to affirmation (the love
of God) must function within a prior and assumed
theology. Where, in any of the films we have
considered, is there justification for Gibson's
theological optimism? Bergman is on a journey, not a
jury to assess human behavior by explicit divine law,
and we find him pushing the limits of Kierkegaard's
aesthetic stage.

Kierkegaard's aesthetic stage is one of unconscious despair which disguises itself as a dispassionate, objective analysis of life or as a passionate, childish life of immediate self-gratification. Each, for Kierkegaard (and now for Bergman), an expression of an inauthentic existence. The former is sterile, the latter other-directed and meaningless. Ester is a translator, creating nothing new and obliged to remain objective and distant; Anna is merely self-indulgent, sensuously using, never appreciating another--herself being used and never appreciated. Each in The Silence, brings the other to the point of conscious despair. At this juncture, says Kierkegaard, we either turn back to recapitulate our past with cynicism, or we move ahead into the Ethical Stage of either/or and decision. David and Tomas also seem to have reached this point, yet not with the understanding of the despair, which Ester and Anna display.

However, it is just this understanding which becomes the incentive for Bergman to continue his journey. Were the film to have only Ester and Anna as its protagonists, then surely the journey would be over, the quest ending in unresolved despair. But we have not taken Johan into consideration yet. Justification for giving Johan a position of importance comes from a number of things. Cinematically we are given this idea by seeing much of the movie from Johan's point of view. The camera is often shooting from his eye-level so that we are led to see things as he does, to identify with him in his perspective. Johan's prominence in the unfolding of the narrative is another reason for considering him

important.   Nothing   in   a   film by Bergman is simply
accidental--least   of   all   role   prominence.   What is
Bergman   saying   in   and   through   Johan?   And finally,
though   there   is   little   of   Bergman's   traditional
symbolism in this film, an important symbol is used in
connection with Johan's action and the resolution of
the film.

As   an   introduction   to   the symbol-connection for
Johan,   it   would   be   helpful   to identify some of the
negative Christian symbols in The Silence, which we
alluded   to   earlier.   In   the   film, church bells do
ring, but their ringing seems to be meaningless. They
do not seem to chime the hours, and if they are a call
to   some Divine Service or Mass, no one seems to be
going or paying attention. We do see from the hotel
window   the   physical   building   of a church, but it is
dark   and   forbidding,   its   entrance shrouded in
darkness.   The only activity that takes place within,
which we know for certain, is Anna's first sexual
encounter with the bar waiter; they went into the
church because it was cool and dark. This, I believe,
is one of Bergman's most devastating images. There
seems   to   be   no anger or defiance in Anna's act; only
sheer   indifference   and creature comfort. Fornication
in the presence of the Host was the blasphemous act of
the   Black Mass. Now all of that has been dismissed as
meaningless.   The   Church   no   longer represents a
meaningful force, nor is it even worthy of being
considered an adversary. It is only a convenience.

Another   symbol   that   Bergman gives us is that of
the   junk cart drawn, not by an emaciated horse as
Robin Wood suggests, but by an emaciated donkey! On
the   cart,   as it moves into the city, is a potted palm
tree, but one could hardly imagine a less triumphal

entry than this. In the midst of the rush and crush
of the city, this antediluvian, pathetic conveyance is
shown us, burdened down with broken and useless
furniture and junk. So, Bergman seems to be saying,
is the Church. Weighted down with centuries of
outmoded practices, ideas, rubrics, and tradition, it
is simply an anachronism in the contemporary world.
Yet in the development of this image, Bergman saves
his punch-picture until late in the film. We then see
the cart again, moving back the opposite way, still
loaded with the piles of junk that it originally had,
but now missing the palm plant. Palm Sunday for
Bergman is even more of a misunderstanding than it was
for the earlier followers of Jesus: though disciples
did not get a Davidic king, they were granted the more
miraculous gift of a risen Lord. For Bergman, the
tomb is not empty; the stone has not been rolled
away. The palm is the herald of nothing...

If Bergman were totally consistent, that's where
the story of Christian symbolism would end; but
Bergman is not "totally consistent" and would no doubt
be angry with anyone who, at this stage, would claim
that as a necessary virtue. Total consistency implies
a closed logical system which is the mark of the
classical metaphysical stance of which he is trying to
free himself. Therefore Bergman shows no shame in
employing the resurrection motif a few minutes later
in connection with Johan and with his own religious
journey. On the second day in the city, the day of
their departure, Anna and Johan had left the hotel to
get a meal before entraining. During their absence
from the hotel, Ester has a severe attack of her
illness, which just about takes her life. As the
attack subsides, Ester lies back in bed and pulls the

sheet up over her face so that she looks like a corpse. When Johan returns and sees this, he goes to the bed and pulls down the sheet from Ester's face. Ester opens her eyes and gazes at him, then says: "Don't be scared. I'm not going to die." Johan nods silently. It is clearly a resurrection image, the only one by Bergman we have so far encountered. The implication is that he still has hope, that the journey is still to continue. Ester then says to Johan: "I've written you a letter, as I promised. It's lying on the floor, if you can find it. Johan! It's important, d'you understand! You must read it carefully. It's all...It's all I...You'll understand."

Beyond what is said and written, the context itself is important here. Hope seems to have some connection with innocence, but the connection is a precarious thing. Innocence, which implies potential-yet-undistorted, is all too quickly destroyed by contact with the neurotic and twisted world of adults. Stuart Kaminsky sees this as one of Bergman's major and tragic themes: "In the films of Ingmar Bergman, children live in a world of tormented innocence. They are surrounded by tortured adults who cannot or will not communicate to them the reasons for their anguish. Distrustful, the children seek their own answers by observing and eavesdropping on the adult world. They try, as they develop understanding, to personify and simplify good and evil. Like heroes of Greek tragedy, they are driven by curiosity, a need to know. Bergman's children are constantly reaching out to touch and communicate with an adult world which they cannot understand. If the child does make contact, either by his own experience or a shared experience, his protective innocence is torn away and he must face the insight which he has only vaguely sensed. He must face the realization that God does not exist or does not communicate, that terrible things are possible because man is unprotected, that death exists as a frightening and final end. This, to Bergman is what it means to become an adult. As an adult, the former child can only find solace for his lost innocence in the acceptance of love, a love which Bergman tells us can range from pure animal passion to almost spiritual devotion."[193]

This had to be written with Johan of The Silence in mind. Time after time one can see the erosion of innocence as Anna and Ester artfully destroy each other in his presence. Consequently Ester's affection and gift is of so much importance. It becomes one of the few non-cynical, unselfish gestures that Johan perceives. "For me," states Bergman, "the important thing is that Ester sends a secret message to the boy. That's the important thing: the message he spells out to himself. To me Ester in all her misery represents a distillation of something indestructibly human, which the boy inherits from her."[194] It would appear that despite the hatred and distrust that exists between the two women, Bergman has not altogether given up on love.

But there is more to this message than just the affection of the one who sends it. The words themselves are important, made more important by the fact that the film version excludes the words Bergman had originally included in the script. In the script we are told that she has recorded three words "spirit," anxiety," and "joy." Critics have made much of the fact that this is her legacy to Johan. But I

find that far too romantic and actually antithetical
to the message of the film. In The Silence we watch
Ester record two words from the porter--her only
contact. The words are "hand" and "face." These seem
like reasonable words to obtain easily in a language
of which one has no knowledge. Abstract terms like
"spirit," "anxiety," and "joy," would be virtually
impossible to ascertain in such a short time. Again,
"hand" and "face" bring together the two aspects of
life which Anna and Ester seem to represent: the
emotional-physical and the intellectual-spiritual.
The other three terms are intellectual concepts,
universals right out of the world of classical
metaphysics.

But this observation brings up two related points
about which Bergman himself has comments. In an
interview, Torsten Manns says to Bergman: "As far as
I can see, quite a few things have become shitty--if I
may use the expression--in The Silence. The spiritual
has been replaced by the physical. One gets terribly
close to these two women. The other thing is that
language no longer functions." Bergman responds:
"No, that's quite right, language has ceased to be a
means of communication: they can't talk to one
another. There aren't many lines of dialogue in The
Silence."[195] What does it mean to say, "Language
has ceased to be a means of communication?" I think
that Bergman understands full well that if a genuine
metaphysical shift has taken place in our
understanding of the world, all of our language is
freighted with outdated and misleading meanings. As
Sweeney complains in one of T. S. Eliot's poems: "The
trouble is, I gotta use words when I talk to you."
But how difficult it is for words to be used to

redefine themselves, yet such seems to be the task we face.

Though we have had hints in earlier films, The Silence shows us that Bergman's understanding of the function and meaning of language does coincide with that of Heidegger. The language of common exchange and conversation has deteriorated to the point that it either fails to communicate anything but superficialities or misleads because it has lost its ground in reality. Were these two the only properties of language, there would be no hope for authentic exchange; all would be relative. But, Heidegger and Bergman both believe that language is grounded in what Heidegger calls "pre-understanding"--a common awareness of being in which our words are grounded, from which they are derived, and whose power they embody. For both Heidegger and Bergman such pre-understanding is an expressive silence without which language could not function at all.

It is clear that Bergman is indicating to us (with T. S. Eliot in "Burnt Norton") that presently "Words strain,/Crack and sometimes break, under the burden,/Under the tension, slip, slide, perish,/Decay with imprecision...;" that we are not ready for words; that he, Bergman, is taking us back to silence in this film. The one universal communication which Bergman permits, which gives promise of retrieval and restoration, is related to music. The name J. S. Bach is shown us in the otherwise incomprehensible language newspaper of Timoka, and it is Bach's music which both Ester and the hotel porter mutually identify.

This semantic-philosophical problem would seem to be precisely the subject of the following trialogue among Jonas Sima, Stig Bjorkman, and Ingmar Bergman:

JS: So, when shooting <u>Winter</u> <u>Light</u>, you felt you needed to penetrate some aspect of your idea of God?

IB: It was more or less like this--as Torsten so rightly says--everything had gone to pieces. All this is so deep down in me, there was no question of 'penetrating' it. <u>The</u> <u>Silence</u> is simple. It tells its story by simple means, not with symbols and such antics.

JS: I'm inclined to see something positive in your capitulation--your insight into God's silence as expressive of some maturation process.

IB: Yes, in itself I believe so too, and I think it's to be seen already in <u>Winter</u> <u>Light</u>. Though it's very hard to say anything definite about this...Out of all man's misery and conflicts and his insufferable condition is crystallized this little clear drop of something different--this sudden impulse to understand a few words in another language. It's remarkable, all that's left, the only positive thing. Just as the only positive thing in <u>Winter</u> <u>Light</u> is the clergyman standing up and holding his service--even though there's no one there to hear it.

> <u>SB</u>: And this curiosity, one feels, is
> not merely momentary. It's
> something to build on.
>
> <u>IB</u>: Quite. And for me it's the one
> essential positive thing in <u>The</u>
> <u>Silence</u>.[196]

"To understand a few words in another
language...." at first sounds too petty to be
considered the denouement of the film, but not when
those "few words" indicate a new world-view, a new
understanding of one's perception of the world. Jerry
Gill believes that the "Words in a Foreign Language"
given to Johan are symbolic of two things: "First,
the list of words clearly emphasizes the importance of
communication, which Bergman has been at pains to
underscore. Second, Johan's interest in, and attempt
to understand, these foreign words suggests that there
is a possibility of hope for him, and perhaps for all
mankind, if he can avoid the limitations of the two
ways of life to which he has been exposed."[197] I
believe these are valid conclusions on Gill's part,
but he has omitted the most important conclusion of
all--that the relation between person and person and
(be there one) the relation between a person and God
is on the level of <u>existence</u> and not of reason. The
words were "hand" and "face" and <u>not</u> "body" and
"soul." The kind of Greek dichotomy that is evident
in the latter two words is not applicable to the
former. In the existential understanding to which
Bergman is turning, there can be no classical
separation between appearance and reality, accident
and essence. Life must be understood as
confrontation, not contemplation. <u>The Silence</u> ends
with the words "hand" and "face;" the next film

<u>Persona</u>, begins with these words translated by Johan
into gestures.

Persona (1966)

"How do you want us to live, then?
After all, we own everything in common."
The <u>Silence</u>

"Artistic creativity has always manifested itself
in me as a sort of hunger. I have observed this need
in myself with some gratification, but I have never in
all my conscious life asked why this hunger should
arise and demand to be satisfied. In the last few
years, as it has begun to ease off, and been
transformed into something else, I have begun to feel
it important to try to establish the reason for my
'artistic activity.'

*   *   *

"Now to be completely honest, I regard art (and
not only the art of the cinema) as lacking importance.

"Literature, painting, music, the cinema, the
theater beget and give birth to themselves. New
mutations and combinations emerge and are destroyed;
seen from the outside, the movement possesses a
nervous vitality--the magnificent zeal of artists to
project, for themselves and an increasingly distracted
public, pictures of a world that no longer asks what
they think or believe. On a few preserves artists are
punished, art is regarded as dangerous and worth
stifling or steering. By and large, however, art is
free, shameless, irresponsible and, as I said, the
movement is intense, almost feverish; it resembles, it
seems to me, a snakeskin full of ants. The snake
itself is long since dead, eaten out from within,

deprived of its poison; but the skin moves, filled
with busy life.

"If I now observe that I happen to be one of these
ants, then I must ask myself whether there is any
reason to pursue the activity further. The answer is
yes...[the] reason is <u>curiosity</u>."198

Though the journey we have been taking with
Bergman up to now has been primarily and
self-consciously a religious one, there is little
doubt--as such critics as Simon, Steene, Samuels, <u>et
al</u> have been at pains to tell us--that there is a
parallel level of artistic struggle for justification
in his films, which is autobiographical. I would
certainly not deny this or dismiss its relevancy out
of hand; it is just that that particular level of
interpretation can be discussed by those whose
interest focuses on that concern. However, because I
do believe that the artistic theme is more prominent
in <u>Persona</u>, it deserves mention and consideration, not
just in terms of itself but in its relation to the
religious themes we have been following.

By the end of the film <u>The Silence</u>, the
existential critique of life has brought us to the
point of accepting the totality of life as important,
not just man's reason, mind, or soul. If that is the
case, then art, as an expressive interpretation of
life, must also be scrutinized through the existential
lens, for it may be our way back to meaningful,
religious expression and communication.

In <u>The Snakeskin</u>, quoted above, Bergman does just
that. Art, as well as religion and philosophy, has
been affected by the existential critique. The
ordinary structures which have governed the graphic
and performing arts--such classical Greek structures

as "beginning, middle, and end," "harmony and measure," "omniscient author," a discernible "past, present, and future"--have disappeared as necessary parameters. Such imposed structures made the gift of artistic presentation at least once removed from reality; the resulting art was not, as Bergman sees, vital to life (a rather ironic agreement with Plato's assessment of art here!). But released from such external structuring, much contemporary art has not become self-critical or innovative, but self-indulgent. It is carrion for the critics to pick over, but not genuinely creative.

Bergman seems to believe that there is a real danger in all this: though the structure and direction are gone, the power of art remains, but it is now at the mercy of the monstrous forces that seem to govern everything in the absence of any transcendent meaning. Such art, captured by mass media, can pose a genuine threat to society by its destructive influence. William Barrett, like Bergman, is concerned with this turn of events: "The last gigantic step forward in the spread of technologism has been the development of mass art and mass media of communication: the machine no longer fabricates only material products; it also makes minds. Millions of people live by the stereotypes of mass art, the virulent form of abstractness, and their capacity for any kind of human reality is fast disappearing."[199]

Coincidentally, Bergman would seem to be saying that traditional religion and its surrogate, traditional art, are both misleading and therefore destructive in their attempts to interpret life to contemporary man. We need a new mythology, but its shape, its nature, its expression is not yet known or perceived. Without that, we are left only with curiosity, an unstructured exploration of life as we live it, not know it to be. Our approach to understanding, now, must be receptive and responsive, not calculating and regulative; philosophically speaking, it must be existential-phenomenological.

The Silence left us rather bleak prospects. The Source, be there one, at the heart of reality is silent; we can feel the oppressiveness of a stifling Nothingness which threatens us with its only discernible characteristic--death. The threat of this anxiety makes us defensive, suspicious, and self-centered and consequently isolates us from our fellow human beings. Under these circumstances, love is seen as sado/masochistic, a way of possessing another, not a sharing or giving of oneself. It is a credit to Bergman's honesty as well as to his existential approach, that this bleak prospect is not turned into a governing principle by which all else is then described or interpreted.

In The Silence the caustic circle has been drawn, but reality has again broken through. Ester's affection for Johan is definitely not sado/masochistic, but altruistic and gentle, and Johan is yet innocent enough to respond. The gift of two words may not be much, but it is significant as a gift, given and received, as Bergman indicated earlier. It must have been obvious to Bergman, by the end of The Silence, that he had not fully explored the relationships that might exist between two people, had not fully understood all that is implied by the word "love." This needed further exposure to his "curiosity."

Any exploration of the themes of communication, love, and language, would seem to presuppose some understanding of the nature of the self and of that elusive relationship of "selves" we experience as integral to our own psyches. Ingeniously, Bergman incorporates both explorations into his next film, Persona; ingenious not because Bergman pulls it off, but because he sees that the two problems are so interrelated that he cannot in any way separate them. To know myself is to know myself in-relation-to-another; to know another is to know that other through myself. The religious dimension of this equation in Persona is there by negation, an existential dialectic which makes me aware of God not by His presence but by His non-presence. As the Death-of-God theologians once put it, one is aware of the presence of the absence of God, rather than the absence of the presence of God.

Bergman is able to reflect these interests by employing the double reference to the Latin term persona. In classical theater, persona referred to the character played by an actor who wore a distinguishing mask; so, even now at most plays, we are given a program which identifies the dramatis personae--the characters and the actors who play them. By the use of masks it was possible for one actor to play more than one part, simply by putting on another mask. This point was not lost on our classical forbearers who often described the Trinity in such fashion: God was one substance but three personae..."God in three persons, blessed Trinity." The fact that we often turn that into a social trinity, three gods, is our mistake, not the Church Fathers'.

The second reference to _persona_ comes from its usage in Jungian psychology. Torsten Manns, interviewing Bergman, comments on this possibility: "Originally _Persona_ means the mask used by actors in classical drama. It can also mean the various personages in a play. But Jung has a definition which I think suits your film admirably--I'd like to hear what you think about it. 'The consciously artificial or masked personality complex which is adopted by an individual in contrast to his inner character, with intent to serve as a protection, a defense, a deception or an attempt to adapt to the world around him." Bergman replies: "It sounds good, and fits well in this case, too. There's something extremely fascinating to me about these people exchanging masks and suddenly sharing one between them."200

As one can readily see, the possibility for variations and nuances on the themes of these references and their interaction is almost endless. John Simon's summary is good at this point, though his elaboration proves wanting in terms of the interests of this study: "Hence we are to see the film, first as a dramatic conflict, a construct, a movie; secondly, as a psychic contest between two people; and thirdly, as the spiritual anatomy of a person or persons, a study of interior human style. But the three levels--dramatic, psychic, philosophic (or, if you prefer, metaphysical)--can be viewed in another way. In that case, the conflict is, first, between acting and being, art and life, illusion and reality; secondly, between sickness and health, lies and truth, concealing and revealing; and thirdly, between being and non-being, creation and destruction, life and death. And all of these things seen in a constant flux, a coming together and a breaking apart, just as Alma and Elisabet experience and enact it in the episodes of the film that so intransigently resist coalescing into a single simple story."201   But before we can go further, and despite Simon's justifiable warning, we must indicate the development of the plot.

During the last performance of Electra, the famous actress Elisabet Vogler stopped speaking. Despite cues she remained silent for about one minute, then finished the play. Afterwards she apologized to her friends and said, 'I got this terrible fit of laughter.' That evening she returned home to her husband and small child, Johan, and everything seemed normal. The next morning, however, she refused to get up for rehearsal, refused to speak. As we are introduced to her on screen, she has not spoken for three months. The psychiatrist working on her case finds nothing mentally or physically wrong with her and assigns a young nurse, Alma, to accompany Elisabet for a summer's stay at the seashore. Elisabet remains silent; Alma chatters incessantly. Slowly the situation begins to change. It appears that Alma is more patient than nurse and that Elisabet is the therapist. By a possible contrived accident, Alma is able to read a letter of Elisabet's to her doctor in which Alma is referred to in a patronizing, if not deprecating way. The result is a confrontation, accusations, and finally violence--all of which seem to clear the air for a recognition of a kind of fusion that has taken place between the two women. Bergman then gives us a series of dreams and fantasies, in which it is impossible for us to separate illusion and reality, perhaps questioning the ultimate separation

of these two. The film ends with the end of summer.
Both women pack to leave the island, Alma to go back
to nursing, Elisabet (we assume) back to the stage,
but we are given to believe that both women have been
profoundly changed by their relationship with each
other.

This film which is so intimately involved with the
nature and development of identity, begins with what
Bergman calls a cinematic poem. At first viewing, it
would appear to be simply a history of his cinematic
career, but it is, in fact, more than that. What
Bergman is giving us is the development of his own
cinematic identity, his own spiritual journey: "Well,
while I was working on Persona, I had it in my head to
make a poem, not in words but in images, about the
situation in which Persona had originated.   I
reflected on what was important and began with the
projector and my desire to set it in motion. But when
the projector was running, nothing came out of it but
old ideas, the spider, God's lamb, all that dull old
stuff. My life just then consisted of dead people,
brick walls, and a few dismal trees out in the
park."202   These last images reflect Bergman's own
hospital experience between The Silence and the
filming of Persona, but they likewise reflect his
spiritual state at the time: "I was in the hospital,
the view out of the window was a chapel where they
were carrying out the bodies of the dead, and I knew
that house was full of dead people. Of course, I felt
it inside me somewhere that the whole atmosphere was
one of death, and I felt like that little
boy...."203

We pick up with <u>Persona</u> where we left off in <u>The</u> <u>Silence</u>. The boy, Johan (reading, by the way, the same book of Lermontov's that he was seen reading in <u>The</u> <u>Silence</u>) is surrounded by death, holding on to the hope of his two words, "hand" and "face." So Bergman begins the credits for the new film with Johan's face and hand extended inquiringly toward a wall or screen of glass on which the face of a woman appears in gigantic proportions; but not one face, rather two, as the image slowly fades from Elisabet into Alma and back again. The distinctions are so minimized, the images just enough blurred, that we are never sure whom we are seeing. Then we are shown flashes of scenes that point simultaneously both forward and back--forward in that they are images of things that will appear again in the film: sensuous lips shown vertically; a Buddhist monk immolating himself; a tree dwarfed, twisted, wasted; barren rocks on the seacoast. These images also look back because they symbolize the monstrous forces that haunt our lives: the forces of sensuality, death, disease, and sterile isolation.

"That the boy's condition in this prologue," writes John Simon, "between death and life, sleep and waking, is Bergman's view of his and our lives, is confirmed by his remark in an interview with Nils Petter Sundgren: 'The reality we experience today is in fact as absurd, as horrible, and as obtrusive as our dreams. We are as defenseless before it as we are in our dreams. And one is strongly aware, I think, that there are no boundaries between dream and reality today.'"204 By the gesture of Johan's hand to Elisabet's image on the glass screen, Bergman gives us the longing for communication Johan experiences and

the barrier that seems to prevent any rapprochement
between himself and his mother. Each is isolated;
each alone, each threatened by the monstrous forces
that continue to shape our reality. For those who
have not seen his previous films, or followed his
journey up to now, Bergman gives us a series of
vignettes to prepare us for understanding the forces
that are at work in the film.

We are told from the beginning that Elisabet's
illness is not an "illness" in the ordinary sense of
that word. The psychiatrist, in making the assignment
of Alma to the "case," tells Alma that Elisabet has
been silent for three months: "She has been given
every conceivable test. The result is clear enough.
So far as we can see, Mrs. Vogler is perfectly
healthy, both mentally and physically. There is no
suggestion of any hysterical reaction, even." It is
clear that Bergman does not want to make the mistake
of creating another Karin of Through a Glass Darkly,
who can be dismissed as insane. Elisabet's silence is
an act of will. Alma quickly understands this and is
hesitant to accept the assignment because she does not
believe that she has enough "spiritual strength" to
meet such a test--an admission that tells us two
things. One, Alma is unsure of herself, despite her
training and apparent competence; and two, the issue
is one of religious, i.e. ultimate, importance and has
to do with the nature of personal identity.

This scene is followed shortly by one in hospital
in which Alma turns on the radio to entertain
Elisabet. What follows, particularly in Bergman's
more complete textual versions, is a masterful
emotional and philosophical recapitulation of The
Silence: a rather melodramatic female voice is

saying, "Forgive me, forgive me darling, you have to
forgive me. All I want is your forgiveness. Forgive
me so that I can breathe again--and live again."
Elisabet's reaction is to laugh at what apparently
sounds to her like histrionics. The voice then
resumes, "What do you know of mercy, what do you know
of a mother's suffering, the bleeding pain of a
woman?" Again Elisabet laughs and increases the
volume on the radio as the voice swells, "Oh God, God,
somewhere out there in the darkness that surrounds us
all. Look in mercy upon me. Thou who art love...."
In the face of Elisabet's continuing laughter,
Bergman's script instructions say that Alma turns off
the radio "in terror." John Simon's judgment here,
with which I would agree, is: "Mrs. Vogler is
rejecting what seem to her melodramatic outbursts
about love, maternity, and God."205 Simon comments
that Elisabet's laughter "must be the same sort of
outburst of laughter as the one she had after her last
performance in Electra."206 Thus, the
recapitulation of The Silence: love between Ester and
Anna is reduced to a sado/masochistic relation; the
maternal relationship between Anna and her son Johan
dissolves in the face of Anna's egocentric
indulgences; and God is silent, assumed absent.

Bergman now gives us each of these contexts of
estrangement in Persona. Alma reads Elisabet a letter
from her husband which apparently Elisabet has been
unable to bring herself to read. In it we are given
to understand that Mr. Vogler, unable to visit
Elisabet, is trying to make some contact. In the
letter, Mr. Vogler says, "As far as I know, we were
happy recently, surely we have never been so close to
each other. Do you remember saying: I'm only just

beginning to understand what marriage really means.
You have taught me that we must look upon each other
as two anxious children full of good will and the best
of intentions, but governed by forces that we do not
entirely control.' Do you remember saying all that?
We were out walking together in the woods and you
stopped and caught on to my belt..." We are not
permitted to hear the rest of the letter. Elisabet's
obvious distress has stopped Alma's reading. It is
evident that the language quoted betrays her present
feelings, that the naivete and innocence of children
proposed in the letter is not really possible, that
the gestures of intimacy are inauthentic and
hypocritical. There is no love between them, only
isolation which she has now consciously admitted but
that he has not--though it's there for him; his first
words, "As far as I know....," are a dead giveaway.

In the letter is a picture of Elisabet's son.
Elisabet takes a long look at the photo and then tears
it vertically in half. She is seemingly rejecting the
responsibility as well as the relationship, separating
herself from him. The third context, God, has already
been given us in the image of a father-rejection. I
do not think it is accidental that Elisabet is playing
Electra when the silence begins. It is as though
Electra's devotion to her father, i.e. Father, for
which Electra really sacrifices her whole life even
after his death, suddenly strikes Elisabet as absurd.
If God is dead, then why this devotion; mourning very
much does not become Electra as far as Elisabet is
concerned. It is this startling revelation of the
death of God and what the implications of that are
which makes Elisabet withdraw from every relation,
question all meaning, question even her own integrity,
authenticity and, ultimately, identity.

Such a claim might be difficult to substantiate were it not for corroborative evidence. First of all, it fits in with the developing themes which Bergman has been pursuing all along--the loss of metaphysical structure is, among other things, a loss of personal orientation. Second, Bergman has used before, particularly in The Silence, the designation "father" as both human sign and divine symbol. Third, shortly after Elisabet and Alma go to the psychiatrist's summer house by the sea, this exchange takes place between the two. Alma says, "May I read you something from my book?...It says here: 'All this anxiety we bear with us, our disappointed dreams, the inexplicable cruelty, our terror at the thought of extinction, the painful insight we have into the conditions of life on earth, have slowly crystallized out our hope of heavenly salvation. The great shout of our faith and doubt against the darkness and silence is the most terrifying evidence of our forlornness, our terrified unexpressed knowledge.'" Elisabet nods in agreement. Our "terrified unexpressed knowledge" is, of course, the death of God. But it is important to note also that this so-called "knowledge" is at the root of all other knowledge and relation. To consciously acknowledge that we have accepted the death of God is to acknowledge to ourselves the darkness and silence of our own isolation. In the face of this radical insight, any persona we adopt to encounter the world becomes relative and finally meaningless. Add to this Sartre's point that my radical freedom prevents me from realizing any final essence or fulfillment prior to death, and we reach the reason for Elisabet's catatonic state.

Alma's position becomes the more ironic when we have really understood Elisabet's silence. The only real difference between them is that Elisabet's understanding of "reality" has become a conscious one; Alma's is still unconscious. One example should suffice. We know that Elisabet has acknowledged the strain, the lack of fundamental understanding, which exists between herself and her husband. Alma has a similar relationship with her fiancé, but does not admit it to herself. In a moment of casual self-examination she says to herself: "You can go about almost any old way, do almost any old thing. I'll marry Karl-Henrik and we'll have a couple of kids that I'll bring up. That's all decided, it's in me somewhere. I don't have to work things out at all, how they're going to be. That makes you feel very safe. And I'm doing a job I like. That's a good thing too--only in a different way. I wonder what's really wrong with Mrs. Vogler." A short time later Alma tells Elisabet about an affair she had with an older man, her first and most romantic affair, before Karl-Henrik is in the picture; then she says: "I like Karl-Henrik a lot and--well, you know, maybe you only fall in love once. But I am faithful to him, of course. Otherwise in our job there are other...possibilities, I can tell you..." She then relates with a kind of intoxicated excitement an orgy on a remote beach in which she, a friend, and two teenaged boys participated, even after her engagement to Karl-Henrik. We have been left with no doubt of her self-deception, the same unconscious despair that haunted Ester and Anna in The Silence.

Elisabet's conscious understanding of her own problem--which is not a psychosis--reveals another dimension to Bergman's understanding of the human condition. From the time of The Seventh Seal, Bergman has suggested that life cannot be understood or governed on the basis of a rational or metaphysical explanation; emotions, moods, neuroses, dreams, etc. must be taken into account as expressive of our reality. Now a new dimension enters--or, perhaps, it is more correct to say that another popular claimant to omniscience is being questioned: psychology.

If it can be said that reason has been demoted as the reigning mythology (a reign which began in the eighteenth century) then for many in the West its place has been taken by psychology. Of course most psychologists did not make the claim, but many of us, as laymen, made the claim for them: psychology was to be the answer to all of man's personal, emotional, and interrelational problems. "Every man needs a shrink," seemed to be the maxim for the day. Although Bergman is much indebted to the insights which psychology has given us into the nature of the human psyche, he still believes that psychology, like reason, is a one-dimensional approach to the understanding of the human condition, the human predicament. In Persona, in which he is so indebted to Jung for his expertise, Bergman also rights the balance by giving us, in all of its incompleteness, the psychiatrist's diagnosis of Elisabet's case. The most obvious point, supposing one could find no fault with the diagnosis, is that knowing cannot be equated with cure, cannot establish rapport. The result is that the officious pronouncement by the psychiatrist tends to undermine what therapy there might be in the analysis. Though

John Simon does not really discuss this point, I am in
agreement with his assessment of the psychiatrist:
"The woman psychiatrist is a curious figure: knowing
yet somehow repellent of aspect; perceptive, but in
some smug way repulsive about it."213   The text of
her analysis is as follows:

> I do understand, you know.   The
> hopeless dream of being.   Not doing,
> just being.   Aware and watchful every
> second.   And at the same time the abyss
> between what you are for others and
> what you are for yourself.   The feeling
> of dizziness and the continual burning
> need to be unmasked.   At last to be
> seen through, reduced, perhaps
> extinguished.   Every tone of voice a
> lie, an act of treason.   Every gesture
> false.   Every smile a grimace.   The
> role of wife, the role of friend, the
> roles of mother and mistress, which is
> worst?   Which has tortured you most?
> Playing the actress with the
> interesting face?   Keeping all the
> pieces together with an iron hand and
> getting them to fit?   Where did it
> break?   Where did you fail?   Was it the
> role of mother that finally did it?   It
> certainly wasn't your role as Electra.
> That gave you a rest.   She actually got
> you to hold out a while more.   She was
> an excuse for the more perfunctory
> performances you gave in your other
> roles, your 'real-life roles'.   But
> when Electra was over, you had nothing

left to hide behind, nothing to keep
you going. No excuses. And so you
were left with your demand for truth
and your disgust. Kill yourself?
No--too nasty, not to be done. But you
could be immobile. You can keep
quiet. Then at least you're not
lying. You can cut yourself off, close
yourself in. Then you don't have to
play a part, put on a face, make false
gestures. Or so you think. But
reality plays tricks on you. Your
hiding place isn't watertight enough.
Life starts leaking in everywhere. And
you're forced to react. No one asks
whether its genuine or not, whether
you're true or false. It's only in the
theatre that's an important question.
Hardly even there, for that matter.
Elisabet, I understand that you're
keeping quiet, not moving, that you
have put this lack of will into a
fantastic system. I understand it and
admire you for it. I think you should
keep playing this part until you've
lost interest in it. When you've
played it to the end, you can drop it
as you drop your other parts.

This _is_ a perceptive analysis on the part of the
doctor, but one is led to take some exceptions. It is
the part of Electra which triggers Elisabet's response
of silence, for, as we noted above, it is in Electra's
role that the transcendent implications of life's
absurdities strike Elisabet. Again, contrary to what

the doctor says about the ending of the Electra role
and the looming void, we have already been told that
Elisabet's failure to show up for a rehearsal was the
occasion of her will-to-silence being discovered, not
her unemployment. And finally, if all human behavior
is to be reduced to role-playing as suggested in the
doctor's final remarks, then such relativities must be
accorded to the doctor herself. The implications of
this last point are grim which, I believe, is just
what Bergman intended. By _Face to Face_ this
observation has been twisted into a witticism: "A
lunatic quack psychiatrist once wrote that mental
illnesses are the worst scourge on earth, and that the
next worst is the curing of those illnesses. I'm
inclined to agree with him." Psychology can be of
great help but it cannot be confused with God or
existential _being_.

In this state of anxious silence by which Elisabet
dramatizes her isolation from husband, son, doctor,
nurse, and indeed, the world, there is one comforting
experience for her--the music of J. S. Bach. Bergman,
who himself is very responsive to music, begins to use
music in a prominent and interpretive way in _Through a
Glass Darkly_. There the poignancy of Karin's illness
and Minus' struggle to understand are given voice by
the use of solo cello playing Bach's "Suite No. 2" in
D minor. In _The Silence_, as noted in the previous
chapter, J. S. Bach is the one phrase and his music
the one experience which Ester and the old hotel
porter can share, which need no interpreter. So in
Persona the one tranquil experience we are shown of
Elisabet's hospital experience is her listening to
Bach on the radio.

John Simon finds this scene significant and its implications therapeutic: "We know that Bergman loves Bach and music in general, and it seems reasonable to assume that the mistrust of the word expressed in Persona by so many diverse means is deliberately contrasted with this trust in music. Does some art, then, have a therapeutic value after all? I would call this scene, with its ambiguities, a key scene--except that Persona is made with such absolute economy that every scene in it is a key scene. The implication here, if I am interpreting correctly, is that art cannot attack the most deep-seated problems frontally, as the radio play would, but only by indirection, insinuation, abstraction, as Bach's music does."208 By and large one must agree with Simon here, but I think the implication a bit too presumptive for the part of music. It would appear to me that Bergman is using music as a universal symbol; or maybe one should say Bergman is using music as a symbol (or promise) that there is some universal meaning to life after all, if we could only find it. It is a hint, a guess, an intuition. It is just possible that there is harmony, rhythm, and time which can tie life together.

On the role of words, Simon is absolutely right. Bergman still mistrusts them because he believes they originate in an outmoded, ineffective metaphysics, i.e. structure and meaning are no longer reciprocal. Alma, at one point, says to Elisabet:

> It's not easy to live with someone who
> doesn't say anything. I promise you.
> It spoils everything. I can't bear to
> hear Karl-Henrik's voice on the
> telephone. He sounds so artificial. I

can't talk to him any more, it's so
unnatural. You hear your own voice too
and no one else! And you think 'Don't
I sound false.' All these words I'm
using. Look, now I'm talking to you, I
can't stop, but I hate talking because
I still can't say what I want. But
you've made things simple for yourself,
you just shut up. No I must try not to
get angry. You don't say anything,
that's your business, I know. But just
now I need you to talk to me. Please,
please, can't you talk to me, just a
bit? It's almost unbearable.
(A long pause. Elisabet shakes her
head. Alma smiles, as if she were
trying not to cry.) --I knew you'd say
no. Because you can't know how I feel.

The dilemma is severe. Simon, considering the
problem, finds himself even entertaining the paradox
that in our lying is our truth. In describing a scene
which is the aftermath of a quarrel, he writes:

After washing up, calming down, and
accepting some coffee from Elisabet,
Alma tries suasion once again. Must
speech be honest and truthful, she
asks; need life be free from quibbling
and making excuses? "Isn't it better
to be silly, lax, babbling and lying?
Don't you think one improves a little
even by letting oneself be as one is?"

What Alma presents here is, though
simplistically expressed, a not
uninteresting notion: that in our
lies, our machinations, our sloppiness,

is our truth; that by yielding to them
we become more ourselves and, in a
sense, better.209

I think what Bergman wants to communicate to us is
not the confusion of the lie-syndrome but the more
profound lament of words' loss of meaning. When Alma,
near the end of the film, breaks down and speaks
nonsense phrases, Bergman offers this explanation:
"She has been driven nearly insane by her resentments
so that words, which are no longer useful, can no
longer be put together by her. But it is not a matter
of psychology. Rather, this comes at the point inside
the movement of the film itself where words can no
longer have any meaning."210   Until Bergman can
relate words to being rather than to metaphysical
form, the paradox will persist.

The film's most significant development takes
place at the seashore, not in the hospital or in the
psychiatrist's office.   Here the two women are
isolated, and we have only their action and
interaction on which to concentrate.   Although
Elisabet continues to be silent, an intimacy begins to
grow between them.   They are obviously communicating
by body and facial language though not in words.
Bergman shows us this ambiguity in a number of ways.
When picking mushrooms the two women are seen walking
along behind a small stone wall.   When one stoops to
pick, the other is erect and vice versa.   It is like
"seeing" the counterpoint of Bach.   When sorting and
identifying the mushrooms they both are (seemingly
quite unconsciously) humming--not the same tune, but
in harmony.   They are at this point not dressed alike,
though they do wear the same kind of large straw sun
hat, Alma's dark and Elisabet's white.   Elisabet takes

Alma's hand (significant after <u>The</u> <u>Silence</u>) and compares it to her own, but Alma quickly withdraws hers, nervous about the portent of such a comparison. So a series of episodes, actions, gestures, and props begin to suggest an intimacy between the two until Alma finally says, "I've always wanted a sister." Alma then presumes such a sibling relationship and tells Elisabet the rather intimate details of her early love life (which she admits sounds a bit like soap-opera), her relationship to Karl-Henrik, and finally of her beach-orgy with the teenage boys which was followed by an intense sexual relation with Karl-Henrik that same evening. The result was pregnancy followed by an abortion arranged by a medical friend of Karl-Henrik.

Alma's relating of the abortion is done with tears which Bergman describes as "a confused sobbing, filled with pleasure." Most importantly, it leads to the following speech of Alma's, which poses the central theme of the film: "It doesn't fit, nothing hangs together when you start to think. And all that bad conscience for things that don't matter. You understand what I mean? Can you be quite different people, all next to each other, at the same time? And then what happens to everything you believe in? Isn't it important at all?" John Simon's analysis of Alma's questions makes an important contribution toward our understanding, and I begin with that: "In the screen play, she (Alma) now asks tearfully: 'can one be entirely different people, right next to   , at the same time?' Where I left a blank, the text reads <u>vartannat</u>, which is mysterious. We expect 'each other,' for which the correct Swedish word would be <u>varandra</u>; <u>vartannat</u> is the neuter form and applies to things rather than people. Unless this is simply a slip of the pen or a compositor's error, it is baffling. In any case, the film changes this to: "Can you be one and the same person? I mean two people?" This cri de coeur of Alma's fairly summarizes the whole film: can two people become one? But, under emotional stress, Alma expresses herself badly, and her wording is significant: can one person even be a consistent whole and not split into two or more people?"211

In this very complicated and insightful film of Bergman's we are dealing with at least three different possibilities, each of which deserves to be considered: it is a psychological study of character development; it is an explication of Sartre's en-soi, pour-soi; it is a phenomenological description of Buber's I-Thou relation. We shall look at each of these in turn.

Perhaps the most popular interpretation of the film is the first of these possibilities, the last suggestion of Simon's above: "...can two people become one?...can one person even be a consistent whole and not split into two or more people?" Following the psychology of Carl Jung, which Bergman seems to favor at this point, many people have thought of Persona as the interplay between Jung's two basic personality types: Elisabet, the Introverted Thinking Type, who appears to be emotionless, aloof, and distant, who wants to be alone, who is headstrong, stubborn and unapproachable; and Alma, the Extraverted Feeling Type, who is effusive, emotional, gregarious, and moody, who needs an appreciative audience. A good case could be advanced for such an interpretation in Persona, but it is the second half of Simon's suggestion that has captured the interest of more viewers.

Because there is in the film an eventful, visual fusion of Elisabet's and Alma's faces, do the two women really represent opposite "forces" or attributes vying for control within one given individual? Again Jung provides ample insights for such speculation. The women may represent, for example, the tension which exists between an ego's "persona" (Alma) and her "shadow" (Elisabet). The "persona" is the expression of the conformity archetype which seeks acceptance by adopting a sociable mask, an acceptable and beneficial corporate, public image. The "shadow" is the powerful and creative expression of one's basic "animal" nature, the source of spontaneity, creativity, strong emotions, and deep insights. For Jung, each of these contributes to the "self," and one suffers if either takes total control. In fact, it is the tension between these forces which produces the energy we characterize as "being alive."

There are other possibilities. The polarities represented by Elisabet and Alma might also be those of "persona" and its "animus"--Alma's public "face" versus those expressions of aggression and strength in Elisabet which characterize the male side of the female psyche. Again, the polarities may be those of the "shadow" and her "animus." Simon's own suggestion would seem to be a variation related to these last two possible polarities: "To begin with, Alma and Elisabet stand for innocence and experience, the naive and the raffiné; in a certain sense, perhaps even for body and mind. This duality can be embodied in two persons, as it is here, but it has a distinct relevance to the contradictory aspects of a single

person. As complementary opposites, they need and
seek each other out following the principle of
polarity; but as conflicting, antithetical forces,
they end up by clashing."212

It is impossible to gainsay the above
interpretations, but they do leave some questions
unanswered, some inconsistencies unexplained if the
two personalities are one woman. One has trouble, for
example, explaining the hospital scenes at the
beginning and ending of the film; it is also difficult
to account for Elisabet's relationships to her son and
her husband--particularly since Alma has neither.
Advocates of this interpretation point to two symbol
forms which Bergman gives us, which they contend
support their thesis. The film begins and ends,
literally, with the movement together and final
separation of two carbon elements between which the
arc produces the light for the film. The second
symbol is even more explicit. At the climax of the
film, Bergman merges the facial images of Elisabet and
Alma into one composite picture. There are other
symbolic interpretations, however.

A more likely explanation, I believe, is that
Bergman is here following the existential lead of Jean
Paul Sartre. Knowing that Bergman has been greatly
influenced by the existentialists, particularly Sartre
and Camus, it is not surprising to see Bergman using
Sartre's en-soi, being-in-itself, and pour-soi,
being-for-itself, as descriptive categories. A short
word of explanation is necessary to show just how
Bergman employed this distinction within human
existence. Being-in-itself is unconscious being, like
the being of a stone or a pencil. Each is what it is
and no more. Its being always coincides with itself.

<u>Being-for-itself</u> is conscious <u>being</u>, and it is the nature of consciousness to be aware of its continuous freedom, its necessity to choose, its need to re-create itself each moment--all of which make human existence a continuous act of self transcendence. For Sartre human existence has meaning only in terms of the future toward which one projects oneself, towards what one is choosing to <u>be</u> rather than what one already is. To try to identify the two, <u>Being-in-itself</u> and <u>Being-for-itself</u> is what Sartre calls an act of "bad faith," an attempt to fix or secure my identity in defiance of time and choice. Examples might be helpful here: it is as though I could say: because I have been a good man in the past, I shall, without question, be a good man in the future; or, because my marriage has been happy for ten years, it will necessarily be happy for fifty. The ambiguity to which Sartre points not only permits such acts of "bad faith" to occur; it also indicates their invalidity. Without knowing the philosophy of Sartre or the jargon of existentialism, we still know that for any man who claims, "I'm the greatest," it's only a matter of time....

In <u>Persona</u>, if we are following this second possible interpretation, Elisabet has discovered this ambiguity of Sartre's--that in conventional or classical terms it is impossible to be a person of "integrity" or "authenticity," if those terms refer to some static definition of self. Elisabet for years had tried to be superwoman--wife, actress, mother, lover--but in each case she was trying to fix her identity, to make <u>Being-for-itself</u> conform to some preconceived notion of <u>Being-in-itself</u>. When she makes this discovery, the discovery of inauthenticity or just plain phoniness, she suddenly becomes silent. It is a desperate attempt to avoid deception. What she learns during the course of her stay on the island with Alma, is that she _must_ choose to be, that being silent is, indeed, a choice in itself. What Alma learns, at great emotional cost, is what Elisabet already knows--that her life up to this point had been mere role-playing, an act of "bad faith." Thus, at the end of the film, both women have learned that life is continuously being threatened by Nothingness and that one's only recourse is to choose to be. It may be that this is why the final word between the two women, said at last by each, is "nothing."

The same analysis applies if, following Simon's suggestion, we are dealing with one woman, not two. Elisabet then becomes the elusive personification of Being-in-itself, Alma the continuously distraught Being-for-itself who finally acknowledges her inability to unify the two--to identify completely with Elisabet. The heart must be a lonely hunter. There is much to commend this Sartrean interpretation, not the least of which is one of the central messages of the next film, Shame: under the pressures of war and in the presence of meaningless chaos, choice is singular and self-centered.

It is the third possible interpretation, however, which is the most inclusive and most probable one for me, yet I am quite sure that Bergman would not recognize it under its formal guise, the existentialism of Martin Buber. I think Bergman probably thought that he was exploring the Sartrean interpretation discussed above but that, descriptively, it proved to be inadequate and unconvincing. I think, likewise, that Bergman is such an honest artist that he will not adjust his observations to fit his theories. If things just don't hang together, if there are loose ends, ambiguities, or contradictions, Bergman will simply include such discrepancies without apology. "Life's like that." A good existentialist attitude. But let us look at Martin Buber's existential stance and see if it does not better suit Bergman's Persona than the previous two attempts.

Martin Buber believes that Western philosophy since Descartes has made a fundamental error in isolating man within the subjective limits imposed by his own perception and understanding of Being. Once locked into the interpretive apparatus of my mind, solipsism and all its kin are a constant threat to any objective, knowable world. Buber's response to this isolation is as simple as it is radical. When Western philosophy begins with "I", i.e. the perceiving, thinking subject, it fails to understand that the basic "word" or term for reality is not "I" but I-Thou. One begins, Buber believes, in relation; and only through the continuing experiences of encounter does one begin to differentiate and distinguish the "I" from the "Thou."

Even our language gives evidence of this corporate beginning. The pronoun "I" cannot even be defined without reference to the "Thou." "I" and "Thou" are correlative terms and express a generic necessity. But our expression and experience of Being is not singular but always twofold, as Being itself is twofold. The basic words are really I-Thou, I-It. The first relationship tells me who I am (a subjective claim), the second, what I am (an objective claim). Though both of these are fundamental to Being, the ontological priority is with I-Thou. My intimate, personal relationships to others through love are I-Thou; my public, objective relationships to things or even others in function or use are I-It; my relation to my "Thou" is subjective, i.e. involving my total self as distinct person; my relationship to "It" is objective, not involving the personal, intimate self, but a public standard or norm.

Under the rubrics of these fundamental distinctions, it should be pointed out that people may be either "Thous" or "Its" depending upon whether they meet me in the intensity of my subjectivity or in terms of some function or service. A lover is Thou; a store clerk an It. The difference, while qualitative, is not a value judgment. Both relationships are needed to give expression to the respective subjective and objective aspects of our lives. Problems arise when either of these categories pretends to the characteristics of the other. Thus a salesperson who calls me by my first name at first meeting is trying to exploit the power of the intimacy of the I-Thou relation for the purpose of getting a sale (In the I-Thou relation I am totally vulnerable to my "Thou"); an "It" I can leave or take according to its objective merits. On the other hand, objectivity is highly desirable in certain areas where subjectivity would be suspect. We expect, for example, a judge to be impartial, unbiased in his pronouncements from the bench. Consequently, we do not expect a judge to rule in cases which involve his own family where love might deprive him of his objectivity.

With this hastily sketched background, we can now see a way around the problem that John Simon raised for us earlier. Alma says, "Can one be entirely

different people, right next to each other, at the
same time?" Simon seemed puzzled because the word
used for "each other" was neuter, but if we follow
Buber's lead here, we can say, "We would expect it to
be neuter; it is descriptive of an I-It situation."
Alma had just told Elisabet about her love for
Karl-Henrik and, in the next breath, her orgy on the
beach. But this poses no problem for Buber, for,
ostensibly, one relationship is I-Thou the other
I-It--each has its own distinct character. So is each
of us a "different" person as we move from the
intimacy of a "Thou" relation to the objectivity of an
"It," from the intimacy of family to the objectivity
of the office.

Because Buber is an existentialist, one must take
the phrase "different person" seriously. Each
encounter I have, whether "Thou" or "It," tells me
something new about myself, in fact, creates a new,
more comprehensive identity, so that one avoids the
identity-problem that Simon discusses. The only
problem that really exists here is that of duplicity.
Alma does not really love Karl-Henrik; she merely says
that she does because that is the kind of relationship
one is supposed to have with one's fiancé. Though
Alma has not articulated it (most likely is not even
conscious of her self-deception), she seemingly can't
understand why her relationship with Karl-Henrik does
not fulfill her expectations, indeed, leaves a sense
of emptiness, a void. She has experienced two "It"
relationships but has tried to give them different
names.

The real I-Thou relationship which Alma has is
that which is beginning with Elisabet. Just after the
speech of Alma's which we have been discussing, Alma

says to Elisabet: "That evening when I had been to
see your film, I stood in front of the mirror and
thought 'We're quite alike.' (Laughs) Don't get me
wrong. You are much more beautiful. But in some way
we're alike. I think I could turn myself into you.
If I really tried. I mean inside. Don't you think
so?--And you wouldn't have any difficulty, of course,
turning into me. You could do it just like that. Of
course, your soul would stick out a bit everywhere,
it's too big to be inside me. It would look all sort
of odd."   This is the language of love.   Alma is
talking about "inside" and "soul"--the intimate,
creative exposure and trust which characterize love.
(One further disclaimer should be made at this time:
this "love" that we are talking of, for Buber and for
Bergman, is a much larger term than sex. Sex may be
one expression of the physical relationship of love,
but it is only one of many.) It is at this point in
the film that we first hear Elisabet's voice, but
because the camera is on Alma, we, like Alma, are not
sure. Was it Alma's imagination or does Elisabet
truly respond to her--a response which the next
morning, under Alma's questioning, she will deny?
Elisabet says, "You'd better get off to bed, otherwise
you'll fall asleep at the table." Startled, Alma
repeats the words but changes the pronouns to pertain
to herself. Alma doesn't know, we don't know, and, I
believe, Bergman himself doesn't know whether Elisabet
really speaks or not. Response is what Alma longs
for; it is what we all long for, for life without love
is incomplete--a desert, as T. S. Eliot would call it.

This burgeoning I-Thou relationship between Alma
and Elisabet also explains the violent reaction Alma
has when she accidentally finds out that Elisabet has

been observing her, using her as an object of study.
Hell hath no fury like a lover scorned. We may be
disappointed when an I-It relationship fails, we may
even be angry at some miscarriage of justice or
evident fraud; but we feel personally betrayed when
the I-Thou relation is violated. At this point
Bergman even portrays the film (a picture of Alma)
catching fire--a fury, an immolation of self which
must remind Elisabet of the betrayal which motivated
the immolation protest of the Buddhist Monk in
Vietnam. Alma's revenge for Elisabet's betrayal is to
leave broken glass where Elisabet will step on it,
cutting her foot, and to fantasize making love to
Elisabet's husband in Elisabet's presence. Both
attempts fail for both are inappropriate and
childish. I-It can never suffice in a situation which
demands an I-Thou response--the truth of which a
revenge-frustrated Hamlet might have warned her.

The ruptured relationship with Alma produced a
confrontation with reality which Elisabet could no
longer keep out. One cannot participate in the I-Thou
of love without the responsibilities of that love
being accepted. Elisabet has responded to Alma; now
it is too late, with impunity, to try to withdraw.
John Simon remarks about a similar episode which
happens at the same time: "...Bergman suddenly
confronts Elisabet and us with an image of human
suffering drawn from real life--the Warsaw Ghetto, an
anguished woman and a frightened boy. Elisabet, too,
has a boy who is suffering--at her hands. The reality
of Warsaw, Elisabet's reality, and our own
merge."213

Elisabet puts back together the two torn pieces of her son's photo, which indicates that the experience with Alma has affected her--in Buber's terminology, _effected_ her.   Elisabet and Alma have both been changed by the encounter; both have become indissolubly part of the other. Bergman portrays this with a series of very powerful scenes--some real, some fantasized. We are shown a scene in which Elisabet and Alma, now dressed alike, sit opposite each other. Alma tells, with surprising, intimate detail, Elisabet's conception of and relation to her son. While this monologue goes on we are watching Elisabet's face and its acknowledgment of guilt. Then the monologue is repeated, but we are watching Alma's face and realize that she is really giving an autobiographical account of her own feelings about pregnancy and subsequent abortion.   At this point, Bergman merges the two faces of the women; the two have become one--or something of each has become inextricably part of the other. Alma tries shortly thereafter to verbalize it but fails: "I don't feel like you, I don't think like you, I'm not you, I'm only trying to help you, I'm Sister Alma.   I'm not Elisabet Vogler. It's you who are Elisabet Vogler. I would very much like to have--I love--I haven't--." Objective words must always fail to be adequate in a description of the subjectivity of the I-Thou relation, as any lover knows--quarreling or not.

The denouement of Persona is faithful to Bergman's journey; it does not resolve the ambiguities with which we have been faced all along, but it does assert that what meaning to life there is resides in relation. In a fantasy scene which recapitulates the film for us, Alma, again dressed in her uniform,

confronts Elisabet. Alma takes her fingernails and
scratches her own arm so that it bleeds. Elisabet
places her mouth over the wound and sucks Alma's blood
so that a blood-bond is symbolically established. But
there is seemingly no exchange here, and critics have
likened Elisabet's action to that of a vampire or,
more appropriately, a blood-sucking spider--the
"monstrous forces" reappearing under a different
guise. As Alma watches this happen, she becomes more
and more enraged until she finally lashes out at
Elisabet, flailing her with both arms, the violent
fury of betrayal. In reality, the two pack their
belongings and leave the island separately.

Yet Bergman has one more instance of the ambiguity
of their relationship to show us. As Alma is ready to
leave the summer house, she pauses to look at herself
in the mirror; suddenly, in the reflected image,
Elisabet's face is there beside her own. Elisabet
strokes back Alma's hair in a gesture of intimacy
which we have seen earlier in the film. Alma shakes
off the apparent reverie and goes about her business,
but Bergman has let us know that Alma will always see
Elisabet when she looks in her mirror. The negative
aspect of this ambiguity is given us when we next, and
for the last time, see the two together. The scene is
back in the hospital. Alma is coaching Elisabet:
"Try to listen. Please. Can't you hear what I'm
saying. Try to answer now. Nothing, nothing, no
nothing." Elisabet responds, "Nothing," to which Alma
replies, "It'll be alright. That's how it must be."

What we have witnessed in the film is an I-It
relationship which has developed into an I-Thou
encounter and then disintegrated into an I-It
relationship again. But because the I-Thou is an

existential and creative relation, the "I" which
resumes an I-It is different than that of the original
I-It relation. Behind this whole process, for which
Buber has given us a vocabulary, Buber maintains there
is an Eternal Thou who stands subjectively in relation
to every person at every moment. It is the one
relation which cannot be reduced to I-It even though
one may, at times, try to think of or respond to God
as an object. It is the I-Eternal Thou relation which
is the ground of all human I-Thou relations and is
mystically manifest in all those relations.

Arthur Gibson arrives at a similar but more
radical conclusion by using a different symbol
system. Gibson suggests that God's intimate and
personal confrontation with man is symbolized by
Elisabet whose silence then becomes symbolically
necessary.214 The result of her confrontation with
Alma is deicide:

> The Persona...of Elisabet Vogler is the
> theophany of the true God. He has
> never needed this creature whom he
> admits to his intimacy; he can admit
> that creature only on condition that
> the creature will surrender himself
> entirely to a radically new dimension,
> different from any in which he has
> familiarly moved; God calls that
> creature gently but firmly and promises
> him not the comfort of satisfaction but
> the glory of transformation allied to
> the continued drama of created
> freedom. When man falters or recoils
> from this invitation in all the
> fullness of its implications, the

result can only be that atheism which
is simultaneously deicide.[215]
As in The Silence I find that I am unable to justify
Gibson's symbol assignments. To make Elisabet the
God-figure of the film puts too much strain on the
total portrait which Bergman creates for us, and it in
no way corresponds to what he himself has said about
the structure and meaning of the film. That the film
ends with atheism and deicide is too definitive a
statement for Bergman. One has to admit that Bergman
does not give any hint of a relationship with an
Eternal Thou, but in the I-Thou relation between Alma
and Elisabet the potential does remain available for
his continuing journey.

From the above analysis of the film, I think that
Bergman would basically agree with the logic of
Buber's point, but is distressed that existentially he
is thus far unaware of that divine manifestation.
That is the power of the ambiguity we have just
discussed. Either human love reflects or points
beyond itself to some eternal reality, some ultimate
meaning which we call God, or it is a sham, a
"nothing," which destroys us by its insidious
pretense. The next film we shall discuss, Shame, is
really an exploration of this latter alternative. But
in Persona itself, the theme is continuously present.
It is Elisabet's response to her role in Electra which
prompts her silence. If there be no meaning, no
ultimate reality, no Father, then all is vanity--as
Ecclesiasticus once told us. If everything is to end
in Nothingness, then all that leads up to this demise
is nothing, too. Any affirmation is a cruel hoax
perpetrated by a fraudulent future.

Outside the cottage where the two women stay is a
pole on which is mounted a ship's figurehead. The
face of the figurehead is strikingly like that of
Elisabet's Electra.   It is a face of anxious
waiting...wondering. The wood has cracked below the
right eye so that it looks like tears flowing down.
It is in front of this statue that Alma's angry
confrontation with Elisabet takes place. The camera
angle is such that even though we know that she is
talking to Elisabet, it looks as though she is
addressing the figurehead. What she says in this
instance continues one of the themes we heard so
strongly in <u>Winter Light</u>--the plea that God would have
a use for us. Now Alma says: "That's what it has
come to--Now you don't need me any more, so you throw
me away."   At this point Alma takes off the dark
glasses she has been wearing in that scene and throws
them down. The time has passed to see through a glass
darkly, but Elisabet, the figurehead, and God remain
silence.

Bergman leaves us with ambiguity, mundane and
transcendent.   In the face of traditional western
manners and morals, the radical individualism of the
existentialist seems heroic, until one is confronted
by the suffering of the Jews of the Warsaw Ghetto.
The holocaust has a corporate face, pleads with
corporate hands.   In the face of popular Western
religion, the radical agnosticism of the
existentialist seems courageous, until one is faced
with the monk who willingly immolates himself for his
belief.   Bergman notes: "The monk scares her
(Elisabet) because his conviction is so enormous he is
willing to die for it."216 The question of God, for
Bergman, remains open though the arguments have become

increasingly negative. <u>Persona</u>, however, has introduced a new element. A new way to expect God to reveal Himself; perhaps a new way to look for God in the first place. The metaphysical God has disappeared; the God who is <u>Eternal</u> <u>Thou</u> may yet appear. For Bergman this is not a statement but a feeling. Birgitta Steene seems to come to this same conclusion, though her categories of reference are different than our present ones: "The metaphysical perspective of <u>Persona</u> seems to me, however, of minor importance; while a film like <u>Winter</u> <u>Light</u> cannot be meaningful without a religious frame of reference, <u>Persona</u> does not benefit much from an 'allegorized' interpretation. But there is certainly in the film an expressed need for a belief of some kind, for a definite and stable point of reference, within which the individual can function."217

Bergman says: "Persona is a tension, a situation, something that has happened and passed, and beyond that I don't know."218

Shame (1967)

> "Give me something to stupefy my
> senses, or beat me to death, kill
> me, I can't do it any longer, I
> can't. You mustn't touch me, it's
> shame, a dishonour, it's all
> counterfeit, a lie. Just leave me
> alone, I'm poisonous, bad, cold,
> rotten. Why can't I be allowed
> just to die away, I haven't the
> courage."
>
>

Persona

In a famous passage in The Republic, Plato is
trying to establish the assertion that justice is of
such value that it is its own reward. But, in order
to prove this, it is necessary to strip away from the
exercise of justice any compensation whatsoever which
may cast doubt on the purity of motive. In fact, the
just man must even be considered unjust by his
friends--then one could determine whether the exercise
of justice is its own satisfying reward. By the time
we get to Shame in Bergman's spiritual journey, I
believe that he, too, has reached this reductionist
point of investigation. The rational proofs for the
existence of God have proved invalid; the mystical
claims for God's existence have proved to be
unverifiable; the apotheosis of love has proved to be
sentimental and unjustifiable. By the time that we
reach Shame man stands alone and anxious in the
universe, unprotected by the certainty or certitude of
God. The shift from classical theism to atheism first
hinted in Persona seems now to have taken place; we
are no longer experiencing the absence of the presence
of God but the presence of the absence of God.

So the question arises: if man is stripped of his transcendent resources and support, what is the nature of his existence, what is the "religious" character of his life to which there may be response if God should appear? William Barrett and Bergman are of one mind in the necessity of this reductionist stance: "The whole man is not whole without such unpleasant things as death, anxiety, guilt, fear and trembling, and despair, even though journalists and the populace have shown what they think of these things by labeling any philosophy [or film!] that looks at such aspects of human life as 'gloomy' or 'merely a mood of despair.' We are still so rooted in the Enlightenment--or uprooted in it--that these unpleasant aspects of life are like the Furies for us: hostile forces from which we would escape. And of course the easiest way to escape the Furies, we think, is to deny that they exist. It seems to me no accident at all that modern depth psychology has come into prominence in the same period as Existentialism and for the same reason: namely, that certain unpleasant things the Enlightenment had dropped into the limbo of the unconscious have begun to backfire and have forced themselves finally upon the attention of modern man."219

Bergman calls the Furies of classical Greek literature the "monstrous forces," and there are few places where these monstrous forces are more evident than in modern warfare: its brutality, impersonalism, lack of rationality, confused motivation, senseless destruction, and human desensitization.   "Shame originates in a panicky question: How would I have behaved during the Nazi period if Sweden had been occupied and if I'd held some position of

responsibility or been connected with some
institution.? Or had even found myself threatened as
a private person? How much civic courage would I have
been able to muster up under the threat of violence,
physical or spiritual, or in the war of nerves in an
occupied country? Every time I've thought about such
matters I've always come to the same conclusion:
physically and psychically I'm a coward--except when I
get angry."220

Shame is a Sartrean study of the individual under
the threat of arbitrary death; it is the struggle to
stay alive in a hostile and meaningless world; it is
an attempt to explore the anxiety which characterizes
all human existence confronted by
Nothingness--"Anxiety before Nothingness has many
modalities and guises: now trembling and creative,
now panicky and destructive; but always it is as
inseparable from ourselves as our own breathing
because anxiety is our existence itself in its radical
insecurity. In anxiety we both are and are not, at
one and the same time, and this is our dread. Our
finitude is such that positive and negative
interpenetrate our whole existence."221

This is the second of the Alternatives, the
Sartrean, discussed as possible interpretations of
Persona. At the end of Persona Elisabet and Alma
part, the love relationship which they shared has
ended--with even some question about whether it had
ever occurred. At the film's end, the carbons parted,
the arc light was extinguished, the word between them
was "nothing." If the relationship between them was
not love, in Buber's sense of I-Thou, then it was
sado-masochistic in the Sartrean sense. It is this
strand of interpretation from Persona that Bergman
picks up for Shame.

Eva and Jan Rosenberg, married for seven years, are professional musicians. A civil war, senseless to both, has forced the disbandonment of their orchestra, and the two have fled to a subsistence-level farm on an island. Their hope to avoid the conflict proves futile; the civil war comes to the island. Their attempt at isolation and neutrality is seen as conspiracy and collaboration by both sides, and they are forced, finally, to take an active role to save themselves. By this time Eva and Jan have lost any sense of idealism, loyalty, dignity, or honor; it is now a matter of survival. With everything they own destroyed, they attempt to flee the island only to find themselves helplessly adrift in a lifeboat, surrounded by the floating, bloated corpses of soldiers whose identity is unknown. The film ends with this nothingness, the meaninglessness surrounding them all; the camera retreats from the scene until nothing distinguishable remains.

Judith Crist believes that "Shame stands as perhaps the most unrelenting in its theme, going beyond the chilling exploration of a loveless humanity in Winter Light and The Silence to cry shame upon the God who has reduced man to bestiality and his civilization to nihilism. It is late in the creative day to be anti-war in specific terms, but Bergman's genius translates the specifics into universals: his is a nameless and continuing civil war in which only the animal instinct for survival motivates human relations. The destruction of the human elements is progressive...."222 Crist's description is very good, with the exception of her reference to "cry shame upon the God who has reduced man to bestiality...." In this film Bergman's growing nihilism is as complete as it gets, so that the shame is not God's but man's.

Bergman seems to use the idea of shame in two ways. The first way, and undoubtedly the way Judith Crist understood the film, the shame refers to man's inhumanity to man, his bestiality, his loss of all those virtues--like Laurence Binyon's "Mercy, Courage, Kindness, Mirth"--which gave man his sense of dignity and worth. So the film cries out, "for shame!" Certainly the impact of the film on the viewer supports this understanding, and one can agree with Crist that it must have been on Bergman's mind, too. But to the extent that that is true, it is anachronistic; it is inconsistent with Bergman's emerging existentialist position. This "for-shame" position depends for its power on the essentialistic notion that man has a metaphysical model, a set nature, a discernible character from which he can part only at his own peril. It is only over and against such a fixed hierarchy of value that one can judge any specific act or demeanor as evil, wicked, or bestial. The essentialist position gives us an idealistic yardstick for such measurements. But if one has rejected such an ideal portrait of mankind as unavailable or nonexistent, then such judgments made in terms of the portrait are simply invalid--at least as universals. If I try to turn my judgments into verifiable responses to some universal moral law, then I am acting sentimentally and illogically. Bergman, in Shame, may be guilty of some such sentimentality--or he may be guilty only of playing on such sentimentality in his audience, counting on their traditionalism to give power to his message. My judgment is that both of these elements are

unconsciously there in Bergman's script, but to dwell
on that or to count it as central would be to miss the
major thrust of his film--the exploration of the
Sartrean understanding of shame and its implications
for each of us.

Eva and Jan live in an absurd world. They are
grubbing away on a poor farm, a life for which neither
of them is suited physically, temperamentally, or
intellectually. They are professionals deprived of
their profession, yet very unprofessionally have let
their virtuosity on the violin deteriorate by
abandoning even practice (Eva, we are told, was first
violinist in the Philharmonic Society Orchestra). The
loss of the consolation and promise of music is an
ominous note for Bergman to sound. The social context
in which they find themselves is no better: their
phone continually rings early in the film, but no one
responds when they answer, a Kafkaesque touch. Their
car won't start--for no apparent reason. Church bells
ring, but it is not Sunday nor do they seem to be
chiming the hour or even sounding an alarm; when Jan
asks what they mean, Eva says, "Nothing"--a
transcendent reference as well as a reference to the
conclusion of Persona. In the town which they visit
to deliver strawberries, announcements are constantly
being made on public address systems, none of which
seem to make any sense--the breakdown of language
which we have inherited from The Silence and Persona.
Communication does not really occur.

No one really knows what's happening in this
country gripped by civil war. Part of the absurdity
is that the war is a "civil" one where political and
social motives and goals have long been forgotten and
cliches like "peace" and "democracy" are being freely

used by both sides. When asked by a military
interviewer whether she preferred democracy or a
dictatorship, Eva responds: "Hasn't the war been
going on far too long for us to know which is which?"
Again, their two best friends (which may be too strong
a designation) are Philip and Jacobi; both visit them
at their house; each represents a different side of
the civil war--though we are never told why. If one
is looking for an explanation, one's efforts are bound
to be frustrated, for the whole context is absurd.

Eva and Jan, themselves, are companions--not
lovers. They have been married seven years, but from
the dialogue (which admittedly becomes a little
strained at times) there has not been much real
communication between them. At one point Jan tells
Eva the story of the maker of his very fine violin, a
strange thing to be happening in the seven-year-old
marriage of two professional violinists. The couple
has no children, which indicates a physical
incompleteness comparable to their social and mental
separation. What they have established is the
sado-masochistic relation which Sartre describes. The
non sequiturs of mutual disinterest seem to be right
out of an Edward Albee play: Jan: "I had the
weirdest dream. Do you know what I dreamed...?"
Eva: "Aren't you going to shave today either?" Or,
Jan: "I think I'm getting a wisdom tooth...Can you
see anything?" Eva: "Did you pay the telephone
bill?" Again this basic lack of communication,
compounded by their psychological tensions:

> Jan: You're right to nag me. But I
> was a good musician, you have to
> admit it. And when we were in
> the orchestra--those were good

years.   You always say I'm weak
and give in.   When it comes down
to it, there's nothing right
about me.   Sometimes I just don't
understand why you don't leave
me.

Eva: You've said that a thousand times
and you don't really mean it.
(Laughs)   I'm sick to death of
you.   You're tired of me too.
Aren't you?

Jan: Yes, I'm pretty tired of you.

Eva: People shouldn't talk about
feelings and things.   It's such a
waste of time...

             *   *   *

Jan: When you stood down there talking
to Philip, anyway, I was in love
with you.   You were so beautiful.

Eva: At a distance, you mean.

Throughout the first half of the film, Jan is
portrayed as both weak and cowardly.   He breaks into
tears over nothing, whines about a sore tooth, faints
when accosted by marauding paratroopers; is unable to
kill chickens to take with them as they prepare to
flee the farm; blames himself when he discovers that
Eva is maintaining a sexual relation with Jacobi.   It
is only when their second "friend" Philip appears at
their house and forces Jan to kill Jacobi or be killed
himself (Jan agrees reluctantly both out of fear and
out of revenge against the man who had cuckolded him)
that Jan reverses his role.   He ceases to be the
masochist and now becomes the sadist.

In Sartrean freedom, such a switch is possible, but Bergman's position is more than just an exercise of Sartrean theory, however justified. It is also based upon the existential insight so eloquently described by both Dostoevski and Nietzsche--that under the nondescript surface of bureaucratized modern man lurk the monsters of frustration and resentment which can at any time erupt in powerful and unaccountable ways. "What Dostoevski saw," writes Barrett, "in the criminals he lived with is what he came finally to see at the center of man's nature: contradiction, ambivalence, irrationality.   There was a childishness and innocence about these criminals, along with a brutality and cruelty, altogether not unlike the murderous innocence of a child.   The men he knew could not be categorized as a criminal type and thus isolated from the rest of the species, man; these criminals were not "types," but thoroughly individual beings: violent, energetic, intensely living shoots from the parent stalk.   In them Dostoevski was face to face with the demoniacal in human nature; perhaps man is not the rational but the demoniacal animal.   A rationalist who loses sight of the demoniacal cannot understand human beings; he cannot even read our current tabloids."223

This understanding of man is the existential ground on which Bergman can justify the radical change in Jan and Eva, a change so many find inexplicable. But Jan is Dostoevski's Underground Man come to the surface, now expressing his hostility toward a universe that he finds alien and threatening. The frustration that results in his trying successfully to cope with that universe imposing itself upon him while, concurrently, endeavoring to realize his

Being-in-himself by Being-for-himself, is the source of his shame. One's experience at not being fully in control of one's life is what Sartre terms "shame." Such an interpretation is not limited to Jan. Eva says, while waiting for an interrogation to which she and Jan are forced to comply, "Sometimes everything seems like a long strange dream. It's not my dream, it's someone else's, that I'm forced to take part in. Nothing in properly real. It's all made up. What do you think will happen when the person who has dreamed us wakes up and is ashamed of his dream?" My impotence in self-realization because of external circumstances over which I have no control results in the experience of shame.

The film ends on just such a desolate note. Jan the masochist, the compulsive sufferer has turned sadist. He murders a young boy just to take his shoes.224 He rejects Eva, telling her that it would be simpler for him if she didn't come along on his planned escape from the island. He is curt and silent, prompting Eva to say, "What's it going to be like if we can never talk to each other any more?" The small lifeboat (ironic in itself) is filled with equally indifferent, self-seeking people. The boat, it turns out, is piloted by Philip who had coerced Jan into shooting Jacobi. Now Philip is helping Jan to escape--providing he can pay. Ironically the money used is Jacobi's, given to Eva, commandeered by Jan. Philip, after the boat's motor breaks down, slips over the side, committing suicide. As noted earlier, the film ends with the boat floating on a horizonless sea, becalmed, surrounded by the floating dead of war. All is silence and despair.

"Bergman's recent work," writes Robin Wood, "especially The Silence, Persona, and Shame, seems to me to be among the most essential investigations in any art form of the contemporary condition of what it really feels like to be alive today."225   So it is, but does it have a religious dimension? If so, as described, it would be that of despair.   There are enough conventional signs in the film to suggest that Bergman's religious approach in this film is nihilistic--well, almost.   But we need to consider that qualification.

First, one should note the negative symbols we are given, one of which we have already mentioned. The church bells ring on the island, but they no longer have any significance; their ringing makes as much communicative sense as Alma's nonsense words at the end of Persona. Again, out of Persona, the figurehead which Bergman associates with Electra and the Father-image, now appears as a relic in an antique shop which Eva and Jan visit--God or waiting for God has become quaint at best, meaningless and forgotten by most. A third image that Bergman gives us (but now only in the published text) comes via Eva's grandfather's grave. While in town, before the actual fighting surrounds them, Jan and Eva visit the grave on the anniversary of the grandfather's death. The grave is in a dark, remote corner of the lot. Grass has grown high all around the stone which is now at an angle:

> Eva: We ought to straighten it up.
> Jan: What good would that do?
> Eva: Perhaps not. (Reads) David
>   Fredrik Egerman, born 25 August
>   1914. Died 18 July 1968. God is
>   my strength.

The silent, neglected witness is devastating.

The most powerful, ubiquitous, and consuming symbol in the film is that of the spider-god, the monstrous forces of hate and death that overpower us and ravage the world. Bergman's device in identifying these forces of destruction and death with the spider is most subtle, and were it not a continuous theme and recurring symbol, we would no doubt miss or discount it. In the partisan raid on Rosenberg's house, led by Philip, Jan has refused to divulge what he has done with the money given Eva by Jacobi. On a search-and-destroy order, the soldiers ravage the house, one partisan senselessly shooting up the interior before the house is torched. In a vivid and obviously structured shot, Bergman has the soldier shoot out a mirror reflecting his image. The bullet shatters the mirror, leaving a hole with grotesque jagged striations. The spider image which Bergman wants is unmistakable. War, with its useless, senseless killing and wanton destruction is another expression of the monstrous forces of death, of the spider-god.

Although Bergman could not attend the world premiere of Shame in Italy, he sent a message in which he stated his intentions. He wants him film "to show unpretentiously how humiliation and the rape of human pride can lead to the loss of humanity in the victim himself...As an artist I am horror stricken by what is happening in the world, and I cannot side with any political system. I hope that in Shame I have been able to convey the intense fear I experience."226

Bergman really seems to have buried God in this film--except for one slim but important hope given credence by his statement above. It is Eva's dream which she relates to Jan while they drift helplessly in their lifeboat:

> I had a strange dream, it was absolutely real. I was walking along a very beautiful street. On one side were white, open houses, with arches and pillars. On the other side was a lovely park. Under the big trees by the street ran cold dark-green water. I came to a high wall, that was overgrown with roses. Then an aircraft came, roaring down and set fire to the roses. They burned with a clear flame and there was nothing particularly terrible about it, because it was so beautiful. I stood with my face against the green-water and I could see the burning roses. I had a baby in my arms. It was our daughter, she was only about six months old, and she was clutching my necklace and pressing her face to mine. I could feel her wet open mouth against my cheek. I knew the whole time that I ought to understand something important that someone had said, but I had forgotten what it was. I pressed the baby close to me and I could feel that she was heavy and wet and smelled good, as if she had just had her bath. And then you came on the other side of the street and I thought that you would be able to tell me about the important thing that I had forgotten.

This beautiful dream raises all sorts of images of love, affection, innocence, creativity, beauty--all the good, positive, affirmative human traits and experiences which the film had virtually destroyed. This would be a dramatic device of the most poignant irony were not the images those with a long history in the Judeo-Christian tradition. The burning roses which are not consumed may be a reference to the Mosaic burning bush and what Eva could not remember is that it is God (not Jan) who will address her at such a holy place. A more likely reference here is to the experience which the early Christian mystics called "exquisite purgatorial anguish." What Eva had forgotten was that the experience represents a purification which one endures before standing the presence of God. Burning roses are also symbols of the anguish of the crucified Christ in his redeemer's role. What Eva does not remember is that such suffering traditionally understood, is an atonement for the whole world, which is certainly what is called for if Bergman's description of the human predicament in Shame is accurate.

Bergman himself describes the dream in more humanistic terms, but the mystical overtones are present nevertheless. "Eva says: 'I had a feeling there was something I ought to have remembered, which I've forgotten.' It's about the burning roses and the child she feels against her cheek. It's about everything that is--water, clear, green running water, like a mirror. It's a dream I've had myself, a pure visual experience of something beautiful and delightful that has happened; something unattainable and which has been carelessly wasted. It must have something to do with love, I suppose."227   While this might be interpreted in terms of the Sartrean en-soi and pour-soi and the inevitable feeling of shame, I believe that it more likely is an expression of Bergman's subconscious hope that there is a "meaning to it all" and the character of that meaning is love. I find that there is a remarkable similarity, at least in tone, between this dream and the stated end of T. S. Eliot's spiritual journey in The Four Quartets: "And all shall be well and/All manner of thing shall be well/When the tongues of flame are in-folded/Into the crowned knot of fire/And the fire and the rose are one."

When one moves back from a more detailed consideration of the film Shame, one is struck by the fact that this film, more than any of Bergman's others to date, creates a mood. One comes away from the film not so much impressed by plot development, character delineation, fine acting, or brilliant directing but rather possessed by an apprehension about oneself and oneself-within-the-world, by what Martin Heidegger would call a mood. Mood, as noted in the Introduction, is not just a psychological feeling or an internal state. It is rather the responsive nature of our "being-there" in the world, so that we are joy or dread; these moods are not what we experience but who we are, here and now. In Shame the mood is one of anxiety (Angst), which is the most fundamental and revelatory of all moods for Heidegger. In experiencing Angst we are acknowledging the hereness and nowness of our existence in all its contingency, acknowledging that life can finally be understood only as being-toward-death.

IB: More and more I've a feeling that people, under the tremendous pressure they're being exposed to today, are acting in panic. Acting out of only one motive: self-interest. And that's what the film's about...

SB: Its chief characters lack any ideals or ideology. They are unable to choose. Unable to make up their minds which side they're on...

IB: I, too, think a faith, whether religious or political, is helpful in critical situations. It immunizes against psychoses.

JS: The film's pessimism offers no concrete alternative. When Eva and Jan put to sea and flee--what awaits them then?

IB: Nothing. We've disinherited ourselves. We're on the slippery slope. There's no stopping developments--things have gone too far already. The opposing forces are too few, too badly organized, too nonplussed, too helpless. What's going on in the West is all to hell. And we know it. And it's getting worse.[228]

In Shame we are made to feel our contingency, our helplessness in the presence of the monstrous forces which continuously threaten our lives; and our hope for redemption, for affirmation, in the face of this anxiety remains a dream.

A Passion[229] (1969)

"Are you just...ideas circulating round
each other and taking hold of each
other and talking to each other?   Or
are you living people who touch each
other the whole time?"

Shame

There was a kind of "finality" in the infinite
stretch of nothingness which surrounded the little
lifeboat at the end of Shame. Mankind, surrounded by
death, had nothing external by which to locate itself
in the universe--either physically or spiritually.
Robin Wood marks this point by observing a change in
Bergman's metaphor of journey: "...for a great deal
of its [Shame's] length the leading characters are in
the home that has become their permanent one (even if
they are still, essentially, displaced persons);
journeys in the first half of the film are abortive
attempts at flight, all of which end in a return to
the house, and the journey at the end is a voyage to
nowhere."230
 In the non-essential universe of the
existentialist there is no where to go; there is only
someone to be. But Bergman is obviously not satisfied
with this description of reality. The futility in
Shame is such that its sheer void robs even the idea
of futility of its power. However, there is for
Bergman an alienation, a lostness, an isolation which
does get its power from relation, and, if that
relation cannot be supplied by place or time, then it
must be found within the nature of being itself.
Thus, any journeys that Bergman may want to take from
here on would seemingly have to be deep within one's
self.

But here another problem arises: if, as an existentialist, Bergman has accepted the fact there there is no essential self, no permanent identity granted us by God, fate, Being-Itself, or what-have-you, then whence this sense of lostness? As he has before, Bergman seems in A Passion to turn to some form of Buber's I-Thou, I-It relation to supply that locus for orientation. My lostness, my isolation is in terms of others, or maybe of God, which would seem to indicate that Bergman is beginning to recognize (as Buber does) that one begins in relation to the world and others; one does not work towards it or finally achieve it, unless one means by that renewal or redemption.

This is a rather long and philosophical way of saying that Bergman has discovered what others have about Sartre (insightful and helpful as he may be): he cannot account for the common and most fundamental human experience of them all--love. Vernon Young is close to the mark when he states that "the moral point of the film...is that you cannot read another person without adequate love or knowledge."231 I assume that the knowledge to which Young refers here is that knowledge which is and can be born only of love. The knowledge of observation, i.e. objective knowledge, can tell you little if anything real about a person--which turns out to be one of the themes of A Passion, a constant theme which begins with the Knight's futile efforts in The Seventh Seal to have a "knowledge" of God. Love or its absence is not only the moral point of the film; it is its philosophical-theological point as well.

On first viewing or by superficial analysis, A
Passion would seem to have made no progress or
indicated no change from Shame, yet in light of the
above, A Passion presents the most significant change
in Bergman's film since The Seventh Seal. It is in A
Passion that Bergman shifts from an existential
context to an ontological one, i.e. from a context
where the encounter is only with Nothingness to a
context in which the encounter is with Being or
Non-Being, with others or with God--present or
absent. But it is now necessary for us to turn to the
film to see how Bergman accomplishes this and what
significance it will have for our spiritual "journey"
within...

As in Shame, the story takes place on an island
off the Swedish coast. Andreas Winkelman, who is
divorced or whose wife and child have abandoned him,
lives in a small cottage near the shore, not unlike
the cottage of Jan and Eva Rosenberg. The cottage is
surrounded by a stone wall symbolically reminiscent of
the circle that David constructed about himself in
Through a Glass Darkly, only now the circle has become
angular, fixed, and harsh. Here, because of a
telephone failure at the sometime home of Eva and Elis
Vergerus (who are distant neighbors) Andreas meets
their house guest, Anna Fromm. Through this and later
chance contacts, a relationship develops among the
four which leads to a short affair between Andreas and
Eva Vergerus, an extended liaison between Andreas and
Anna Fromm, and a relationship of varied dependence of
all three on Elis Vergerus. Each recognizes his
fundamental need for another or others, yet no one of
them can commit himself to another with sufficient
love to finally overcome the distance between them.

Thus, instead of saving each other, they end up
tormenting each other. The sense of lostness is as
profound as it is at the end of Shame, but we now
better understand it's genesis.

As in Shame, the film is suffused with violence,
both present and potential, explicable and
inexplicable: Bergman states: "The relationships in
A Passion grew out of the setting of Shame, and for me
this had a curious meaning. The war which was going
on in Shame now manifested itself for me in the same
milieu but in a more surreptitious way. In the cry of
the animals, the lambs stabbed to death, the burning
horses, and the bird which flies against the
windscreen. Meanwhile the real war--the war I can
find no formulation for--has moved over to the TV
set....The war in Shame, A Passion's background of
violence, was in my mind all the time."232 When
Bergman is interviewed by Charles Samuels, he not only
reinforces this connection with Shame, he also
suggests an even more organic link: "You know, the
atmosphere in A Passion is exactly like that of
Shame: killing, brutality, anonymity, people's sense
of their utter helplessness before brutality. Liv
Ullmann plays the same role in both films, and the
woman in Shame might have dreamed the same dreams that
Anna dreams."233 Indeed she might. In fact, the
dream which Anna has in A Passion has as its context
the final lifeboat scene of Shame--Anna, dressed as
Eva Rosenberg, comes ashore when the boat drifts close
to land. In the dream the shift from Sartrean
Nothingness to Christian alienation, from existential
nihilism to ontological mysticism (the relation to
Being) is symbolized, a point to which we shall return
in more detail later.

In order that our concentration might be focused on the developing relationships among the characters, Bergman does a number of cinematic tricks. One is to break into the plot structure of the film and have each major actor turn to the audience and discuss his or her own understanding of the part being enacted. With some hindsight, Bergman tells Charles Samuels that he is not convinced of the wisdom of such a ploy--only the women actors ad-libbed the way he had hoped all would do."234 The effect, at any rate, is to break into the story-line and make us engage more seriously in an analysis of who these people are rather than in what they are doing. This, in itself, shows Bergman's growing awareness of Buber's distinction between the natures of I-Thou and I-It.

A second device Bergman uses is related to the above distinction but is more subtle philosophically. It, too, is germane to his spiritual quest. Bergman utilizes his growing awareness of the ambiguity of time. Clock-time, G.M.T., seems to be one kind of comprehending context, one that governs the physical relation of things. In Buber's terminology this is the objective relation of I-It, of cause and effect, or of the relation between any number of things observed objectively by a self. Identity-time, by contrast, is the durational extension of conscious self-awareness. As such it is something quite different than clock-time. Identity-time is the subjective relation of I-Thou or the subjective awareness of one's personal identity in which minutes, hours, and days are of secondary importance. Clock-time is something one uses to give quantitative expression to the nature of one's identity; identity-time is the qualitative dimension of such an expression. Bergman effectively uses the two concepts so that we are never quite sure how much clock-time has elapsed between episodes or whether, in fact, things or experiences are actually repeating or extending themselves through identity-time. It is this latter possibility which has captured Vernon Young's imagination. Anna's first husband's name is Andreas; Winkelman's name is also Andreas. Anna's first husband is a scientist; Winkelman is also a scientist. Elis Vergerus says his wife had a brief affair with Andreas Fromm; Eva has a brief affair with Andreas Winkelman. Anna's first husband and child are killed in an accident when Anna was driving; Andreas Winkelman seems to know this and, in fact, seems almost to be victimized in the same way. There are other comparisons, but that should be enough to support Young's contention that Andreas Winkelman and Andreas Fromm are actually one and the same; that there is only one Andreas in the film: "What Bergman has done in this film is to abdicate from the conventional conception of time and duration, even more radically than he did in _Persona_. This is _limbo_, or, if you like, purgatory. This has all _happened before_. _It will happen again_. Time is spiral. Andreas and Anna and the others are _re-enacting_ a convoluted, unending torment out of the time-space continuum we are prepared to accept."235

While it is true that Bergman has become increasingly concerned about time (the ticking of clocks and watches, their presence in rooms or around wrists is more and more evident), it is with time's inevitability, its intractableness as a physical measure, that he is obsessed. Were this the only concept of time in _A Passion_ then Bergman would be

victimized as Young suggests--doomed to repetition.
But Bergman's use of identity-time, time in terms of
who we are rather than what we are, would seem to be
making a different point in A Passion. Instead of
saying that the two Andreas are really one and the
same, it would seem to indicate the wisdom of
Ecclesiastes: "Vanity, vanity, all is vanity; there
is nothing new under the sun." The point which
Bergman wants to make for us is that human nature,
influenced as it is by the "monstrous forces" (Anna,
in a dream, calls them "forces from underneath"), is
doomed to repeat the violence of the past if there be
no way of breaking out of our isolation and
establishing a relationship in love.

Love as a motivating, subjective force can alter
the objective sequence of cause and effect--as anyone
whose life's been changed by "falling in love" or
religious conversion knows. Put into Bergman's
current metaphor: the only way to break the
deterministic tyranny of clock-time is through the
incursion of a transforming identity-time. Support
for this interpretation, as opposed to Young's
common-identity hypothesis, comes from the fact that
we do see a picture of the first Andreas, Andreas
Fromm, who is quite different in appearance from
Andreas Winkelman. It is also supported by the very
end of the film, a picture of Andreas Winkelman pacing
back and forth in one spot, only to disappear
altogether in a fade-out, while the narrator's voice
states: "This time his name was Andreas Winkelman."
It is obvious that Bergman wants us to say, "Right,
but next time it will be me...or another."[236]

Another thing which makes this film different from
Shame and, indeed, from all Bergman's films since
Winter Light is the reintroduction of traditional
Christian symbolism. Without this he is unable to
convey both the hope of deliverance and the power of
alienation, the hope of resurrection and the pervasive
power of the Fall. His use of this symbolism remains
negative, but the nature of its origin remains
positive. The film begins, while the credits are
given, with the sound of sheep bells. Of course that
in itself would not be enough to say that Bergman is
introducing the idea of suffering and sacrifice, the
symbol of the paschal lamb, the lamb of God, the
Christ; but when it is seen in concert with the other
symbols of the film that likelihood is enhanced.

The narrative of the film begins with Andreas
observing three suns--"parhelions." "Such celestial
phenomena," says Bergman, "have been omens of violent
events or catastrophes of various sorts. For me it's
an old familiar sign."[237] So, too, for us who have
followed Bergman's films: it also appeared in The
Seventh Seal. A Passion follows just such a
catastrophic course. Andreas finds a puppy which has
been hanged but is not dead--our introduction to the
fact that a maniac is loose on the island who seeks,
for no apparent reason, to torture and kill animals.
So just before Easter we are shown sheep that have
been brutally killed and dismembered, and the symbol
of the paschal lamb, the suffering of innocence at the
hand of evil and/or irrational powers, is brought home
again. A rather pathetic island recluse, Johan
Andersson, is accused by his nameless and faceless
neighbors of being the killer, though Bergman has
already given us enough inside information to doubt

seriously any such accusation. Andersson is attacked, beaten, brutalized, and humiliated. He is forced to claim responsibility for the crimes, before his tormentors leave him unconscious. Unable to live in such a world, faced by such hostility, Johan hangs himself, leaving a note of explanation to Andreas who has befriended him. His stoning and subsequent death bring not only the martyr Stephen to mind, also Christ himself. When we are permitted to see his body, he has been laid on his own bed, over which hangs a picture of Jesus with the traditional come-unto-me gesture. The symbolic irony is powerful.

Identified with this event, though earlier in the film, is another symbol from the Biblical Passion story. Andreas and Anna are watching the TV and have just seen the famous footage of the South Vietnamese officer taking out a pistol and shooting a bound young prisoner in the head. Just at that moment a bird strikes the window of Andreas' cottage and is stunned, perhaps seriously hurt. Andreas and Anna go out; Andreas says that he must put the bird out of its misery, so he bashes in its head with a stone. He then proceeds to follow the Pilate precedent and washes the blood off his hands.

Bergman has implied a universal symbol by linking together these three extraordinary events: the Vietnam War, Andreas immediate response of violence, and the stoning and hanging death of Johan—in each case the epitaph "in cold blood" could apply. Where there is no love, there is not simply a vacuum—there is violence. Where love is sado-masochistic the same potential for violence holds true. An old letter from Anna's first husband, which Bergman permits us to read early in the film, asking for a separation,

apprehensively describes just such a relationship:
"It is best that we don't meet. I will only give in,
as despite everything I am in love with you. But I
don't want to give in because I know that we shall
only involve ourselves in new complications which in
their turn will bring on terrible mental disturbances,
as well as physical and mental acts of violence."
Just so did their "reconciliation" bring violence and
death.

The curse of the Fall--however that expulsion and
elimination is described--is isolation. It is a
defensive posture that makes even my neighbor,
finally, my enemy in my fight for survival and
supremacy. The only way out of this dilemma is
redemption, forgiveness, and reconciliation; but at
this stage, Bergman seems to believe that there is
none to be found. That is the message of Anna's
Easter dream--that dream which began with Eva in
Shame. In the dream Anna goes ashore and appeals to a
young girl for help but is told that she can expect
none--"We mustn't have guests any more. It's
forbidden. We have changed the locks on all the
doors." The dream continues with Anna meeting a group
of women, one of whom sits apart. Anna learns that
that woman's son is to be executed: "She is on her
way to the place of execution," Anna is told. "It is
to take place in public. We've tried to persuade her
not to go, but she says she wants to see it all...she
wants to be with him...." Anna tried to beg the
woman's forgiveness, but receives instead a look of
scorn. So ends the Easter dream; again, the
crucifixion with no resurrection, no forgiveness, no
redemption, only the lingering sense of guilt.

Against this background of the dream, Anna's prayer, given as a soliloquy in the text, but not in the film, gives the context we have been describing:

> God, formerly I lived near You.
> I put out my hand in the dark and
> touched You! You punished me and knew
> why. You enclosed me in Your
> forgiveness and I rested. Away from
> You I am worried, always hunted, never
> safe. I try to do right but do wrong.
> I want to be truthful but live in a
> lie. I make an effort to think clearly
> but move about in a confusing gloom.
>
> God have mercy on us all. Do not
> turn away from our cry. If You are
> ashamed of Your creation and want to
> obliterate it, then do not destroy us
> in this slow way. Hurl Earth from its
> orbit and let it fall into the void
> beyond Your knowledge. Put out our
> light, silence our screams, and let us
> be annihilated in a moment.
>
> God, free me from myself, free me
> from my prison, free me from life's
> fever.

But the Lutheran paradoxes of law and grace, belief and unbelief, freedom and bondage so evident in the above prayer are also characteristic of Anna's whole approach. She also believes in truth, but her truth turns out to be her own subjective judgment of the situation, despite the objective facts involved. Anna tells us several times of her love for her first husband, of how well they communicated with each other. Each time that Anna does this, Bergman flashes on the screen that portion of her husband's letter which speaks of "complications which in their turn will bring on terrible mental disturbances, as well as physical and mental acts of violence." The discrepancies between Anna's subjective truth and objective truth and the tensions that result, have always been Anna's undoing, even in her conceived relationship to God, which Bergman's text makes clear: "I long for God, long to be able to kneel down. Sometimes I pray merely because it feels unbearable not to pray. I find it so hard to live without God. I'm not a believer. I can't believe. But I know that when I say there's no God, I'm only saying half the truth and denying something important that I don't understand or don't want to understand. For me, it's insoluble. No Christ can console me. Do you understand me, Andreas?"

Andreas does understand her--at least one side of her. When Anna goes to pray after hearing of Johan Andersson's death, this exchange takes place:

She was kneeling with hands clasped. I asked her what she was doing.

"I am praying for Johan," she replied without looking up.

I told her to stop that damn silly acting. Anna asked me to leave her alone. I lost my temper still more and sat down on the stairs.

"You're only praying for your own sake."

"Go away," Anna shouted, "go away and leave me in peace!"

"Awful acting," I said and went
slowly down to the kitchen.

Bergman says this about Anna: "She's always
influencing others, a sort of moral force of nature.
Sometimes she has had a negative effect, sometimes she
can have a positive one--that depends on
circumstances.   Personally I feel she's terrifying.
I'm scared stiff of moralists--I've been one
myself....And she can't manage herself, either.
There's something dreadfully destructive about her
moralism, her incessant demands.   This inability to
accept herself, to accept the outside world, is about
the most dangerous thing of all.   I believe that
before one can start to do anything, one must first
accept oneself."238

Elis Vergerus is Anna's polar opposite and much
like his namesake in The Magician.   We also observe
that the figure-head resembling the tragic Electra
which was so prominent in Persona and relegated to the
antique shop in Shame now appears decoratively on the
door post of Elis' house.   Urbane and cynical, Elis
claims to believe in nothing, least of all what he is
doing as a professional architect.   He is presently
designing a "formidable monument of cultural
affectation" for the city of Milan--"a mausoleum for
the utter meaninglessness with which people of our
kind live."   He is likewise an amateur photographer
whose passion is to take pictures of people in the
grip of violent emotions--"At one time I collected
only pictures of violence and acts of violence."   But
the same cynicism prevails: "I don't imagine that I
reach into the human soul with this photography.   For
God's sake don't think that.   I can only register an

interplay and counterplay of thousands of forces, large and small. Then you look at the picture and give rein to your imagination. Everything is nonsense. Games and fancies. You cannot read another person with the slightest claim to certainty." But in addition to playing the Sartrean cynic to Anna's Lutheran romantic, Elis seems to represent another theological position or possibility for Bergman. Eli in Hebrew means judge or priest, and Elis Vergerus wears a white turtleneck and dark jacket, which looks very much like a priestly costume. As architect, i.e. as creator, he is removed from his creation, the bricks and mortar of it all, by at least one step; he remains objectively apart, emotionally uninvolved with his creation. It is a classic Deist position, the last vestige of a metaphysical concept of God. Elis' soliloquy, given in the text but not the movie, bears this out: "It is hypocrisy to cry over the world's folly. It is absurd to be appalled at human cruelty. It is a waste of feelings to clamor for justice or decency. The sufferings of my fellow creatures do not keep me awake at night. I am indifferent in my own eyes and other people's. I function." Yet Bergman is too fine a director to create for us a sheer stereotype. We do know that Elis cried (the only time that Eva can remember) when medical malpractice resulted in the abortion of his and Eva's child. We know, too, that while travelling he was concerned or jealous enough to call Andreas to check on Eva whom he could not reach by phone. "He is," says Bergman, "a man who's concealing an enormous sensitivity and sensibility behind a highly conscious outward attitude."239

Andreas is developed as a foil for both Anna and
Elis. Fleeing from an unsuccessful professional life
and an unfulfilled personal life, Andreas seems to be
pursued by the world. His stone wall of protection is
breached over and over again in terms of his needs and
the needs of his neighbors. Though we are seduced by
Bergman into liking this man who is kind to puppies
and civil to lonely old men, we learn at the same time
that he eavesdrops on his neighbor; he has been
convicted as a forger; arrested for drunken driving
and hitting a policeman. He represents the futility
of one who has consciously accepted his existential
predicament but can find no way out--a kind of
Sartrean nausea. When Anna tells him that their only
hope together is to leave the island, to go to some
new context, to leave the past behind, Andreas
replies: "Has it ever occurred to you, Anna, that the
worse off people are, the less they complain. At last
they are quite silent. Although they are living
creatures with nerves and eyes and hands. Vast armies
of victims and hangmen. The light that rises and
falls, heavily. The cold that comes. The darkness.
The heat. The smell. They are all quiet. We can
never leave here. I don't believe in any move away.
It's too late. Everything's too late."

In the text, but again not in the film, the
despair is reiterated: "The world rolls over me.
I've no shelter any more. I've no one to turn to in
protest, no one to accuse, not even myself. I am
helplessly exposed. I cannot exorcise or transform
what I see and hear. It goes on incessantly hour
after hour, it bleeds, gurgles, screams, creeps, and
stinks. I look on dispirited, frightened,
paralyzed." "What happens to Andreas?" asks Bergman.

"He dissolves. That man hasn't a chance of existing
in the material world. He's on the way to
dissolution. Whether one sees it in the film or not,
I don't know. He walks to and fro on the road and
finally lies down--just before the image dissolves
altogether."240

Eva is the only one of the four who seems to evoke
some hope, although this does not come through in the
film so much as in the text. Eva, as we first meet
her, is a non-person, empty and without character
unless being supplied by another. When asked if she
believes in God, she responds by telling of the book
she read as a child, which pictured God as one with a
great white beard--a beautiful picture which she still
remembers. She then turns to Elis and asks, "Do I
believe in God?" But Elis cannot answer for her and
seems to show little interest in doing so. One must
assume that it is because she craves his attention for
self-assurance and does not receive it, that she turns
to others like Andreas for affection and attention.
Even with Andreas, Eva talks of Elis: "Elis is
awfully tired of me. I don't know how to put it. I'm
a small part of his big general weariness. The
difference is just that...The world is indifferent to
Elis's sarcasm. But I'm not. No. I wish I could pay
him back. But I can't think of anything. I don't
know what to do, you see. Elis is a fantastic person
and I...The worst of it all is that I love him. I
mean _love_. There's no other word for it. I can't
even show him my love. _What is to become of us,
Andreas?_ Why do we grow like this? What is it that
destroys us bit by bit? What is this deadly poison
that corrodes the best in us, leaving only the shell?"

Eva's answer to this, suggested both in the film and the text, is to give herself to others--not in contrived affairs as with the two Andreases, but to others who suffer this claustrophobic life more acutely than herself--deaf-mutes. In the text this is given a definite Christian symbol of resurrection, but a resurrection within this life, not at its end: "I couldn't endure it [an abortion]: being conscious, seeing with open eyes, knowing what was going on. So I took the remaining sleeping pills and sank into a deep coma. It was crisscrossed by ghastly dreams. I wanted to wake up but couldn't. On the third day they roused me. By then my existence was changed, I thought that my previous being was a little sister who had died long ago and whom I mourned with sadness but no sense of loss. Now I am learning the language of deaf-mutes. It is a liberation, I'd like to call it a reprieve. I have left the past and exist only in the present."241

When Torsten Manns is interviewing Bergman, he tries to defend Anna: "But she's a more meaningful personality than Eva, with all her compromises." Bergman replies: "But Eva's always human, altogether like a human being; while Anna has something of the monster in her, something frightfully dangerous."242 If Eva, whose name is even suggestive, is to be Bergman's model for a new humanity, then the ontological relationship suggested by Martin Buber is reasserting itself. The important thing in a meaningful existence is not Being-in-and-for-itself but Being-with-another. Love, with its genuine desire to give and to unite cannot be dismissed as a minor variation of some sado/masochistic relationship. Meaningful living is not the exclusion of others but the inclusion of others in an intimate and personal way. It is this which Sartre has tried to ignore; it is this which spells out the difference between the despair of _Shame_ and the anxious hope of _A Passion_.

The transition from despair to anxious hope is more than just an exercise in theological gymnastics; it is the agony of dying-to-self in order to be free-for-another. It is the experience which Christians have long associated with the crucifixion--the agony one must endure in giving up one's egocentric world in order to be open to the world for the first time. It is the experience which Soren Kierkegaard calls "repetition." I have (possess) the world; give it up as worthless; I am given the world back and find it the joy of my life. Bergman has certainly not gone this far to date and may never describe it in just these terms, but he recognizes that some transition from our ego-suffocating defensiveness (in which all relationships are _I-It_) is necessary before love can freely grow. He recognizes that this transition is always, for the participant, an anxious, painful risk--a passion, modeled on _The_ Passion. After the Fall, descent into hell precedes ascent into heaven.

Vernon Young's analysis of _A Passion_ in his insightful study of Bergman's films, _Cinema Borealis_, follows somewhat similar lines to those above--at least in acknowledging that a shift does take place between _Shame_ and _A Passion_. But where we differ is equally important. Young sees Bergman returning to religious symbolism but also to the same theological position he had held earlier, a point I would strongly contest. "He (Bergman) assures interrogators," Young writes, "from the press or elsewhere, a dozen times over, that he has done with all that superfluous questioning of God and the silence of God and the riddle of existence. His films become, ever more hermetically, like messages launched in sealed bottles, rephrasings of the original cry for deliverance."243   Young then proceeds to show how A Passion is really the symbolic presentation of The Passion in what appears to me as a strained, literalistic way never intended by Bergman.244   Elis is cast in the role of Pontius Pilate; Eva is Mary, the madonna without child; Andreas seems to have a dual role: Peter the denier and Barabbas the thief; Anna is Mary Magdalen; Johan is a Christ-like good Samaritan. As imaginative as all this is, I find it highly that.   It seems to find more support from Young's quotations from Strindberg than from Bergman. However, my real dissent is not from this strained symbolism but from the implication that Bergman's religious position is retrogressive here, a fixed cinematic ploy which provides him with his artistic milieu.

After noting the negative force present in the Swedish spirit, Young states: "The exception is the Dogged Believer, exemplified by Bergman, a desperate pilgrim on the road to Damascus; he is bound to be desperate, like Strindberg having eliminated the possible alternatives; he is forced to become cabalistic, like Strindberg, for he is the citizen of a via media, here-and-now community and he dare not too freely boast of his complete defection from the pragmatic commandments. The more he becomes convinced that God is nowhere, the less inclined he is to forgive anyone for presuming to take His place and the

more earnestly he strives in his art to expound the
secret doctrine, that man in his freedom is paltry and
helpless."245   But it is just this understanding of
Bergman's so-called pragmatism that leads Young into
the erroneous judgment that Bergman is not truly a
religious pilgrim: "I have been visited by the
suspicion...that Ingmar Bergman is not an
authentically religious figure, despite the evidential
symbols in his films that accumulate to suggest he
is. I would describe him as a retentive personality,
in whom belief has been replaced by obsession. A
religious personality, by the simple definition I
understand, is one for whom there is something
resident beyond him, in the natural world, something
with which he can commune and which, in turn, communes
with him. The ceremony is reciprocal and instills
confidence. I feel nothing like this in Bergman's
movies, nor do I see it hinted in a single avowal he
has ever made."246

Young's problem would seem to be in his "simple
definition."   God, in the Christian tradition,
certainly never resided any<u>where</u> and most certainly
not <u>in</u> the natural world, which would, of course, make
the natural world, not God, sovereign. But the error
here is two-fold. First, Young's definition is a
popular one, not one from an area of competence in
religious thought, and consequently it would be hard
for him to identify Bergman's journey as a religious
one. Second, Young does not seem to be sensitive to
the change in Bergman's theological position--the
rejection of the "natural theology" of <u>The Seventh
Seal</u> and the implication of a new ontological (albeit
negative at present) context in terms of
<u>Being</u>-in-relation. I would say that Bergman is an

"authentic religious figure" for just those reasons that bother Vernon Young. Bergman does reject the God-out-there because such an objective God, so objectively considered, could never be the God who addresses the existential situation in which I and all people find themselves. The best that Young can say for Bergman, religiously, is that he is "a filmmaker of magic with an evangelical point of view--a Druid captured by Lutheranism."247

As charming as that is, it is not the whole story. But the ironic thing is that Young's final word of rejection can be, if we have understood the theological shift that has taken place in Bergman's religious posture, our present word of acceptance: Bergman "is the victim and the beneficiary of a traumatic displacement, a shock of disbelief from which he has never recovered in his soul; that shock is responsible for his impetus and for the intense condensation of his art. He cannot now move freely save within the confines of the belief he has tried to repudiate, the symbols it provides, the rejections it assists, the polarities and correlatives of which it is composed. He must retain the belief, if only in a glass darkly, for it is the sole source from which his own creation is supplied; within it conventions he can move. And one has to respect the untiring sagacity with which he has incorporated himself; he has been able to enact his own father, his own erring son, his own wife, God, the devil, and the saints. He has become his own Passion."248

Read with the shift from essentialism to existentialism in mind, one could hardly write a better summary to this point. But, the confines of Bergman's present belief have little in common with

the confines of the old. Existentially he <u>has</u> become
his own Passion. <u>That</u>, it would seem to me, is the
primary point that Bergman has to show us--that the
superficiality of the objective world, the world of
knowledgeability rather than knowledge, the world of
technique rather than responsibility, of rapport
rather than relation, can only isolate us, fragment
us, and finally lead to our destruction. I believe
that Bergman's films are in full accord with the
following observation by William Barrett "Every step
forward in mechanical technique is a step in the
direction of abstraction. This capacity for living
easily and familiarly at an extraordinary level of
abstraction is the source of modern man's power. With
it he has transformed the planet, annihilated space,
and trebled the world's population. But it is also a
power which has, like everything human, its negative
side, in the desolating sense of rootlessness,vacuity,
and the lack of concrete feeling that assails modern
man in his moments of real anxiety."249

Cries and Whispers (1972)

"Perhaps I am driven by a more
modest hope: a longing for affinity,
a secret dream of understanding."

A Passion

"What it most resembles is a dark flooding stream: faces, movements, voices, gestures, exclamations, light and shade, moods, dreams. Nothing fixed, nothing really tangible other than for the moment, and then only an illusory moment. A dream, a longing, or perhaps an expectation, a fear, in which that to be feared is never put into words."250 So Bergman begins his introduction to the story Cries and Whispers to his colleagues. Like all of his films since Persona it is part of Bergman's inward journey to achieve or find some spiritual self-understanding which can no longer simply be passed off as a psychological condition. The demanding, self-encompassing integrity ("wholeness"--if such a term can be understood without its usual classical/metaphysical implications) of the existential moment is greater than any single scientific or objective attempt to describe it. The journey must be that of a self-conscious self, not that of the self, clinically observed or objectively considered.

To emphasize this, Bergman creates an ancestral home as the setting for Cries and Whispers. Two sisters, Maria and Karin, turn to their childhood home to be with the third sister, Agnes, who is dying of uterine cancer. The whole of the film takes place within the rather dark and ornate Victorian manor

house, with the exception of one flashback at the end
of the film and the credit footage at the beginning.
In these latter two instances, we are in the park
grounds of the estate during the autumn season--with
its beauty but also its promise of death and dying.
The internal focus of this picture by set design and
action is, of course, an effort on Bergman's part to
make us aware of the perimeter of action as well as
the parameters of being, most notably that of
being-toward-death, that understanding of one's life
which includes the acceptance of one's death. The
interior sets for this spiritual exploration are red,
with this explanation by Bergman: "...all our
interiors are red, of various shades. Don't ask me
why it must be so, because I don't know. I have
puzzled over this myself and each explanation has
seemed more comical than the last. The bluntest but
also the most valid is probably that the whole thing
is something internal and that ever since my childhood
I have pictured the inside of the soul as a moist
membrane in shades of red."251

As in A Passion the elusive time and dream
sequences of the film prevent us from concentrating on
any plot development and attempt to force us to
confront the power and facticity of death itself. The
story, hinted above, is not much more extensive than
the hint. Agnes, the middle sister attended by a
devoted servant, Anna, is dying of cancer. Her two
sisters Maria and Karin arrive at the family home to
be with her in her last hours. Agnes dies; the
funeral arrangements are completed; the sisters, along
with their respective husbands who came for the
service, leave the house after settling the estate and
discharging Anna.   In itself, the plot is hardly

enough to keep the mind alive; but the power of the
film is in the interaction of the sisters and Anna,
their character portrayal, and their individual
ability (or inability) to confront death.

Since Shame, Bergman has been narrowing his focus
in this area of monstrous forces which so drastically
affect the meaning and meaningfulness of our lives.
In Shame such forces had to do with irrational
violence and the encounter with Nothingness, the
Void--the absolute loss of standards, values, or
principles by which to measure a meaning in life. In
A Passion Bergman found the Sartrean analysis
inadequate; the irrational forces which seemed to
threaten a meaningless death supersede the place of
Nothingness. Now, in Cries and Whispers, he comes to
the conclusion shared, indeed, by Scripture and,
philosophically, by Martin Heidegger, that death is
the final enemy. Death is the only event which
inevitably poses the ultimate question of life, for
death is the only thing that moves us beyond the
existentialist's despair.

I believe that Bergman's use of symbols supports
the transition indicated here. Time has always
bothered Bergman. In some films, like The Silence,
Bergman seemed to take us out of time so that we could
focus on the human interaction within the film. So,
too, the effect of most of his "island" films which
isolated us from the mainstream of getting and
spending in the frantic time-world of superficial
schedules and meaningless rituals. In Shame, the
striking of clocks and the ringing of Church
clock-chimes were irrational and meaningless; clocks
were in the antique store to remind us only of an
irretrievable past. Even in A Passion time was an

elusive double matrix within which love and hate, faith and doubt played out their definitive roles. But not so for Cries and Whispers. The role of time is central in this film. The home is filled with clocks, and one is constantly being reminded by sight-more often by sound--of the passage of one's life. There is one clock in the film, among the many, that has ceased to work: the clock in Agnes's bedroom. The contrast is, I am sure, a paradox which Bergman has intended for us to understand. The timeless, perennial problem of death is, at the same time (!) the problem of time itself. Death is not simply a state of Nothingness to confront; it is a state of Nothingness which each one of us must confront, and the ticking of the clocks is a constant reminder that our "time" is coming. The ambiguous use of the word "time" in English is indicative of the point Bergman wants to make. "Time" in English has both qualitative as well as quantitative connotations. The distinction in Greek (well appreciated by the Biblical writers) is much clearer. Kairos is significant time, identity-time, the "time to be born, and the time to die" of Ecclesiastes. But this has little directly to do with chronos, clock-time, the measure of change marked by the movement of the stars. Kairos has to do with my death and its meaning; chronos assures us that we each must die, each must face our own kairos. With such symbolism, clock-time has become identified with the monstrous forces which shape our lives. To emphasize this, one of the clockfaces has been given the spider-god symbol, rays radiating out from the center much in the same way the arms of the fan cage did in The Silence or the bullet hole striations did in Shame.

One can only "second guess" a director at great peril and with the proviso that one is quite possibly wrong, but it would seem likely that the stark confrontation with death in Cries and Whispers is possible for Bergman only because the affirmative (but negated) hope of love in Persona, and the partially realized relationships of A Passion have given him the "courage of his despair." The growth is pari passu. Thus the most starkly negative confrontation is given us in the most positive context we have yet had with Bergman. In Cries and Whispers we experience an assimilation and a partial resolution of many of the themes we have traced throughout this journey with Bergman. But, the best way to analyze the significance of what he is saying is to look at each of the characters in turn.

Karin and Maria represent the complementary opposites which we have dealt with so often in Bergman's films--the Knight and Squire of The Seventh Seal, David and Karin in Through a Glass Darkly, Ester and Anna in The Silence, Elizabet and Alma in Persona, Eva and Anna in A Passion. Bergman does not resolve all these polarities in Karin and Maria, but he does at least have Karin and Maria make contact, acknowledge each other. They do not unite but they do touch.

Maria is the youngest of the sisters. She is married to a financially and socially successful man and has a five-year-old daughter. But according to Bergman, and well documented in the film, Maria "is like a spoiled child--gentle, playful, smiling, with an ever-active curiosity and love of pleasure. She is very much taken up with her own beauty and her body's potentialities for pleasure. She is completely

lacking in imagination about the world in which she
lives; she is sufficient unto herself and is never
worried by her own and other people's morals. Her
only law is to please."[252]   One could add here--to
please herself.

Maria is Kierkegaard's aesthete. She lives in the
present and for the present; kairos would have no
meaning for her. Immediate satiation is always to be
chosen over future promise; she continuously seeks
that which makes her feel alive, needed, or fulfilled
at the moment. Though there may be some descriptive
similarity between that and the existential posture of
the reality of the present, the similarity remains
linguistic. There is in Maria's action no commitment,
no decision which carries the weight of either/or, no
sacrifice for others or even for one's own integrity;
in fact, time has no meaning for her as opposed to
being central to one's awareness of self and its
freedom, as it is for the existentialists. She flees
from any situation which encroaches upon her or
threatens her. Even her death watch over her sister
is avoided by falling asleep. One has the feeling
that should death come, Maria wants Karin or Anna to
cope with it, not herself.

Likewise, Maria avoids commitment to other
people. We are given to believe that Maria has had a
long-standing, if intermittent, liaison with the
doctor who is treating Agnes. Maria tries to
proposition him as he leaves the house after visiting
Agnes, but he refuses, a refusal we know she will not
take as final. Later in the film we see depicted an
earlier visit when he doesn't refuse her obsessive
demands upon him, even though at that time he treats
her to a devastating lecture on what selfishness and

self-indulgence are doing to her character. Her response is to say "Your arguments have nearly always bored me...You love saying interesting things. About yourself and other people." "And you love looking at yourself in the mirror," responds the doctor, "Is there any difference? Are there no extenuating circumstances for people such as you and I?" Maria taunts: "I've no need of being pardoned..." But the next morning, when her husband has returned and obviously has realized what has occurred, Maria fantasizes his attempted suicide because of grief. When he pleads with her to help him, she recoils with disgust and revulsion, and says "No." Maria obviously is related to Anna (The Silence), Alma (Persona), and Andreas (A Passion).

But Bergman is not just creating caricatures. There is something which is childishly winsome about Maria who had always been her mother's favorite. When denied other contacts, Maria makes an overture of friendship to her estranged sister Karin. Karin, like the physician, confronts Maria with a very unpleasant picture of herself--"Do you realize how I hate you? Do you realize how absurd I think you are with your coquettishness and your wet smiles? How have I stood you so long, and never said a word? I know who you are, you with your caresses and your false promises..." But despite such verbal abuse, Maria persists and she and Karin share a few moments of rapport and affection. They touch; they kiss--acts which mean too much to Karin and too little to Maria--but, for Bergman it is a beginning of liaison.

After the death of Agnes, one further insight about Maria comes to us through the servant Anna's perceptive dream about the sisters. Anna dreams that the dead Agnes, somewhere in the state between life and death, calls for Maria to come to her, to comfort her. Maria's first reaction is one of horror but she feigns loving willingness. Bergman himself, in the text, describes the rest: "Maria leans closer. She shuts her eyes and face, overcome with cold terror and nausea. Agnes lifts her hand and with a somnambulistic movement removes the combs from Maria's hair. It tumbles down over their faces. Then Agnes puts her hand behind Maria's neck and pulls her violently to her, pressing her lips against Maria's mouth.

Maria screams and wrenches herself away, wiping her mouth with her hand; she staggers backward, spits. Then she flees out into the next room, tries to open the doors to the dining room, but they are shut; tries to open the doors to the hall, but they are locked. The clocks strike and the trees in the park are shaken by another gust of wind."253 When all else seems to let her slip by, death will not. That even Maria cannot escape. In short, Bergman would seem to be saying that the way of the aesthete is not an authentic alternative, i.e. a viable alternative of choice. One sooner rather than later begins to have to pay a price which is contradictory to the whole aesthetic stance.

Karin is another Bergman character with a past who, in Cries and Whispers, moves toward some new resolutions. She is Ester (The Silence), Elizabet (Persona), Anna (A Passion); she is cold, frigid, aloof, proud, and seemingly self-sufficient. Her relationship to people seems to be established through violence, for which she asks forgiveness, yet never receives it. She hates her husband, her senior by twenty years, with a cold fury. In one of her

fantasies she mutilates her genitals in order to spite
her husband, smearing the blood over her face--surely
one of the most startling and grisly scenes that
Bergman has ever filmed. Bergman describes her this
way: "Deep down, under a surface of self-control, she
hides an impotent hatred of her husband and a
permanent rage against life. Her anguish and
desperation never come to light except in her dreams,
which torment her from time to time. In the midst of
this tumult of bridled fury, she bears a gift for
affection, devotion, and a longing for nearness. This
large capital lies immovably shut in and unused."254

The psychological reasons for Karin's neuroses are
due, in part, to Karin's relationship to her mother.
Agnes tells us in her diary that "Karin was always
being scolded, because Mother thought she was so
clumsy and unintelligent." Apparently deprived of
love as a child and ridiculed for her lack of
dexterity, Karin has developed a consuming sense of
guilt. When Maria, as we have noted above, makes an
advance, a gesture of reconciliation, Karin recoils
and withdraws: "I can't. I can't. All that which
can't be altered. All the guilt. It's constant
misery and torment. It's like in hell. I can't
breathe any more because of all the guilt...It's true,
I've thought of suicide many times. I have sleeping
tablets. It's disgusting, it's degrading, I'm rotten
to the core. It's nothing. I mean it's not a serious
problem." At this point she is almost
schizophrenic--one moment raging at the furies which
seem to be destroying her and then an immediate switch
to the controlled, calculating, objective personality
the next. But the sense of guilt would seem to be
more than a matriarchal imposition. We learn in this

tormented exchange with Maria that Karin also has a
"lover:" "Lover indeed. What a silly word. As if
our affair had anything to do with love; it's a dirty
itch and a few moments' oblivion. It's a certain
revenge on Fredrik [Karin's husband]." Guilt, in
either case, would seem to be more than the social
conditioning of the home. The overtones here are
those of Sartre's shame or Heidegger's ontological
guilt--the guilt one experiences at not being the
master of all things including oneself, the guilt at
not being able to fulfill one's potential--to be all
things to all men all the time everywhere.

Though not denying the negative side of Karin's
personality, Martin Buber would probably say that
until Karin is able to love, to give herself to
another, she is doomed to this flight from reality,
fulfillment, and authenticity. Bergman seems to
suggest both the negative and affirmative
possibilities in Anna's dream after Agnes's death. As
with Maria, Agnes calls Karin to come to her. "Agnes
asks her to hold her hands, to warm her, to kiss her.
Agnes says that everything around her is emptiness;
she begs her sister to help her. Agnes asks Karin to
stay with her until the horror has passed.

"'I can't,' Karin says. 'There isn't a soul who'd
do what you ask. I'm alive and I don't want anything
to do with your death. Perhaps if I loved you. But I
don't. What you ask of me is repulsive. I'll leave
you now. In a few days, I'm going away.'

"Agnes listens with her eyes shut.

"Karin leaves the bedroom. The clock strikes the
hour. The trees are shaken by a gust of wind. Then
it is still once more."255

As for Maria, so for Karin: the spider-god of time clangs the bell...There is also, in the wind, a hint of the transcendent, the Spirit, which responds to the rejection of love--though it would be wrong to claim that this is any more than a hint or suggestion at this point.

In contrast to the two sisters whose polar traits we have met and dealt with before in Bergman, he now gives us two others in which there is a much higher degree of personal resolution and affirmation than before. Agnes and Anna. In creating the role of Agnes, Bergman for the first time seems to accept the intricate complexity of life. Rather than experiencing life as an isolated series of struggles and battles against the monstrous forces, he now begins to understand life more in terms of some field of force in which all sorts of charged particles are continuously interacting. As such, life can be described more in terms of textures rather than substantiality. Bergman has stopped seeking absolutes, metaphysical or personal, and has begun to affirm that life is a series of inextricable mixtures and blends; absolutes are a product of mind, only a fragment of the fabric of Being.

For Agnes, writes Bergman, "love has been a confined secret, never revealed. At the age of thirty-seven she has cancer of the womb and is preparing to make her exit from the world as quietly and submissively as she has lived in it...She complains little and does not think that God is cruel. In her prayers she turns to Christ in meek expectation."256 In an almost Nietzschean way, revelation about life comes to Agnes through suffering. Suffering seems to be the inevitable

concomitant of any worthwhile insight. What we learn
of this from Agnes comes through the entries in her
diary. It is obvious from her notes that her likeness
to her father had become a source of estrangement from
her mother (though   it's difficult to tell here
whether we're dealing with a response to an electra
complex or simply to an unhappy marriage).
Nevertheless, the experience of rejection actually
becomes the insight for Agnes' acceptance of her
mother: "I loved Mother. Because she was so gentle
and beautiful and alive. Because she was so--I don't
know how to put it--because she was so present. But
she could also be cold and indifferent. When I used
to come and ask her for affection, she would rebuff me
and be playfully cruel, saying she hadn't time. Yet I
couldn't help feeling sorry for her, and now that I'm
older I understand her much better. I should like so
much to see her again and tell her what I have
understood of her ennui, her impatience, her panic and
refusal to give up." Bergman would seem to be
suggesting here that there is a human camaraderie born
of our recognition of the universal human
predicament. It may be a reflection of Soren
Kierkegaard's observation that if you knew everything
about any given person--all his hopes, dreams,
disappointments, failures, losses, loves--you'd love
him to death, no matter who he is.

Agnes's suffering is not just at the hands of her
mother, however, It is also in the face of
lovelessness and death: "Sometimes I want to cover my
face with my hands and never take them away again.
How am I to grapple with the loneliness? The long
days, the silent evenings, the sleepless nights.
Whatever am I to do with all this time that pours over

me?   Then I go into my despair and let it burn me.
I've found that if I try to avoid it or shut it out,
everything becomes much harder.   It's better not to
shut your eyes or try to dodge it."   And a later
entry: "I used to imagine that my creative efforts
brought me into contact with the outside world, that I
left my loneliness.   Nowadays I know that this isn't
so at all.   In the end all my so-called artistic
expression is only a desperate protest against death.
Despite this, I keep on.   No one but Anna sees what I
achieve...I've no idea whether it's good or bad.
Probably bad.   After all, I've seen so little of
life.   I've never bothered to live among people in
their reality.   Though I wonder whether _their_ reality
is any more tangible than mine--I mean my illness."
Agnes has won through to the insight that meaning is
achieved not by where we are or what we are, but only
by the way in which we live and choose and express our
being.

The film ends with Anna reading, then our seeing
enacted, the last entry in Agnes' diary.   After
expressing her gratitude for her sisters coming to be
with her, Agnes tells of a short and rare outing to
the estate park she took with them and Anna.   "I
closed my eyes and felt the breeze and the sun on my
face.   All my aches and pains were gone.   The people
I'm most fond of in the world were with me.   I could
hear them chatting round about me, I felt the presence
of their bodies, the warmth of their hands.   I closed
my eyes tightly, trying to cling to the moment and
thinking: Come what may, this is happiness.   I can't
wish for anything better.   Now, for a few minutes, I
can experience perfection.   And I feel a great
gratitude to my life, which gives me so much."   The

scene and speech are strikingly reminiscent of
Antonious Block's bowl-of-wild-strawberries-and-milk
declaration in The Seventh Seal: "...it will be an
adequate sign--it will be enough for me."   As we
observed, it was not enough for the Knight, but
Agnes's moment of happiness is enough for her.   The
difference is the distance we have travelled with
Bergman on his journey.

Here the paradoxes that have so often haunted
Bergman's characters are reconciled: pain and
happiness, time and eternity, the closeness and
distance of her sisters, the servitude and love of
Anna.   It is clear that Agnes has triumphed over the
terrors of the monstrous forces that beset her and has
lived an authentic life in the tenuous and temporary
manner in which that can only happen--brief moments of
perfection, happiness and grace, in which the memory
of pain persists but is superseded.   Agnes has done
this both in the realm of relationship and in the
realm of inner personal strength.   Her personal
self-realization, her triumph over the monstrous
forces, has little or no lasting effect on Maria or
Karin who still relate in terms of their conflicts,
insecurities, and guilt.   But, one of the great
advances in this film is that Bergman, in keeping with
the above existential claims, no longer demands the
impossible from a return to innocence or from love, as
he did in the unsatisfactory endings of The Seventh
Seal and Through a Glass Darkly.   Life is now seen as
an existential expression of my being which has the
possibility but not the guarantee of integration,
fulfillment, and authenticity.

Before leaving this discussion of Agnes, two
observations about communication ought to be made. As
opposed to the role of pictures and the inability of
the camera to catch the truth, which was so prominent
in Elis' stance in A Passion, here we are shown
pictures of family, both the sisters and Anna, which
are meant to include us in an attempt to understand
these women. The same is true for language which has
been so suspect for Bergman since The Silence. In
Agnes' diary, which has the healing effect of
resolution, understanding, and acceptance, we are a
long way from David's novel in Through a Glass Darkly,
or Elizabet's letter in Persona, or Andreas Fromm's
letter in A Passion. The intimacy of the diary, that
expression of self for oneself, achieves a directness
and honesty which public communication so often
distorts or destroys. For once we can affirm the
possibility of genuine communication through words.

Anna is Agnes's counterpart, as Maria is Karin's.
It's as though Bergman wanted to emphasize that
resolution of the paradoxes, that triumph over the
monstrous forces, is not dependent upon intellect or
special creative gifts. Bergman's description of Anna
is as follows: "Anna is the maidservant in the
house. She is about thirty. As a girl, she had a
daughter, and Agnes looked after her and the child.
This meant that Anna became very attached to Agnes. A
silent, never-expressed friendship was established
between the two lonely women. The child died at the
age of three, but the relationship between Anna and
Agnes endured. Anna is very taciturn, very shy,
unapproachable. But she is ever-present--watching,
prying, listening. Everything about Anna is weight.
Her body, her face, her mouth, the expression of her

eyes.   But she doesn't speak; perhaps she doesn't
think, either."257

Anna, as the others in this film, has her
ancestral line.   She is the innocence that has
appeared in every film (usually as children) since The
Seventh Seal, but for the first time it is not an
innocence which is pathetically vulnerable, as
Bergman's other representations have been.   The
innocence of Anna is the innocence about which Robert
Penn Warren speaks in his Brothers to Dragons: the
innocence born to our knowledge of our complicity.
Though not articulated, Anna well knows the guilt
involved in the human predicament.   Bergman gives us
this in a graphic symbol early in the film.   Anna,
rising from bed in the morning, lights a candle and
says her prayers.   She then reaches out and picks up a
fine red apple and takes a big bite--one has the
feeling that this Eve knows that she's in quite a
garden.   Anna's prayers are interesting, too, because
they tell us that her relationship to God is
accepting, trusting, simple, and real--even if
unexamined.   She obviously has accepted the death of
her child as the will of an infinitely wise and
merciful God.

Anna's dream is the only one which is directly
connected with present events.   It is a very revealing
one, and whether one credits this to intuition or
intelligence is inconsequential.   What the dream tells
us is that Anna knows she is the only one who truly
loves Agnes.   Earlier we saw that when Agnes calls for
help and comfort because of her excruciating pain,
Karin and Maria either could not or would not hear.
It is Anna who climbs into bed with Agnes and comforts
her as a mother would her infant child.   It is also

Anna who seems to understand (as the sisters obviously
do not) the great loneliness which Bergman thinks is
implicit in the act of dying: "Death is the extreme
of loneliness; that is what is so important. Agnes's
death has been caught up halfway out into the
void...What, once again, is the so-called meaning? I
don't know...All I know is that I am driven by a
desire to lay bare a state of affairs, to create a
space in the midst of a chaos of confusion and
conflicting impulses, a space in which a joint effort,
imagination and the wish for form crystallize a
component in my sense of being alive; the unreasonable
and never-satisfied longing for fellowship, the clumsy
attempts to do away with distance and
isolation."258   When both sisters have fled the
scene (in Anna's dream) out of disgust or fear, it is
Anna who goes to Agnes to comfort her, without
embarrassment or repulsion. The camera gives us a
poignant shot of Anna holding Agnes in the traditional
Pieta pose.

The family's guilt and emotional revenge against
Anna for the obvious closeness she shared with Agnes
is to dismiss her without pension or special
consideration for the devotion she had given Agnes.
They did decide to let her take a memento, which she
declines with a show of dignity the family cannot
match. However, as noted earlier, Anna's innocence is
one instructed by complicity, and .Anna has already
hidden Agnes' diary--the most personal, beautiful, and
revealing possession Agnes had. Anna undoubtedly
thought that none of the family would appreciate it,
and, indeed, she was right: none of them even missed
it. This provides us with another insight into the
validity of language for Bergman. Obviously from

Anna's actions, words communicated to another in love and in trust are meaningful and significant. Though Anna says virtually nothing, one comes away from the film with the belief that she, like Agnes, is a whole person, a mature person who has learned to share herself in love.

After something of a moratorium on specific religious discussion, Bergman reintroduces the religious debate again in _Cries and Whispers_. It is true that it has been present in all the films we have discussed, but since _Winter Light_ he has been rather covert in his symbolism and speculation. Now we get another direct assault by way of the clergyman who is called into the home to take charge of the funeral. The pastor arrives at the house and is described by Bergman as "an old and holy man" who may even be modeled on Bergman's own father. As they all gather around Agnes's death bed, the pastor says this prayer: "God, our Father, in His infinite wisdom and mercy, has decided to call you home in the flower of your youth. Prior to that, He found you worthy to bear a heavy and prolonged suffering. You submitted to it patiently and uncomplainingly, in the certain knowledge that your sins would be forgiven through the death on the Cross of your Lord Jesus Christ. May your Father in Heaven have mercy on your soul when you step into His presence. May He let His angels disrobe you of the memory of your earthly pain."

Having said that prayer, the Pastor moves from the dark side of the room to the opposite side where he kneels by Agnes's bedside to give his second prayer: "If it is so that you have gathered our suffering in your poor body, if it is so that you have borne it with you through death, if it is so that you meet God

over there in the other land, if it is so that He
turns His face toward you, if it is so that you can
then speak the language that this God understands, if
it is so that you can then speak to this God. If it
is so, pray for us. Agnes, my dear little child,
listen to what I am now telling you. Pray for us who
are left here on the dark, dirty earth under an empty
and cruel Heaven. Lay your burden of suffering at
God's feet and ask Him to pardon us. Ask Him to free
us at last from our anxiety, our weariness, and our
deep doubt. Ask Him for a meaning to our lives.
Agnes, you who have suffered so unimaginably and so
long, you must be worthy to plead our cause."

There are some interesting things to note about
these prayers. The first prayer, though more orthodox
and apparently read from a prayer book, is not really
addressed to God at all, but to Agnes. Technically,
one could question whether or not it really is a
prayer. The wording is such that the pastor, while
referring to "our Father," really excludes himself
from any sense of God's presence. He is reduced to
the repetition of ritual, which immediately identifies
him with Pastor Tomas of Winter Light. The plea in
this prayer is for justice: "If anyone deserves to
enter Heaven, it is you Agnes..." The specific
theological concepts in this prayer, e.g. the
redemptive acts of the Christ, the Trinity, etc., are
quite orthodox.

Then the clergyman moves to the other side of the
bed, into the light. The prayer is extemporaneous,
much more fervent, and one has little doubt that it is
a real prayer, although it, too, is addressed to
Agnes. Behind all of the conditional clauses with
which the prayer begins, is a genuine longing for

meaning, forgiveness, and peace. The problem of
language again arises--"if it is so that you can then
speak the language...pray for us"--and we are given
the impression that the pastor believes God to be
somewhere, waiting.

It is interesting to note here that both this
pastor and Tomas seem to be acknowledging the same
doubts and fears, but the impressions they each create
are opposite. With Tomas one believes only the
spider--god exists; for this pastor in Cries and
Whispers, hope--if not belief--has been reborn. The
important new step for Bergman is that the hope is
reborn through the life of Agnes, not through some act
of special divine revelation. In the words of the
Scottish theologian John Baillie, we have an instance
in this film of "mediated immediacy," the paradox of
God's presence and absence evident in the same
revelational experience. The pastor says: Agnes "was
my confirmation child. We often had long and intimate
talks. Her faith was stronger than mine." Bergman
has stopped hoping for some all consuming miraculous
transcendent affirmation and has begun to find the
transcendent in the immanent. In short, as Martin
Buber has suggested, the Eternal Thou is present in
every I-Thou relation, and it now looks as though
Bergman finally knows where he can look for God.

The "cries and whispers fade away" at the end of
the film and there is silence--not the silence which
betrays a void, but the silence which grants us
peace. This is the most affirmative film we have yet
seen.

Face to Face (1976)

> "I think if we helped each other
> we could change everything."
>
> <u>Cries</u> <u>and</u> <u>Whispers</u>

"Dear Fellow Workers:
We're now going to make a film which, in a way, is about an attempted suicide. Actually it deals ("as usual" I was about to say!) with Life, Love, and Death. Because nothing in fact is more important. To occupy oneself with. To think of. To worry over. To be happy about."259   At first glance, that may seem to be a strange series of modifying sentences for "Life, Love, and Death," yet that is just where this journey with Bergman has taken us. The simple and discreet absolutes sought in the earlier films have given way, as we have seen most notably in <u>Cries</u> <u>and</u> <u>Whispers</u>, to complex and ontologically related existential moments: a relation to self which involves a relation to others; a knowledge of self which incorporates a knowledge of others; a reality expressing "then" and "yet" by being <u>here</u> <u>and</u> <u>now</u>. More than introducing new themes, <u>Face</u> <u>to</u> <u>Face</u> gives us the most developed and mature expression of Bergman's perennial but existential concerns yet, about which we are privileged to occupy ourselves, think, worry, and be happy.

Before beginning an actual analysis of the film, it will be helpful to see what Bergman himself has said about it in his letter to his colleagues before production. The idea began with a hope to exorcise an anxiety of his own which was vague and without apparent cause (which, almost needless to say, is the case by definition of any genuine anxiety). "Another person's vicissitudes came to my aid; I found similarities between her experiences and my own, with the difference that her situation was more obvious and more explicit, and much more painful.

"In this way the chief character in our film began to take shape: a well-adjusted, capable, and disciplined person, a highly qualified professional woman with a career, comfortably married to a gifted colleague and surrounded by what are called 'the good things of life.' It is this admirable character's shockingly quick breakdown and agonizing rebirth that I have tried to describe.260

"The first part of the film is almost pedantically realistic, tangible. The second part is elusive, intangible: the 'dreams' are more real than the reality. In this connection let me add a somewhat bizarre comment. I am extremely suspicious of dreams, apparitions, and visions, both in literature and in films and plays. Perhaps it's because mental excesses of this sort smack too much of being 'arranged.'

"So when, despite my reluctance and suspicion, I go to depict a series of dreams, which moreover are not my own, I like to think of these dreams as an extension of reality. This is therefore a series of real events....Although Jenny is a psychiatrist she has never taken this extended reality seriously. Despite her wide knowledge she is, to a pretty great extent, mentally illiterate (a common ailment with psychiatrists: one could almost call it an occupational disease). Jenny has always been firmly convinced that a cheese is a cheese, a table is a table, and, not least, that a human being is a human being.

"This last conviction is one of the things she is
forced to modify in a rather painful way when she
realizes in a flash that she is a conglomeration of
other people and of the whole world.[261] Frankly, I
don't know whether she will be able to bear her
realization."[262]

Although our primary interest will be to see how
Bergman develops these themes, a somewhat more
extensive relating of the plot than what Bergman has
given us above will be helpful in their discussion.
Jenny, a psychiatrist, is spending the summer filling
in for the medical supervisor of the Psychiatric
Clinic at the General Hospital. Her husband, Erik, is
chairing an international meeting in Chicago, so Jenny
has moved in with her grandparents with whom she had
spent her adolescent years from nine on (her own
parents had been killed in an accident). Her daughter
Anna is at camp and then plans to spend the remainder
of the summer at a friend's house.

For Jenny the combination of fatigue, a suppressed
emotional involvement with one of her patients, Maria,
a reawakening of childhood fears and anxieties related
to living with her grandparents, and an attempted rape
produce an anxiety crisis which drives Jenny to
attempt suicide to escape. She leaves a taped message
for her husband (unfortunately excluded from the film)
in which she describes her condition:

> Dear Erik, my dear one. It's easier to
> speak like this to a tape recorder than
> to write a letter. It has always been
> the way with me that whenever I go to
> put something in writing, the words
> escape me. In a little while I'm going
> to take fifty Nembutal. Then I'll get

into bed and go to sleep. I'm afraid
you'll be angry with me for this. As
far as I know we have never discussed
the possibility that one or the other
of us might commit suicide--there has
never been any call to. All the same,
I realize suddenly that what I'm going
to do in a little while has been
lurking inside me for several years.
Not that I've consciously planned to
take my life, don't think that. I'm
not so deceitful. It's more that I've
been living in an isolation that has
got worse and worse--the dividing line
between my outer behavior and my inner
impoverishment has become more
distinct. I remember last Whitsun, for
instance. You and I and Anna went for
a ramble in the forest. You and Anna
thoroughly enjoyed yourselves. I made
out it was wonderful too, and said how
happy I was, but it wasn't true. I
wasn't taking in anything of all the
beauty surrounding us. My senses
reported it, but the connections were
broken. This upset me and I thought
I'd try to cry but the tears wouldn't
come.
This is only one example picked at
random, but the more I think back, the
more I remember. I stopped listening
to music, as I felt sealed up and
apathetic. Our sex life--I felt
nothing, nothing at all. I pretended I

did, so that you wouldn't be anxious or
start asking questions. But I think
the worst of all was that I lost touch
with our little girl. A prison grew up
all around me, with no doors or
windows. With walls so thick that not
a sound got through, walls that it was
useless to attack, since they were
built from materials I supplied myself.
I think you should explain all this to
our daughter. You should explain it
very thoroughly, you must be
unflinchingly truthful. We live, and
while we live we're gradually
suffocated without knowing what is
happening. At last there's only a
puppet left, reacting more or less to
external demands and stimuli. Inside
there is nothing but a great horror.
Erik my dear, I don't feel afraid or
sad or lonely. Please don't feel sorry
for me--I'm quite content, almost
excited, like when I was little and
going on a trip. It may even be that
this is a recovery from a lifelong
illness. I give you my word....263

The attempt is unsuccessful in part because she is
discovered in time by a doctor acquaintance, Tomas, to
whom she had earlier been introduced. Because of his
solicitude and concern, her will to live prevails and
her reassessment of life begins. She relives some of
the basic anxieties uncovered by the extremes of her
experience and her consequent dreams and is thereby

able to accept herself, to break out of the "prison" of self in which she felt confined. She meets with her daughter, only to realize history seems to be repeating itself; Anna already feels isolated and alone. Jenny does not know whether it's too late or not to salvage their relationship. Jenny then returns to her grandparents house, able to "see" them through adult eyes, able to appreciate them for what they are to each other and to her. As the film ends, Jenny is ready to go back to work, back to life.

Bergman, like most of Western culture, has been much taken with the benefits of psychiatry and the advances in clinical psychology. We know, particularly from his sophisticated use of Jung's theories in _Persona_, that Bergman is anything but a philistine about the contributions which psychology has made. But, he is likewise aware of the debate raging in psychological circles these days about the merits of clinical psychology vs experimental psychology; he is also aware of the public's tendency to mythologize psychology, to turn it into a cure-all, despite its internal debates and doubts. So, in _Face to Face_ Bergman both extols and excoriates psychology, as he has done with every rationalized, objectification of the reality since _The Seventh Seal_. Bergman extols psychology by employing the insights of psychology as major components of his story. In Jenny's dreams, which truly are central in the development, she is dressed in her Little Red Riding Hood attire, and the wolves are not hard to find. Bergman indicates Jenny's love-hate relation with her parents; her residue guilt because of their death when she was only nine; her terror of rejection and punishment by her grandmother who then reared her;

her anxiety caused by a quarrel between her mother and
grandmother; her feelings of inadequacy as a
psychiatrist when patients would not respond in a
textbook fashion; her self-immolation, an
ego-destruction device, which (I'd like to think) has
some reference back to Elisabet's watching the
self-immolation of a Buddhist monk in _Persona_. Now it
is self-immolation for life, not death. All of this
is pretty orthodox and constructive.

Bergman excoriates psychology first, and most
obviously, by making Jenny a psychiatrist, a physician
who cannot heal herself, indeed, cannot diagnose her
own symptoms. After the attempted rape, when she
shows some fear of losing control in an attack of
anxiety, she says to Tomas: "If you force everything
to be as usual then it _will_ be as usual. Don't you
agree? That's how it is with me anyway." Tomas
replies, "Is that how you cure your patients?"
Jenny: "No, but they're sick. I'm not." Her
arguments more reflect the willfulness of Anna in _A
Passion_ who also wished to fashion truth to her fancy,
than of a psychiatrist. However, Bergman's most
forward statement about the shortcomings of psychiatry
comes from a discussion between Dr. Wankel, a
colleague and friend of Jenny's and Jenny herself
about the limitations of their profession. Maria has
been the subject of their conversation:

> _Wankel_: You can hand her over to me
> when you've had enough. And
> realized how hopeless it is to
> cure psychoses of her kind. So
> far there are only mechanical
> solutions.

<u>Jenny</u>:   Do you think they deserve to be called solutions?

<u>Wankel</u>: My dear Jenny. A lunatic quack psychiatrist once wrote that mental illnesses are the worst scourge on earth, and the next worst is the curing of those illnesses. I'm inclined to agree with him.

<u>Jenny</u>:   (L a u g h i n g)   You <u>are</u> encouraging.

<u>Wankel</u>: Twenty years ago I realized the inconceivable brutality of our methods and the complete bankruptcy of psychoanalysis. I don't think we can really cure a single human being. One or two get well despite our efforts.

<u>Jenny</u>:   Man as a machine?

<u>Wankel</u>: Exactly! We change spare parts and eradicate symptoms.

Harsh words of self-criticism from the practitioners who themselves never bought the myth under which they publicly labor. I do not think that Bergman in any way believes in the bankruptcy of psychology, but his own search has led him past its messianic illusion.

But the life of willful truth and determined affirmation is not without its anguish; or, as we have noted before, the unconscious despair described by Soren Kierkegaard. Maria, Jenny's "sick" patient, says to her in an important clinical encounter excluded from the film:

> Jenny: I see that you're putting on an
> act.
> Maria: What am I acting?
> Jenny: Anguish.   Fear. Anguish, I
> think.
> Maria: And what am I acting now? Look
> carefully.
> Jenny: I don't know.
> Maria: I was imitating you.
> Jenny: I couldn't tell that.
> Maria: No, you couldn't.   (Pause)
> Poor Jenny!

Whether Bergman should credit Maria with such
observation and insight is a moot point; but the point
that Jenny is suffering from Angst is not.

But it is really her response to the attempted
rape that shatters her composure and self-control. We
learn from her relating the experience to Tomas that
the boy who tried was not so cruel or sadistic as
frantic, nursing at her breast all the while.
Suddenly, she relates, she wanted him to be
successful; she stopped struggling, but he was still
unable to penetrate her--"I was all tight and cramped
and dry." Her trauma was caused not by the fright she
originally experienced or the sense of physical
debasement, but by the fact that she could not control
the situation, could not change at will her response.
It brought home a recollection that her first lover,
before her marriage to Erik, told her that she was
frigid.   We know from her suicide note that her
relation to Erik is also remote and cold, as is her
sexual response to friend Tomas. All of this forcibly
makes her confront her isolation from others, her
feeling of suffocation, her sense of lostness, her
fear of death--physical, psychical, and spiritual.

We have had some preparation in the film for this breakdown. When Jenny first moves into her grandparents' apartment she sees a woman, dressed entirely in black, descending the apartment stair. She carries a white cane. "Her face is strong and very pale. Her right eye socket is staring and empty."264 The woman, we note, is not unlike Jenny's grandmother. The resemblance is close enough to make us uneasy and apprehensive. The first night that Jenny stays in the apartment, she wakes up in the middle of the night feeling completely paralyzed--"Opposite her bed, in the changing, shadowless nocturnal light, she can make out a shapeless, gray, billowing mass. Now it takes form, rising, collecting itself. It is a large woman dressed in gray. One eye has been gouged out and the socket gapes black. With excruciating slowness she turns her terrible face toward Jenny and gazes at her. Then she speaks. The thin black lips form words which Jenny cannot grasp but which seem very urgent, menacing. When Jenny doesn't understand, the expression on the woman's face changes to cruel impatience...Now the woman is standing on the floor, her face distorted with fury. She approaches the bed with flowing, unreal movements.

"Jenny tries to scream but can't make a sound. Just then the apparition vanishes and she (Jenny) wakes up, puts on the light and sits for a long time bolt upright in bed."265 This same apparition appears once more just before Jenny's suicide attempt. Clearly we are back to Bergman's monstrous forces and the ultimate anxiety, death. But now there is a difference. The anxiety about death finds two expressions, has two symbols. It is still, as in

Cries and Whispers, time the destroyer, the inexorable
force which marks the terminus of our physical life,
but now it has also become the anxiety about death as
a "state" of non-being, which is present in our fear
of deterioration and dying. It is this latter aspect
of the anxiety of death that is symbolized by the
grotesque old woman. Thus Bergman extends the area to
which religion must speak, if it is to be heard as an
affirmation of life and death.

To elaborate his point, Bergman gives us a number
of instances. The first (in the text, but
unfortunately cut from the film) comes by Jenny's
chance encounter with the friends of Tomas's, a young
actor named Stromberg. When Stromberg finds that
Jenny is a psychiatrist he takes the opportunity to
pose the question: Do you think someone can commit
suicide out of fear of death? It sounds crazy, but do
you think it's possible?"266 When Jenny concurs,
Stromberg goes on to add: "Suddenly time stops, the
seconds are endless. It's like sitting in an airplane
when the engines fail. Every step I take--every word
I say--every moment...Funny, isn't it? I'm the
luckiest person in the world. It's summer. Elisabeth
is the kindest little mother imaginable. I'm
extremely talented...That's how it is, Jenny! I'm
afraid to go to sleep in case I never wake up again.
And I know it's inevitable. I,I,I, Mikael Stromberg,
will die at any moment, somehow or other. It's no use
crying or running and hiding. If I believed in
something great it would be different. Sometimes I
know just how it smells." Jenny: "Smells?"
Stromberg replies: "The smell of death. The stench
of a corpse. I look at my hand, I put it to my nose,
and I can smell it, sickly sweet and

nauseating."267   In this exchange Bergman not only
prepares us for Jenny's suicide out of her fear of
death, but also introduces the ontological theme of
contingent existence.   What Stromberg has just
realized is that I do not really have control over my
life.   I cannot control my death--but more
importantly, I cannot give any guarantees on my life!

These insights are poignantly reinforced by
Jenny's grandfather, a very proud man who has recently
suffered a stroke.   It has affected his speech and his
memory, and he is painfully aware of both losses.
They have made him utterly dependent upon his wife.
Fears of embarrassing his family in public, fears of
being sent to a nursing home alone obviously haunt
him--"Old age is hell" he says, pathetically, to his
wife.   Later, in a dream of Jenny's after her suicide
attempt, she finds her grandfather standing in a
closed closet.   He whispers to her: "I'm afraid of
dying."   Jenny says, "So am I."   "What can I do?" he
pleads.   "Count to ten.   If you're still alive when
you get to ten, then start again" is her advice.   It
is obvious that both fear and impotency are present,
for herself personally and for others professionally.
That dream and the subsequent ego-destroying dream of
self-immolation mentioned earlier, lead Jenny to
confess her fear of death to Tomas: "As a child I was
afraid of death.   It seemed to be all around me.   My
poodle was run over, that was almost worse than
anything.   Mama and Daddy were killed in a car crash.
I told you that, didn't I?   Then a cousin died of
polio.   I was fourteen then.   We had sat under the
dining table kissing on the Saturday, the next Friday
he was dead.   Grandma made me go to the funeral.   I
begged and pleaded to be let off, but Grandma wouldn't

relent...Grandma told me to go up to him and look at
him and 'bid farewell', as she put it. I imagined he
was breathing and that his eyelids were twitching. I
said so to Grandma. She said it was a common optical
illusion and that I would control myself. When they
screwed down the lid I knew for sure that Johan would
wake up in there in the dark, way under the
earth...." From then on death became an idea to
suppress: "Death didn't exist any more except as a
vague idea, and that was that," but in her mind,
Grandma and death had become indissolubly linked
together.

Yet Bergman has not forgotten time and its
reminder of inevitability. Stromberg first brings it
up--that moment when <u>kairos</u> (identity-time) and
<u>chronos</u> (clock-time) come together at the moment of
anticipated death. Grandpa, too, shares his
foreboding. One night Jenny observes her grandfather
come into the dining room, go to the grandfather [sic]
clock and search for the key to wind it up. Just then
Grandma enters:

<u>Grandma</u>: What are you doing up at this
         hour?

<u>Grandpa</u>: The clock--

<u>Grandma</u>: My dear, we wound it properly
         last night. It's not good
         for it to wind it too often.

<u>Grandpa</u>: It keeps stopping.

<u>Grandma</u>: No, it doesn't. We had a
         w a t c h m a k e r h e r e w h o
         overhauled it and said it was
         one of the best grandfather
         clocks he had ever seen.

<u>Grandpa</u>: It loses time.

> Grandma: It keeps the same time as the
>   other clocks, but if you
>   insist on tampering with it,
>   then it's sure to stop.

Inexorable and universal. Just so, however, is Jenny's concern when she is in her semi-conscious state following the suicide attempt. Her first question is always, "What time is it? What day is it?" None of us can ever quite overcome the sure and certain knowledge that each second that goes by, goes by forever, ever depleting the fixed quantity that we call our lifetime. It is our awareness of our lifetime that determines the times of our life. If there be a salvation, one of its characteristics must be a release from the tyranny of time.

Lest we forget old symbols of the monstrous forces, the spider who first introduced us to them in Through a Glass Darkly, is yet present, but now in a much more domesticated form. It appears, appropriately enough, in the suicide scene. After Jenny takes her fifty Nembutals, she lies back on her bed and the camera assumes the vision for Jenny's eyes. She follows her finger tracing a design on the wallpaper (while, somewhat off tune and time she hums the Brahms' lullaby); then, when the drugs begin to take effect and she starts the downward drift into oblivion, her "eyes" idly take in various objects--pictures, lamps, etc.--around her room. One of these objects, taking up a whole corner, over which our eyes wander is a spider plant, a morass of sharp variegated leaves, silently presiding in the room.

Our one possible reprieve from such horrors, such monstrous forces, in all Bergman's films since The Silence, is love --not sentimental romanticism of

<u>Through</u> <u>a</u> <u>Glass</u> <u>Darkly</u> but rather the more
sophisticated, complex relation which we witnessed, in
its positive form for the first time, between Anna and
Agnes in <u>Cries</u> <u>and</u> <u>Whispers</u>. But one of the
prerequisites for such love is communication, and it
remains a problem in <u>Face</u> <u>to</u> <u>Face</u>. Nevertheless, new
affirmations and insights are here. Photographs, over
which Grandpa pours much of the time now, are treated
as enriching and comforting (as they are in <u>Cries</u> <u>and</u>
<u>Whispers</u>), rather than harsh, disruptive, and
distancing (as they are in <u>Persona</u> and <u>A</u> <u>Passion</u>).
One is reminded of Eliot's <u>Four</u> <u>Quartets</u> here: "There
is a time for the evening under starlight,/A time for
the evening under lamplight/ (The evening with the
photograph album)."

Though I'm sure that it does not signal any
noticeable return to organized religion, church bells
can now be relied upon to tell us, at least, that it
is Sunday, which is more than they signalled in
<u>Shame</u>. Words still bother Bergman, but he makes a
distinction in <u>Face</u> <u>to</u> <u>Face</u> not made heretofore. So
Jenny begins her suicide "note" to Erik as a tape:
"It's easier to speak like this to a tape recorder
than to write a letter. It has always been the way
with me that whenever I go to put something in
writing, the words escape me." Even in her dreams,
Jenny deplores the lack of words, the lack of
communication without which love itself may be
denied: "I'm sure there <u>is</u> something called love. I
even think I've met people who love or have
loved...I've tried to live like everyone else. And
I've failed. Do you think I don't see that myself?
(<u>Cries</u> <u>out</u>) I have no words to say what I mean. It's
hopeless." In another dream she talks with Tomas
about her patients:

Jenny: If only for once I had the
         right words. Just for once.

Tomas: Exactly, Jenny.   They're
         sitting there in the dark, your
         patients, longing for the right
         word. But it must be their
         word, their feeling, not your
         word and your feeling.

Jenny: I   k n o w   t h a t
         l o n e l i n e s s — p e o p l e ' s
         loneliness—that they are brave
         in their loneliness.   Like
         children in the dark who are
         determined not to call out lest
         they grow even more afraid if
         no one should come. They weep
         quietly and restrainedly, in
         their loneliness. (Pause) A
         human head is so fragile.   To
         hold someone's head between
         your hands and to feel that
         f r a i l t y   b e t w e e n   y o u r
         hands...and inside it all the
         loneliness and capability and
         j o y   a n d   b o r e d o m   a n d
         intelligence and the will to
         love and...(Pause)   An old
         person's hand...the day has
         been long and trying but
         evening comes, the hand that
         opens. (Pause) I can't go on,
         no.

The bequest from The Silence, "hands" and "faces" come back poignantly to meet us again, begging to be comprehended, held, expressed. "Do you think I'm crippled for the rest of my life?" Jenny cries out to Tomas, after her dream is over. "Do you think we're a vast army of emotionally crippled wretches wandering about calling to each other with words which we don't understand and which only make us even more afraid?" Tomas's mumbled response is: "I don't know."

Most tragic of all, however, is Jenny's meeting with her daughter who has returned from camp to visit her mother in the hospital. Jenny can't find the words to make her understand what has happened and why. Jenny finally pleads "You must try to forgive me." Anna's cool response is: "I don't know what you mean." Finally this pathetic exchange takes place:

Anna: Will you do that again?

Jenny: No.

Anna: How can I be sure?

Jenny: You must count on me to tell the truth.

Anna: But do you know what you're saying?

Jenny: I think so.

Anna: But you're not sure.

Jenny: (Vehemently) Just what are you getting at? Can't you understand anything?

Anna: You've never liked me anyway...You haven't, you know. Well, I must go now. Don't worry. I'm good at managing on my own. Bye-bye.

And Jenny wonders if it is too late.

But the film does not end so pessimistically, nor is Bergman at the end of his journey. He really has prepared us very well for the agonizing next step of the way. We have seen from the above that the word to be spoken cannot be my word, for _my_ world cannot reach _their_ solitude and isolation. But the word, likewise, cannot be _their_ word, as Tomas was suggesting, because their word (as Jenny noted in her suicide tape to Erik) is part of the prison they have built up around themselves, "with walls so thick that not a sound got through"--either way! And with the conversation between Jenny and Anna, Bergman gives another factor (implied in Agnes' relation to Anna in _Cries and Whispers_, but not formally considered before): the word reflects and therefore depends upon the _being_ of the speaker and the relationship implied to the hearer. Thus the intelligible word, the therapeutic word, the healing word is not _my_ word, not _another's_ word, but _our_ word. The word born out of love.

After Bergman's first attempt in _Through a Glass Darkly_ to affirm life in terms of love turned out to be sentimental, weak, and contrived (not to mention, much criticized), his involvement in existential thought led him to explore Sartre's radical individualism with its sado-masochistic relation to others. This, too, proved to be inadequate to experience, and Bergman once again began to explore the possibilities of compassionate love--even if it meant initially that he described life in terms of the absence of this love. Thus there is an interesting parallel between his search for God and his search for love. Superficially they were identified in _Through a Glass Darkly_; then radically separated. The development of both, then proceeded independently and

by the process of negation. Only in <u>Cries</u> <u>and</u>
<u>Whispers</u> do we get any hint that the two may again be
linked together in Bergman's mind, and <u>that</u> genuine
expression of love in that film is between two who
share a faith-affirmation. Our speculation then was
that Bergman may be coming to the place where he wants
to claim that the Transcendent is really to be found
in the Immanent. I believe this theme is continued
and developed in <u>Face</u> <u>to</u> <u>Face</u>.

The insightful Maria, Jenny's patient who
perceived Jenny's anguish, also perceives that Jenny
is isolated, locked up within herself: "Do you know
what's so incredibly wrong with you? Well, I'll tell
you, because I've figured it out: <u>You're</u> <u>unable</u> <u>to</u>
<u>love</u>!...<u>You're</u> <u>almost</u> <u>unreal</u>." Jenny's response to
her is to suggest that Maria is having a problem with
transference, a common problem of fixation on one's
analyst. She cautions Maria about this and suggests
that Maria leave the responsibility of therapy to
her. Maria's sage response is: "...shouldn't we
share the responsibility--and the risks? Why should I
take all the risks and you something vague and
harmless called responsibility?" I am not sure why
this conversation is eliminated from the film unless
it would too early (for dramatic effect) raise a
question about just who is neurotic. Love with
responsibility and risks is a long way from the grand,
sweeping definition of love in <u>Through</u> <u>a</u> <u>Glass</u> <u>Darkly</u>,
which seemed to be irresponsible, if anything.

Bergman then gives us a series of examples of
inauthentic or inadequate love, all of which have, or
we know will have, deleterious effects. Jenny has
obviously sent her daughter off to camp and then to a
friend's house in order to be free; we already know

what has happened there. When Jenny hears about the
work her Grandmother does to take care of her husband,
Jenny asks, "Don't you ever wish you were a little
freer?" for which she is properly rebuffed: "That
Grandpa was dead, you mean? Having someone to look
after like this, to get cross with or pat on the cheek
or just to talk too-it's important." While Jenny's
husband Erik is abroad for summer seminars, Jenny
takes a 'lover'--which says something about her
marriage, to say the least. When describing the
situation to Tomas, it creates a pathetic picture of
lostness:

> Jenny: My husband is away for three
>   months.
>
> Tomas: So you implied at dinner.
>
> Jenny: Actually I miss him very much.
>
> Tomas: Oh, I'm quite sure you do.
>
> Jenny: All the same I've taken a lover
>   who isn't half as nice. Can
>   you understand that?
>
> Tomas: Yes, up to a point.
>
> Jenny: To put it bluntly, he's a bore.
>
> Tomas: Well then, get rid of him.
>
> Jenny: No, he'll do--until the middle
>   of August. Then Erik will be
>   home.

When Erik does return, upon hearing of Jenny's
attempted suicide, the loveless nature of their
relationship is manifestly evident. They are awkward
in each other's presence. They, indeed, have no
"words" for each other. Jenny finally asks him to
leave, to come back tomorrow, when she would be
feeling more up to the visit. His response is just
about as loving--he has to return to America tomorrow

to chair his meeting. They share a marriage about the
same way they would share a car. Erik's lineage can
be traced to Maria and Agnes in Cries and Whispers.

As in Cries and Whispers Bergman's affirmative
portrayal is not made by the central characters, and I
can only surmise that Bergman is not ready to make
that intimate a statement. It would be, by its very
nature, a very personal, existential confession--the
most excruciating artistic presentation of all. I
imagine that eventually he will be unable to avoid it
unless he decides to settle for being just an
entertainer, which is most improbable.

The affirmation in Face to Face is granted us in
the relationship which exists between Jenny's
Grandmother and Grandfather, and its promise, by the
end of the film, is extended to Jenny. As noted in
our analysis of Cries and Whispers, Bergman has
abandoned any search for absolutes and has accepted
the fact of life's complexities and ambiguities.
Jenny's Grandmother is both villain and heroine, the
inspiration for the spectre of death and the
inspiration for the gift of love.   In the
Grandmother's differing roles with Jenny and in the
Grandmother's relationship to her husband, Bergman
skillfully gives us his perplexing but honest
picture. He does not insult us with platitudes or try
to soothe with placebos. The power of the picture is
its honest presentation of the complexities that
concern us all.

Jenny's relationship to her Grandmother, at the
beginning of the film, had not matured. Grandmother
is still the authoritarian figure, and Jenny is still
the little girl living in rebellion and with guilt
(when she goes to bed, she throws on the floor the

pillows her Grandmother had especially placed on the
bed). As a woman Jenny is isolated and removed from
any openness of mind or heart which might let her
"see" or communicate with her Grandmother. Earlier in
our analysis we mentioned that for the word to be
spoken, it had to be our word, the word of I-Thou, not
my word or another's word. This remains true, but
what Bergman seems to be indicating here is that in
order for me to participate in I-Thou relation, I must
be free to open myself to another so that our word can
be spoken. As an authoritarian, Grandmother appears
as the repressive and repulsive spectre of destruction
and death; as another human being, willing to accept
Jenny as an adult, Grandmother appears as a concerned
and loving companion, freed from the acculturated
responsibilities of authority. We see this, even when
Jenny can't. It is Grandmother who notices at once
that something is the matter with Jenny, that she is
not herself. Jenny passes it off as the aftermath of
flu, which a few vitamins will cure. Grandmother's
loving concern for her husband, which appears as such
a burden to Jenny, is not understood at all by Jenny
who probably attributes it to Grandmother's sense of
duty. It is not until Jenny's ghosts are exorcised
that Jenny can participate in a love relation with
anyone or even manage to see love in others without
discounting it as a psychological dodge.

When Jenny has returned to her Grandmother's
apartment after her hospital ordeal but with her new
sense of self, the changes in her understanding are
really given us through the magnificent camera work of
Sven Nykvist who brings such life to Bergman's
description in the text: Jenny looks at her
Grandmother: "It's as if she saw her for the first

time.   The old woman has sat down on a chair by the wall and the sunlight is shining in her face.   Jenny discovers now that her grandmother is very old, that the clear blue-gray eyes are sad, that the firm mouth is not so firm, that she is not holding herself as straight as usual, that in some way Grandma has become smaller, not very much, but quite noticeably.   And when she turns her face to Jenny and gives a little questioning smile, her head shakes almost imperceptibly but it shakes nevertheless, and the strong broad hands, the capable active hands, lie tired and idle in her lap."268

Jenny's openness, her breaking out of David's circle of Andreas's stone fence, also enables her to see the love which exists between her Grandmother and Grandfather, with its profound meaning for her understanding of death.   Again we are indebted to Nykvist and Bergman's text.   Grandmother has gone in to comfort Grandfather; we have been given indications earlier that death may be imminent.   Jenny watches them from the door of the room.   Speaking of Grandfather, Bergman writes: "The anxious eyes grow calmer and he gives a little nod, then takes Grandmother's hand.   She sits down beside the bed and pats him.   Again and again she pats his hand.

"Jenny stands for a long time at the door looking at the two old people and the way they belong together, moving slowly in toward the mysterious and awful point where they must part.   She sees their humility and dignity and for a short moment she perceives--but forgets just as quickly--that love embraces all, even death."269

On this almost triumphant note the film ends.
Bergman does seem to hedge a bit in suggesting that in
love we overcome death; Jenny, though she is
self-conscious in a way that Agnes is not in _Cries_ _and_
Whispers, is not ready to accept as Agnes does the
fact that reality must be understood in terms of
moments, in states of _being_, rather than in objective,
unequivocal contexts. But we are left with that hope
and even some promise. When Tomas is with the
hospitalized Jenny, spending his last few days before
leaving for Jamaica, they discover much to their
mutual amazement, that they have lost track of time.
Instead of it being five past four as Tomas believes,
the nurse informs them that "outside" it's five past
ten. Without elaborating, Bergman makes a distinction
between what we have called identity-time and
clock-time, between the realm of _I-Thou_ and _I-It_,
between love and causality. This, again, is
reminiscent of Eliot's _Quartets_: "Love is most nearly
itself/When here and now cease to matter." In future
films Bergman may well explore this distinction more
thoroughly.

Jenny's relation in love to Tomas is an
interesting commentary by Bergman. We know that this
relation exists--everything points to it from dialogue
to gestures--but Bergman forces us to affirm this
despite the fact that we have been told by this time
that Tomas is "gay." This is an affirmation which
Bergman makes that may put to rest the savage refrain
of Ester in _The_ _Silence_ and Karin in _Cries_ _and_
Whispers: that love, particularly as it is defined by
sex, is "all a tissue of lies." Love is an intimate
union, a creative union of human beings which may or
may not be expressed through sex. In the two

beautiful and affirmative relationships in this film,
sex (in the narrow sense) plays no part. The maturity
and dignity with which Bergman has given us this is
very moving.

But just as the film ends with two different
affirmations of love, so it makes two different
affirmations of faith related to those of love.
Before Tomas leaves Jenny in the hospital, he tries to
share with her his own credo--an existentialist,
agnostic credo born out of his own lonesome journey.
Because he is as devoted as he is, as gentle as he is,
we take him seriously, as Jenny does:

> Tomas: I do see that life has its
> moments of splendor. With a
> certain objectivity I admit
> that it is even extraordinarily
> beautiful. And generous.
> Intellectually I can grasp that
> it offers all sorts of things.
> I'm only sorry to say that I
> personally think it's a pile of
> shit.
>
> *   *   *
>
> There's an incantation for us
> who don't believe.
>
> Jenny: What do you mean?
>
> Tomas: Now and then I say it over
> silently to myself.
>
> Jenny: Can't you tell me what it is?
>
> Tomas: I wish that someone or
> something would affect me so
> that I can become real. I
> repeat over and over: Let me
> become real one day.
>
> Jenny: What do you mean by real?

Tomas: To hear a human voice and be
          sure that it comes from
          someone who is made just like
          I am. To touch a pair of lips
          and in the same thousandth of
          a second know that this is a
          pair of lips. Not to have to
          live through the hideous
          moment needed for my
          experience to check that I've
          really felt a pair of lips.
          Reality would be to know that
          a joy is a joy and above all
          that a pain has to be a pain.

Jenny: Please go on.

Tomas: Reality is perhaps not at all
          what I imagine. Perhaps it
          doesn't exist, in fact.
          Perhaps it only exists as a
          longing.

I think one can ignore, at least not pick at, the
inconsistency of petition ("Let me become real one
day") to observe that there is a strong existential,
familial resemblance in Tomas's credo to that of Camus
in The Fall. Each experience life in terms of a
longing; each, in the presence of such an
irrepressible longing, has the courage to be in spite
of no transcendent reference. It is to see one's self
and to see life face to face. It is what Jenny has
experienced in the hospital; that confrontation with
self, symbolized for us by mirror images and double
roles, which finally enabled her to truly identify
herself in the presence of others.

The second religious affirmation is that represented by the Grandparents. Not that it is self-consciously religious (Bergman is not ready for that commitment), but it does confirm the religious direction in which Bergman has been moving. Ironically enough, the articulation of this affirmation of faith is given us at the beginning of the text (tragically enough, not included in the film). Jenny says to her Grandmother, while talking of her relationship to Grandfather, "It was a saint who said, 'Love is a state of grace. Those who are in it usually do not themselves know they are among the chosen. Love influences through their actions just as naturally as the rose through its scent or the nightingale through its song.' I think it was St. Francis." Grandmother replies: "A state of grace? Whose grace?" Jenny: "For St. Francis there was no doubt." Grandmother (Respectfully): "Well, that just goes to show. For me life has been mostly practical considerations."

Of course what Grandmother's response shows is that she is living in the state of grace. Grandmother and Grandfather exemplify what Bergman is saying in Cries and Whispers and now in Face to Face: the Transcendent is really to be found in and through the Immanent in the mediated-immediacy of love. It is there, in love, when we meet each other (not ourselves!) face to face, that we come before the Face of God. Once we saw through a glass darkly, but now, in love, we see face to face. Jenny's childhood prayer that her Grandmother's face would be changed back to its loving self has been answered. In response, her own, too, has changed.

It would be folly to try to reconcile these two religious responses for Bergman. It would prove to be an artificial gesture employing the very metaphysical mechanics he has been struggling to escape. Neither Bergman's journey, nor ours, is over yet.

Autumn Sonata (1978)

"Jenny stands for a long time at the
door looking at the two old people and
the way they belong together, moving
slowly in toward the mysterious and
awful point where they must part. She
sees their humility and dignity and
for a short moment she perceives...that
love embraces all, even death.

Face to Face

The polarities of love and hate, loneliness and
companionship, the paradox of life in the presence of
death, with which Bergman's last two films, Cries and
Whispers and Face to Face, engaged us are now restated
and carried forward in Bergman's next film Autumn
Sonata. Both previous films, despite some of
Bergman's most vivid and violent cinematic moments,
end with a sense of gentleness and affirmation--a
fragile, spiritual tranquility after the existential
storm. It is not that Bergman has promised us no more
conflict or personal angst, but that he has at least
given us a glimpse of love successfully confronting
hate, of life affirming itself in the presence of
death. That Bergman should entitle his next film
Autumn Sonata seems most appropriate.

Autumn is the season of paradox and therefore
perfectly suited for Bergman's symbol system: autumn
is serenity but it carries the ominous threat of
winter; it bespeaks maturity but at the cost of age;
it suggests fulfillment but as a prelude to loss; it
designs exquisite and beautiful forms but is
structured by decay; it is vibrant life but in the
presence of death.

When Bergman adds to this powerful, suggestive
symbol the word "sonata," the balance is weighted
toward the affirmative side of polarity and paradox.
Music has always been expressive and promising for
Bergman. When it has been denied, as in Shame where
even musical instruments were broken before our eyes,
there has been no hope for human communication or
love--in short, for human meaning. In Autumn Sonata
Bergman treats us to Bach, Chopin, and Handel. One of
these, Chopin's "Prelude No. 2 in A minor", is played
by mother and daughter, the two major protagonists of
the film. The prelude is, like the word "autumn",
symbolic of the whole personal drama we are watching.
Charlotte, a professional pianist and a mother (in
that order) makes this statement before playing the
prelude for her daughter. "This second prelude must
be made to sound almost ugly. It must never become
ingratiating. It should sound wrong. You must battle
your way through it and emerge triumphant." So the
theme and tenor of the film is set. It is Bergman's
call for integrity and candor as the only way through
human adversity. Only personal authenticity can push
beyond the stultification of cultural convention, the
banality of polite but meaningless behavior, the
blindness of self-deception. Authenticity becomes the
key to relationship and love and, therefore to
redemption.

The plot of Autumn Sonata, like that of so many of
Bergman's earlier films, is simple enough in terms of
time, place, and action; the complexity comes in the
analysis of human motivation, thought, and feeling.

Eva, a sometime journalist living with her husband
Viktor, a Lutheran pastor, has invited her estranged
mother Charlotte, a concert pianist, to come

to her parsonage home on a Norwegian fjord for an
extended visit.   Eva has learned from mutual friends
that her mother's companion of thirteen years,
Leonardo, has died.   Eva hopes that such a visit, at a
time of obvious need, might bring about a
reconciliation between her mother and herself.   Both
have suffered the loss of a loved one--Eva, her small
son Erik who, seven years earlier, drowned at the age
of four, and Charlotte, her lover Leonardo.   As if
that strain were not enough, Eva fails to tell her
mother that living with herself and Viktor is
Charlotte's younger daughter Helena.   Helena is ill
with a progressively debilitating disease which may
have been psychosomatically induced by Charlotte's
neglect occasioned by professional ambition.
Charlotte is to find this oversight on Eva's part
hostile, or naive at best.

Charlotte arrives at the parsonage to find herself
soon confronted by Eva's sublimated fury for the
rejection and humiliation she has received over the
years, by Helena's piteous demands for affection which
Charlotte now cannot fulfill, and by a gentle, placid
but accepting Victor whose good will is ineffectual in
resolving the passionate animosities among the three
women.   The visit climaxes with Eva and her mother
each becoming candid and confessional with the other
for the first time in their lives.   The intensity of
expressed hatred is enough to drive Charlotte away,
but not before she makes clear to Eva her
(Charlotte's) own sense of rejection, confusion, and
fear occasioned by her own mother and father.

The encounter, though destructive, has cleared the
air between the women, though such an accomplishment
is not recognized until after they part.   It is only

then, in a letter, that Eva reaches out to ask
forgiveness, but we are left without knowing whether
the gesture is too late, whether human character is
immutable and therefore doomed to despair, or whether,
now that the ugliness has been exposed, a triumph of
love may be possible. The film ends with a close up
shot of Charlotte, having read Eva's letter, not
knowing how to respond, travelling on and, perhaps,
away.

Bergman's portrayal of this family strife is
presented with his usual honesty, but this film's
honesty is not all destructive; it is the prelude to
affirmation. The theme, mentioned above, of
experientially struggling through to triumph is
portrayed by a series of transformations which take
place in the motifs we have been following in
Bergman's earlier films. The effect is similar to
Soren Kierkegaard's use of the experience of
repetition or what linguists think of as the
hermeneutical circle: events and conditions outwardly
seem to be the same, no change; yet, because of our
existential/experiential insights, they are markedly
different and more complex.

The film's first and final sequences begin with a
long shot of Eva writing a letter to her mother. In
each instance she is observed, at a distance, by a
concerned but unobtrusive Viktor. The first letter,
which an uncertain and insecure Eva asks Viktor to
hear and approve, is Eva's invitation to Charlotte to
come for a visit. It is filled with conventional and
(we later learn) insincere--though desired--words of
endearment: "Dearest little Mother." and "Mother
dearest." It also reads like an advertisement for a
pleasant vacation at a Norwegian country inn--a

description of the accommodations, the natural beauty
of the fjord location, the availability of a piano for
practice, and the luxury of unstructured time. The
letter ends, formally, with the greeting: "Much love
from Viktor and your daughter Eva."

The second letter, with which the film ends, is
given to Viktor to mail. Eva no longer needs Viktor's
approval and isn't really concerned whether he reads
it or not. The content and tone are much different.
It is honest, straightforward, non-judgmental--unless
it be toward herself: "I met you with demands instead
of with affection. I tormented you with an old sour
hatred which is no longer real." The exorcism of
hatred which had characterized the visit had opened up
the possibility of reconciliation, at least for Eva.
Until the venting of that passion, hatred blocked any
true rapprochement between the two women. What Eva
learns, as Marta had learned in Winter Light, is that
her prayer had been answered--she had been given a
"use" by God and set "free from (her) prison." Eva
writes: "Suddenly it dawned on me that I was to take
care of you...I hope...my discovery will not be in
vain. There is a kind of mercy after all. I mean the
enormous chance of looking after each other, of
showing affection." Eva's only fear is that it is too
late. Watching Charlotte's face, as we are permitted
to do, we are not sure of the letter's efficacy; but
we are sure that, finally, real communication has a
chance to begin, relationship a chance to grow.

This development proves to be an important clue to
Bergman's emerging understanding about the place and
validity of words, the vital importance of
communication. Since The Silence Bergman has been
struggling with whether one can ever regain

authenticity in our language, and, therefore, in our
relationships; whether words can ever be trusted to
mean what they say. Eva's sensitivity to this dilemma
and her awareness of a possible resolution appears at
the beginning of the film in the following exchange
between Eva and Viktor:

<u>V</u>: I long for you.

<u>E</u>: Those are very pretty words, aren't
        they?

<u>V</u>: You know quite well what I mean.

<u>E</u>: No. If I knew, it would never
        enter your head to say you long for
        me.

<u>V</u>: That's true.

What Bergman has come upon is the existential claim
that there must be a synonymity between word and
action, that each validates and establishes the
other. Without words, all actions remain ambiguous,
but without action, all words remain empty. When
words betray action or vice versa, we have the
breakdown of any meaningful communication and
relation. "I didn't understand your words," Eva
explains to her mother, "They didn't match your
intonation or the expression in your eyes. The worst
of all was that you smiled when you were angry. When
you were angry with Papa you called him 'my dearest
friend;'when you tired of me you said 'darling little
girl.' Nothing fitted." This exchange between Eva
and Charlotte ends, in the text but not the film, with
Charlotte disclaiming such dissembling and Eva
responding: "What does it matter? Your words apply
to your reality, my words to mine. If we exchange
words, they're worthless."270 Sometime, between
text and take, Bergman became more optimistic about
genuine communication.

The implications of this linguistic understanding for religion are profound and have been reflected in all of Bergman's films since The Silence. The recitation, by rote, of creeds and prayers, the preaching of "acceptable" sermons, the espousal of ethical norms, if not existentially affirmed, are hypocritical and destructive. This analysis explains the affirmative way that Bergman treats the Clergy in Cries and Whispers and Autumn Sonata. In each case the Pastor makes no transcendent claim to knowledge or faith not his, but in each instance lays claim to a faith sustained by a human relationship. In Cries and Whispers it is Agnes' faith and patient suffering which inspire the Pastor. In Autumn Sonata Viktor openly and easily confesses to Charlotte: "The little faith I have lives on her (Eva's) terms." Perhaps this is why Bergman calls this Pastor "Viktor." There is no pretense in the man. He is gentle, kind, winsome, and honest. There is no pomposity; no claim to rank or reverence; no judgment of others by some presumed absolute standard or vocational privilege. The man is a man of faith which becomes evident in the abandonment of all the traditional and accepted marks of ecclesiastical proprieties and manners. He has become victorious over the system; he believes despite his unbelief.

This rejection of norms and creeds as mere words reflects more than Bergman's rejection of religious traditionalism; it is also his rejection of the whole classical, metaphysical "structure" of reality--something we have traced since The Seventh Seal. Reality is that which must be lived rather than known as an act of mind. Indeed, in one film which has not been selected for special study, The Serpent's

Egg, the scientific and technological fruits of such a metaphysical interpretation of reality become identified with the origins of Nazi barbarism and brutality. The point is simple to state: when principle supersedes person, and Truth is equated exclusively with scientific method, inhumanity in all its ugly manifestations results. Whether one is dealing with religious "truths" or political "truths" makes no difference. The result is demonically the same.

In Autumn Sonata the destructive power of such metaphysical "truth" and its eventual transformation through love characterizes Eva's confrontation with her mother. After accusing her mother of causing Helena's illness by her wanton disregard and rejection of Helena, Eva says to her: "There are no excuses, Mother. There is only one truth and one lie. There can be no forgiveness." Only when Eva, after her mother's departure, realizes her own guilt in disregarding and rejecting her mother, does she drop the arrogance of absolute rights and wrongs and herself plead for forgiveness--"I don't think it is too late. It must not be too late."

The reality which simultaneously integrates and makes possible such a transformation is that of a dynamic, inclusive interrelatedness. It is the expressive world of Being Itself in its ontological wholeness. It is no longer the world of Sartre, in which one must totalize one's self, the world of pour soi, en soi which we explored in Persona. Rather, it is the world as it is, in its timefulness and giveness, within which I find myself interrelatedly as a part. I am, as Heidegger says, "being there," not "in the world" but "of the world."

Bergman dramatizes this development in two ways. The first is more traditional and more expected. It comes in an exchange between Eva and her mother. Eva wants to explain why she derives great comfort from sitting quietly in the room that her son Erik used as a nursery.[271]

> Right inside I felt from the outset that he was still alive, that we were living close beside each other. I've only to concentrate, however little, and he's there. Sometimes, just as I'm falling to sleep, I can feel him breathing against my face and touching me with his hand. Do you think it sounds neurotic? I can perhaps understand if you do. For me it's quite natural. He's living another life, but at any moment we can reach each other, there's no dividing line, no insurmountable wall. Sometimes, of course, I wonder what it looks like--the reality where my little boy is living and breathing. At the same time I know it can't be described, as it's a world of liberated feelings...To me, man is a tremendous creation, an inconceivable thought; and in man there is everything, from the highest to the lowest, just as in life; and man is God's image; and in God there is everything, vast forces, and then the devils are created and the saints and the prophets and the obscurantists and the artists and the iconoclasts.

> Everything exists side by side, one
> thing penetrating the other. It's like
> huge patterns changing all the time, do
> you know what I mean?   In that way
> there must also be countless realities,
> not only the reality we perceive with
> our blunt senses but a tumult of
> realities arching above and around each
> other, inside and outside. It's merely
> fear and priggishness to believe in any
> limits. <u>There</u> <u>are</u> <u>no</u> <u>limits</u>. Neither
> to thoughts nor to feelings.   It's
> anxiety that sets the limits don't you
> think so too? When you play the slow
> movement of Beethoven's Hammerklavier
> Sonata, you must surely feel you're
> moving in a world without limitations,
> inside an immense motion that you can
> never see through or explore.

It is both interesting and instructive that in the
text Bergman adds the following comment by Eva:

> It is the same with Jesus. He burst
> asunder the laws and the limitations
> with an entirely new feeling that no
> one had heard of before--love.   No
> wonder people were afraid and angry,
> just as they nearly always try to sneak
> off in alarm when some big emotion
> overwhelms them, though they eat their
> hearts out pining for their withered
> and deadened feelings.[272]

One can speculate here that through love, through
interrelatedness, Jesus again becomes accessible to
Bergman.   By contrast, the Christ who does the

miraculous, who is expected to return trailing clouds
of glory, is simply part of that magical world of
make-believe which Bergman has rejected. The Jesus
who loved, was humiliated, and who died at the hands
of other men, Bergman understands and relates to.
Theologically what seems to be developing at this
point is a sense of God's immanence accompanied by a
very "low" Christology. Jesus is an example of
extraordinary authenticity and spiritual sensitivity,
not God incarnate.

The second way that Bergman affirms the
interrelatedness of his reality is to end the film at
the graveyard where Erik is buried. As Eva finally
rises to leave, she soliloquizes about Erik (at least
for the camera): "Are you stroking my cheek? Are you
whispering in my ear? Are you with me now? We'll
never leave each other, you and I." If we apply Eva's
own test of the validity of words, which we have noted
her using on Viktor, then some question may be raised
about the validity of her experience--if it were so,
would she need to be asking the question? However,
the final statement is not a question but a
declaration, and I believe represents that important
next step beyond the speculation in Cries and
Whispers. It is confirmation that the I-Thou relation
of love conquers even death itself and now expresses
itself in another dimension of reality.

Bergman has described his journey in search of
meaning as a "longing for affinity," and it would
appear, in Autumn Sonata that he has ascertained that
affinity is spiritually and temporally possible. Eva
is quoted by Viktor as having once written: "If
anyone loves me as I am, I may dare at last to look at
myself." By the end of this film and journey, Eva

would be saying, "If I can give myself to another, I
will never have to look at myself again." It would
appear that existentially Bergman has arrived at the
Biblical insight that she who seeks to save her own
life will lose it, but she who gives herself to or for
another will save it. However, such affinity demands
as its price that candor and honesty with another (or
God) which is the most difficult and dangerous
relation to effect.

Despite early efforts to the contrary, Bergman now
believes that interrelatedness can never be a matter
of indifference. Relations with another or with God
are characterized, obviously, by power--not just in
the Sartrean sense of sado/masochism, but in the polar
possibility of love. All genuine relationships are
achieved and sustained at some cost. The scriptural
notion that he who is not for me is against me is
closer to the truth of the nature of relation than
Sartre, but even in the former, some graduation is
evident. Bergman, throughout the films we have
surveyed, has indicated those monstrous, spider-god
forces that beset the physical, social, and spiritual
modes of our existence--forces such as death, war,
disease, time, technocracy, hatred, etc. But the net
effect of such blights on our existence is to deprive
us of meaning and purpose, harmony and love, and
rewarding relationships. As we have noted above, he
has arrived, now, at the conclusion that only human or
divine love can overcome such forces and that,
consequently, any deprivation of such love is not only
tragic but itself the worst of the monstrous forces we
must face.

The negative side of this human equation which claims that my deliverer can also be my demon is nowhere more graphically or powerfully portrayed than in Bergman's From the Life of the Marionettes. The protagonists, Peter and Katarina, have each violated the personal commitment of their marriage; each has lost that sense of sexual excitement which had attracted them in the first place, so that even sodomistic practices fail to satisfy or arouse them. The love which might have sustained the relationship and kept vital their sexual life is non-existent. Peter, searching for that love but mistaking it for the excitement of sexual encounter, goes to a brothel. There he witnesses a prostitute putting on a show on a stage-in-the-round. The naked woman is on the floor of the stage, gyrating in a spider-like fashion, spreading and closing her legs, inviting the voyeurs into her spider's nest. There could have been no more graphic portrayal of Bergman's notion of the beautiful and healing power of love transformed into the monstrous and destructive force of carnality. That which should have been the final and most complete expression of love and unity has become the initial and most complete expression of exploitation and alienation. The grossness of the image has been rivaled only by Bergman's scene of animalistic copulation in The Silence. Peter, working out the extreme logic of Sartrean sado/masochistic sexuality, then murders one of the prostitutes (whose first name is Katarina, like his wife, and whose surname is Kraft, the German word for power or force) and commits necrophilia. Peter is confined to a hospital, a mental hospital we can assume, where he now spends his time, we presume waiting for death, playing chess with

a computerized set--an update on Bergman's Seventh
Seal. The last hospital scene we see is a light
flashing on the side of the chess set stating "You
missed the mate." So he had. When impersonal
sexuality is substituted for love, the force unleashed
is monstrous and not redemptive.

In Autumn Sonata this confrontation and confusion
is between mother and daughter, not husband and wife.
The generational alienation and hatred we were shown
in Face to Face is recapitulated between Eva and
Charlotte. It is obvious that Charlotte has
sacrificed her family for her art and in so doing has
emotionally crippled both her daughters. Again the
spider image appears. Eva, on the night of her
mother's arrival, is coaxed into playing the piano for
her mother. Music, like sex in From the Life of the
Marionettes, should be the power, the love, which
binds them together; but, in this instance, it becomes
the symbol of the force of hatred between them.

When asked to critique Eva's playing, Charlotte
gives a little lecture and then plays the Chopin
prelude herself. The camera zooms in on Charlotte's
fingers which are moving ominously and spider-like
over the keys. The web is woven in music. Eva's hope
for a full and meaningful life rests with her
relationship to her mother, but it is her mother who
is presently denying her that reconciliation and
love. At the same time, Charlotte's hope to end her
Odyssean wandering and return home depends upon Eva's
willingness to forgive and accept her unequivocally.
Each has tried a substitute, but to no avail. Eva has
taken on the burden of caring for Helena, yet, as
noble and satisfying as that may be, it cannot obviate
the primal relationship which must be resolved between

herself and her mother. Charlotte, for her part, has
tried to substitute her agent Paul for the lost
Leonardo and the alienated Eva, but Paul, with about
as much character as silly putty, cannot be a
surrogate for her daughter. It is only when Eva and
Charlotte both have expressed their alienation and
need that the possibility of love appears. The way to
salvation is confessional, personal, and existential.

It is evident that for Ingmar Bergman there can be
no one formula or one answer to the problem of one's
meaning, purpose, and happiness, but each of these
depends upon our recognition of our primal need for
love of another. Such love demands openness, honesty,
and candor, the fulfillment of which alone can tell us
who we are and what contribution we can make. I am
sure that Bergman, for our own search for life, would
have each of us say, "I am going to persist! I won't
give up, even if it should be too late. I don't think
it is too late. It must not be too late."

EPILOGUE

New films have rarely received the initial critical attention accorded _Fanny and Alexander_, but that is because few directors have the stature of Ingmar Bergman. Add to this Bergman's claim that _Fanny and Alexander_ is his last film, and one can understand why the world has rushed to greet it. It is touted to be the summation of Bergman's contribution to cinema and a consummate expression of the art. In terms of this present study, the latter may be true, but certainly not the former, despite Bergman's own claim that the film represents "the sum total of my life as a film maker."273

Fanny and Alexander is a radical break from the mainstream of Bergman's art and a departure from the existential insights through which he has brought us over the last thirty years. Critics, applauding the film, are inclined to associate it with earlier films like _Smiles of a Summer Night_ or his recent production _The Magic Flute_ and apply such descriptive adjectives as "Dickensian" and "Victorian." It is true that many of the themes Bergman has dealt with over the years are acknowledged--humiliation, fear, sexual promiscuity, death, wicked and/or inept clergy, useless religious practices--but all of these are caricatured to the point of fantasy, and a child's fantasy at that. It may be great cinema, but it does not help to advance Bergman's spiritual pilgrimage of understanding.

Pauline Kael puts such a judgment succinctly: "Nobody is really religious, nobody is in any way spiritual; in fact, Alexander's idealized family is so hearty and indulgent it's gross." Kael goes on to observe: "What it ['Fanny and Alexander'] has is lovingly placed warm gingerbreading, which I fear will lead audiences to take it as a healing experience. They can come out of the movie beaming with pleasure at the thought of Ingmar Bergman's finally achieving harmony with himself. But the conventionality of the thinking in "Fanny and Alexander" is rather shocking; it's not modern conventionality--it's from the past. And that may have a lot to do with why the film seems healing. It's as if Bergman's neuroses had been tormenting him for so long that he cut them off and went sprinting back to Victorian fantasy, and it may win Ingmar Bergman his greatest public acceptance. Coming from Bergman, banality is bound to seem deeply satisfying--wholesome. It can pass for the wisdom of maturity."274

Nowhere in Fanny and Alexander is this more accurately portrayed than in Bergman's description of the Ekdahl family at the beginning of the film: "While we are looking at the colorful picture of Christmas dinner in the Ekdahl's kitchen, I will tell you about the families' mutual attentiveness. They touch each other, shake each other, slap each other's backs, pat, fondle, and hug one another, give each other wet smacking kisses, hold each other's hands, gaze into each other's eyes, and ruffle each other's hair. They enjoy dramatic squabbles, they burst into tears and abuse one another and seek allies, but they make it all up just as readily, uttering sacred vows and endearments. One thing is just as sincere as the other."275

Such is the fantasy land from which the film derives its power and charm but because of which it removes itself from this study of Bergman's religious insight. In his film _Autumn Sonata_ the family is portrayed in its agonizing struggle for love, affection, and caring, which speak to us existentially. _Fanny and Alexander_ merely entertains us.

There is, perhaps, a theological reason for this hiatus in Bergman's religious quest. The very nature of existential religious thought is such that unless it is _lived_ it cannot be claimed or even authentically described. Bergman can no more make up religious insight than he can suspend a juggler's ball in mid-air. Bergman's critique of spiritual reality in such films as _Winter Light_, _Shame_, and _Cries and Whispers_ is so devastating and captivating simply because Bergman has reached deep into our psyches, beyond our learned and borrowed defenses, to confront us with our authentic selves. It is at this level of encounter that our genuine religious predilections and faith become apparent and operative. Bergman is able to do this for us because he is drawing on his own harrowing and heroic struggles.

From _The Seventh Seal_ on, we have acknowledged with Bergman that our religious faith, whatever it may be, cannot be a matter simply of objective, mathematical reason or inherited tradition. Faith must be an expression of ultimate personal importance and ultimate creative source, which only together can give integrity to the living of our lives. The cultural expression of such an existential faith demands a commensurate synonymity in our words and deeds. But Bergman discovered that most of us are so

immersed in our psychological fantasies and narrow
cultural accommodations that there is no truth in us,
that we are hopelessly lost and alienated in the world
and from each other. The only personal harmony
Bergman can begin to find is in human love and the
only worldly harmony in music. Gradually, as we have
seen, Bergman's understanding of human love has grown
from that of a desperate need, in The Passion of Anna,
to a desperate need to give in Autumn Sonata--a
theological growth from the atheism of Sartre to the
theism of Kierkegaard. Music has continued, for
Bergman, to relate to the mystery of our unity and, as
such, can really be said to be revelatory for him.
The harmony of God's universe is symbolized in the
harmony of music.

It is difficult at this stage to determine how
personal the experience of God may be for Bergman. If
one means by "God" that metaphysical entity of
tradition, then one would have to conclude, at this
point, that such a "God" is not only impersonal but
dead. If one means by "God" a sense of personal
presence which permits us to claim an identity and to
be present to those whom we love--living or dead--then
one could conclude that Bergman truly is a man of
profound faith. Bergman's own integrity about words
and pictures may prohibit him from praying to such a
personal Presence, yet, like Marta and Eva, his
prayers may have been answered, nevertheless.

ENDNOTES

[1]Bergman, as quoted in *Bergman on Bergman*, Stig Bjorkman, Torsten Manns, and Jonas Sima, trans. Paul Austin, (New York: Simon and Schuster, 1973), p. 169.

[2]Bergman, as quoted in *The Films of Ingmar Bergman*, Jorn Donner, (New York: Dover Publications, Inc., 1972), p. 144.

[3]William Barrett, *Irrational Man*, Anchor Books, (Garden City, New York: Doubleday and Co., 1962), p. 18.

[4]Bergman has announced that his next film is to be his last. After its release, he intends to return to the theater which is his first love. Whether he holds to such a determination is a matter of much speculation. His "final" film, so far as we can tell, is about childhood and the formative years. No doubt we will be given new glimpses with Bergman's own child-view, but I doubt that the substance of this film will significantly alter the subject matter or direction of this present study.

[5]Ingmar Bergman, *Four Screenplays of Ingmar Bergman*, trans. Lars Malmstrom and David Kushner, (New York: Simon and Schuster, 1960), p. xvii.

[6]Birgitta Steene, *Ingmar Bergman*, (New York: St. Martin's Press, 1968), "Preface."

[7]Donner. *The Films of Ingmar Bergman*, p. 8.

[8]Ibid., p. 6.

[9]T. S. Eliot, *Selected Poems*, (Harmondsworth, Middlesex: Penguin Books Ltd., 1948), p. 75.

[10]Bergman, *Four Screenplays of Ingmar Bergman*, p. xiv.

[11]Ibid., p. xix.

[12]Bergman, as quoted by Charles T. Samuels, "Ingmar Bergman, An Interview," *Ingmar Bergman, Essays in Criticism*, ed., Stuart Kaminsky with Joseph Hill, (New York: Oxford University Press, 1975), p. 100.

[13]Bergman, _Four Screenplays of Ingmar Bergman_, p. 14.

[14]Bergman, as quoted by Robin Wood, _Ingmar Bergman_, (New York: Frederick A. Praeger, Inc., 1970), p. 24.

[15]Ibid.

[16]Bergman, as quoted in _Bergman on Bergman_, p. 219. _TM_: "You mention Sartre and the religious syndrome. I'd like to get on to the question of what view you take of the father, of authority, of the primitive father-image...Many people have called you a Freudian; but they're wrong. You're really a Jungian. It's Jung who has these atavistic, primitive archetypes--which were originally individual and private, but have acquired a universal validity."

[17]Bergman, as quoted by Stig Bjorkman, et al., pp. 80-81.

[18]Ibid., p. 239.

[19]Ibid., p. 62.

[20]Barrett, _Irrational Man_, p. 57.

[21]Ibid., p. 49.

[22]Bergman, as quoted by Stig Bjorkman, et al., p. 62.

[23]Bergman, as quoted by Steene, p. 19.

[24]Ibid., p. 20.

[25]Bergman, as quoted by Samuels, p. 130.

[26]Strindberg, as quoted by Gunnar Brandell, _Strindberg in Inferno_, trans. Barry Jacobs (Cambridge: Harvard University Press, 1974), p. 15.

[27]Ibid., p. 33.

[28]Strindberg, as quoted by F. L. Lucas, _The Drama of Ibsen and Strindberg_, (New York: The Macmillan Co., 1962), p. 324.

[29]Strindberg, as quoted by Brandell, p. 21.

[30]Strindberg, as quoted by Lucas, p. 327.

[31]Strindberg, as quoted by Brandell, p. 24.

[32]Bergman, as quoted by Steene, pp. 23-24.

[33]Ibid., p. 22.

[34]Barrett, Irrational Man, p. 45.

[35]Bergman, as quoted by Stig Bjorkman, et al., p. 130.

[36]Ibid., p. 66.

[37]Ibid., p. 210-11.

[38]Ibid., pp. 218-19.

[39]Bergman, Four Screenplays by Ingmar Bergman, p. xxii.

[40]Bergman, as quoted by Eugene Archer, "Bergman: 'I try to Write Subconsciously, to Let My Dreams Flow,'" New York Times, April 2, 1967, Sec. D., p. 11.

[41]Bergman, as quoted by Stig Bjorkman, et al., p. 164.

[42]Ibid., pp. 245-46. Also, Barrett, Irrational Man, p. 53.

[43]Bergman, Four Screenplays, p. xxi.

[44]Bergman, as quoted by Charles T. Samuels, p. 121.

[45]Ibid., p. 103.

[46]Bergman, as quoted by John Simon, Ingmar Bergman Directs, (New York: Harcourt Brace Jovanovich, Inc., 1972), p. 15.

[47]Ibid., p. 38.

[48]Bergman, as quoted by Steene, "Preface."

[49]Bergman, as quoted by Stig Bjorkman, et al., pp. 104-5.

[50]Bergman, as quoted by Steene, pp. 22-23.

[51]Bergman, as quoted by Stig Bjorkman, et al., pp. 106-7.

[52]Bergman, Four Screenplays, p. xix.

[53]Bergman, as quoted by Stig Bjorkman, et al., p. 220.

[54]Bergman, as quoted by Robin Wood, p. 51. Of "Sawdust and Tinsel." "One is free to interpret the circus as in some sense symbolic of the Human Condition, although the film doesn't seem to me to insist on it;...If one sees the sequence showing the erection of the Big Top in the pouring rain as expressive at once of human achievement and human wretchedness, this is not a matter of say 'imposed symbolism' but of meaning growing naturally out of naturalistic and powerfully tactile images."

[55]Bergman, as quoted by Samuels, pp. 102-103.

[56]Bergman, as quoted by Simon, p. 11.

[57]Bergman, as quoted by Steene, "Preface."

[58]Bergman, as quoted by Simon, p. 12.

[59]Bergman, as quoted by Stig Bjorkman, et al., p. 172.

[60]Liv Ullmann, Changing, (New York: Alfred A. Knopf, 1977), p. 214.

[61]Bergman, as quoted by Stig Bjorkman, et al., p. 224.

[62]Nykvist, as quoted by David Denby, "The Man Who Films Bergman's Nightmares," New York Times, Sec. II, April 25, 1976, p. 15.

[63]Bergman, as quoted by Stig Bjorkman, et al., p. 224.

[64]Nykvist, as quoted by David Denby, p. 15.

[65]Bergman, as quoted by Steene, p. 22.

[66]Bergman, as quoted by Simon, p. 18.

[67]Bergman, as quoted by Stig Bjorkman, et al., p. 225.

[68]Ibid., p. 95.

[69]Stanley Kauffmann, Ingmar Bergman, Essays in Criticism, ed., Stuart Kaminsky with Joseph Hill, (New York: Oxford University Press, 1975), pp. 224-225.

[70]Bergman, as quoted by Stig Bjorkman, et al., p. 146.

[71]Ibid.

[72]Donner, The Films of Ingmar Bergman, p. 11.

[73]Ibid., p. 13.

[74]Bergman, as quoted by Steene, p. 23. Though there is some reason to believe that Bergman has been misunderstood here--See Bergman on Bergman, p. 177--there is no reason to quarrel with the general intent of Brigitta Steene's statement. Before Bergman can dismiss the metaphysical question, he feels the obligation to confront it.

[75]Donner, The Films of Ingmar Bergman, pp. 10-11.

[76]Ibid., p. 219.

[77]Donner writes: "I maintain that B's inspiration is Christian, but that his film dramas can apply to all people. The question of what he believes in, or if he believes in anything, therefore becomes of no concern, so long as the non-believer or the believer in something else manages to penetrate into B's world, the world of his characters. The moral discussion in his films, the question of the possibilities of choice, often builds on Christian conceptions and is worked into a Christian symbolism. B's art, however, would lack universal validity if its problems applied only to Christians." Ibid.

[78]Jerry H. Gill, Ingar Bergman and the Search for Meaning, (Grand Rapids, Michigan: Eerdmans, 2969), p. 42.

[79]Bergman, as quoted by Stig Bjorkman, et al., p. 177.

[80]Donner, The Films of Ingmar Bergman, p. 203.

[81]Bergman, as quoted by Stig Bjorkman, et al., p. 64.

[82]Bergman, Four Screenplays, p. 21.

[83]Ibid., p. 22.

[84]Bergman, as quoted by Stig Bjorkman, et al., p. 40.

[85]The Revelation to John 6:12-17, R.S.V.

[86]Ibid., 8:1.

[87]Job, 3:23-26. Archibald MacLeish, who uses Job as the model for his drama, J.B., puts the question of theodicy in a more succinct form: "If God is good He is not God/If God is God He is not good..."

[88]Bergman, Program Note for The Seventh Seal, as quoted by Steene, p. 62. Steene, herself, finds the allegory philosophically more ambiguous!

[89]Peter Cowie, "The Seventh Seal," Films and Filming, January 1963, p. 29.

[90]Donner, The Films of Ingmar Bergman, p. 136.

[91]Barrett, Irrational Man, pp. 24-25.

[92]Bergman, as quoted by Steene, p. 64.

[93]Bergman, Introductory description: "The Seventh Seal," Four Screenplays, pp. 138-139.

[94]Ibid., p. 139.

[95]Ibid., pp. 149-151.

[96]Barrett, Irrational Man, pp. 88-89. "The West has thought in the shadow of the Greeks: even where later Western thinkers have rebelled against Greek wisdom, they have thought their rebellion through in terms which the Greeks laid down for them...Reason, Aristotle tells us, is the highest part of our personality: that which the human person truly is. One's reason, then, is one's real self, the center of one's personal identity. This is rationalism stated in its starkest and strongest

terms--that one's rational self is one's real
self--and as such held sway over the views of Western
philosophers up until very modern times. Even the
Christianity of the Middle Ages, when it assimilated
Aristotle, did not displace this Aristotelian
principle: it simply made an uneasy alliance between
faith as the supernatural center of the personality
and reason as its natural center; the natural man
remained an Aristotelian man, a being whose real life
was his rational self."

97Ibid., pp. 83-84. "...the young Plato,
tormented by this vision [the doctrines of Cratylus],
desired at all costs a refuge in the eternal from the
insecurities and ravages of time. Hence the enormous
attraction for him of the science of mathematics,
which opens up a realm of eternal truths. Here at
least, in pure thought, man can find an escape from
time. Hence, too, the tremendous emotional force for
him of the theory of eternal forms or Ideas, since
these latter were an everlasting realm to which man
has access. We have to see Plato's rationalism, not
as a cool scientific project such as a later century
of the European Enlightenment might set for itself,
but as a kind of passionately religious doctrine--a
theory that promised man salvation from the things he
had feared most from the earliest days, from death and
time."

98Villy Sorenson, as quoted by Donner, The
Films of Ingmar Bergman, p. 145.

99Bergman, as quoted by Stig Bjorkman, et al.,
p. 117.

100Ibid.

101Bergman, as quoted by Steene, p. 65.
Donner makes the statement that "The scene with the
strawberries is one of the moments that man has at his
disposal to manifest his moral center. It comprises
the center around which the entire film revolves."
Donner, The Films of Ingmar Bergman, p. 149. Granting
an importance to the scene, I find no evidence for
centrality Donner ascribes to it here.

102Donner, The Films of Ingmar Bergman, p.
146. Internal quote: Colin Young, Film Quarterly,
XIII, No. 3 (Spring 1959), p. 42.

103Gill, Bergman and the Search for Meaning,
p. 17. Jerry Gill's assessment is corroborative:
"The traveling actors, Jof and Mia, with their son
Mikael, portray a personal, simple, somewhat mystical
approach to life...The basis of this simple calmness
seems to be twofold: their love for one another, and
their lack of awareness of the kind of questions that
the knight insists on asking. The knight must ask
them, the squire will not ask them, and the couple is
unable to ask them."

104Donner, The Films of Ingmar Bergman, p.
146.

105Bergman, Four Screenplays, p. 161.

106Barrett, Irrational Man, pp. 75-76.
"Protestantism later sought to revive...face-to-face
confrontation of man with his God, but could produce
only a pallid replica of the simplicity, vigor, and
wholeness of this original Biblical faith. Protestant
man had thrown off the husk of his body. He was a
creature of spirit and inwardness, but no longer the
man of flesh and belly, bones and blood, that we find
in the Bible. Protestant man would never have dared
confront God and demand an accounting of His ways."

107Donner, The Films of Ingmar Bergman, p.
150.

108Vernon Young, Cinema Borealis, (New York:
Avon Books, 1971), p. 186.

109Robin Wood, certainly one of Bergman's most
perceptive critics, does take Bergman to task (a bit
harshly, I believe) for failing to achieve the
synthesis just indicated: "Bergman achieves a horror
sequence full of 'Gothic' images calculated to
unnerve, which we watch without losing our composure
or detachment for a moment. Besides a horror sequence
that doesn't horrify, The Face boasts comedy that
doesn't make us laugh and anguish that entirely fails
to move. The film's distinctive flavour arises from
the discrepancy between our much too acute awareness
of what Bergman is trying to make us feel, and our
almost total failure to feel it. One could, I
suppose, talk about 'alienation effects'; but the
actual experience is closer to boredom, relieved (if
that is the word) only by an embarrassed discomfort."
Robin Wood, Ingmar Bergman, pp. 93-94.

110Wood, _Ingmar Bergman_, p. 92.

111"Closer to the predicament of Vogler is...Pirandello's Henry IV, who is forced to continue playing a role he had once assumed arbitrarily. Bergman himself told Sjoman, quoted in L 136 that the connection between his theater production and his films was a close one and that...intimations of Pirandello in _The Magician_ should not be overlooked." Vernon Young, Ingmar Bergman, _Essays in Criticism_, ed., Stuart Kaminsky with Joseph Hill (New York: Oxford University Press, 1975), p. 210.

112Arthur Gibson, _The Silence of God_ (New York: Harper and Row, 1969), pp. 74-75.

113Wood, _Ingmar Bergman_, p. 95.

114Gibson, _The Silence of God_, pp. 68-70.

115Young, _Cinema Borealis_, p. 183.

116Bergman, as quoted by Steene, p. 84.

117Bergman, _Four Screenplays_, p. 310.

118One is reminded here of the now famous quotation of President Eisenhower: "Our government makes no sense unless it is founded in a deeply felt religious faith--and I don't care what it is." Quoted by Will Herberg, _Protestant Catholic, Jew_, p. 84.

119Donner _The Films of Ingmar Bergman_, p. 184.

120Bergman, as quoted by Samuels, p. 125.

121"The possibilities of interpreting _The Magician_ are many. George Sadoul has compared it with the Passion play. Vogler may be Christ. As Carl-Eric Nordberg says: 'By his presence he makes everybody strangely disturbed, he exercises an irrestible fascination on his environment, whether it reacts with hatred or with love.' The same critic is reminded by Mrs. Egerman of Pilate's wife, who says she has 'suffered much in the dream for his sake,' for the sake of the Crucified One. Stig Wikander, the historian of religion, has rendered the most thoroughgoing interpretation. He believes that Vogler's history corresponds point by point to the early Christian legend of Simon Magus, Simon the Magician. It is true that Vogler wears a Christ mask. But he is not Christ, neither is he a false savior, but a Gnostic savior: 'Early Christian literature has strange things to tell of the meeting between the Apostle Peter and Simon the Magician, with Emperor Nero as referee. It turned out in about the same way as when medical counselor Vergerus and Doctor Vogler in the film meet before police chief Starbeck, a small-time Nero." The final change to victory receives the following natural explanation: "When the King's Son, the One sent forth, has been as deeply humiliated as is possible, there is a turn in the tide. Then comes, says the Gnostic, the Letter, the Royal Letter from the world outside of our reality, and conveys the King's will: That his son will be rehabilitated and enter into the glory of his Father.'" Donner, The Films of Ingmar Bergman, p. 179.

[122]The Pleasure Garden (1961).

[123]Stig Bjorkman asked Bergman: "When you had made Through a Glass Darkly, did you know instinctively you would carry on the film's line of reasoning? Was the trilogy already planned? Or did each film arise spontaneously? And at what point in time did you feel justified in placing the three films together as a trilogy?" Bergman responds: "Not until all three were finished. But then I was a bit astonished myself to see how unified they were. It must have been Vilgot Sjoman who first pointed it out to me. But when I was actually making them I no such intention, no." Stig Bjorkman, et al., p. 172.

[124]Bergman, Stockholm, May, 1963, as quoted in Three Films by Ingmar Bergman, (New York: Grove Press, 1970), Title Page et seg.

[125]Lucas, The Drama of Ibsen and Strindberg, p. 454.

[126]Bergman, as quoted by Stig Bjorkman et al., p. 168.

[127]Barrett, Irrational Man, p. 155.

[128]Bergman, as quoted by Stig Bjorkman, et al., pp. 190-191.

[129]I believe this understanding is closer to Bergman's intent than Jerry Gill's assertion: "...that after The Seventh Seal, Bergman gave up

trying to formulate his questions and answers concerning God and human existence in the terminology of traditional Christianity. In a way, this trilogy can be viewed as the secular, or modern, translation of these questions and answers." Gill, Bergman and the Search for Meaning, p. 25.

[130]Bergman, as quoted by Stig Bjorkman, et al., pp. 190-191.

[131]Ibid., p. 195.

[132]I Corinthians 13:11-13, RSV.

[133]Bergman, as quoted by Stig Bjorkman, et al., p. 163.

[134]Wood, Ingmar Bergman, pp. 108-109.

[135]Ibid. Robin Wood states: "In anyone's memory of the film, it is Karin and her Spider-God that remain: David and Martin evaporate. Minus remains, as yet, a mere shadowy presence."

[136]Young, Cinema Borealis, p. 204.

[137]Gene D. Phillips, S. J., "Ingmar Bergman and God," in Essays in Criticism, ed., Stuart Kaminsky, pp. 48-49.

[138]Gill, Bergman and the Search for Meaning, pp. 27-28.

[139]Gibson, The Silence of God, p. 86.

[140]Donner, The Films of Ingmar Bergman, p. 214.

[141]Bergman, as quoted by Steene, p. 101.

[142]On the narrative level of interpretation one must agree with Steene's interpretation, but on the mythological level Donner's critique takes precedence.

[143]H. Richard Niebuhr, The Responsible Self (New York: Harper & Row, 1963), p. 140.

[144]It is true that we are introduced to this idea of the healing of love in The Magician, but Granny is such an ambivalent character, that we do not accept it as a major theme.

145Bergman, as quoted by Stig Bjorkman et al.,
p. 167.

146Bergman, as quoted by Steene, p. 102.

1471962. The Communicants is the original and
preferred title of the film.

148Bergman, as quoted by Simon, pp. 17-18.

149Simon's interview with Bergman is not
dated, but I would judge from the publication date of
Simon's book that the interview probably took place in
1971.

150Bergman, as quoted by Stig Bjorkman, et
al., p. 175.

151Barrett, Irrational Man, pp. 28-29.

152Bergman, as quoted by Steene, p. 103, who,
in turn, refers to Vilgot Sjoman, L 136, p. 28.

153Bergman, as quoted by Stig Bjorkman, et
al., p. 219.

154Stuart Kaminsky with Joseph Hill, Essays in
Criticism, (New York: Oxford University Press, 1975),
pp. 106-107.

155Jorn Donner sees a continuity here with
David in Through a Glass Darkly: "The author David
and pastor Tomas Ericsson seem to symbolize the
breakdown of the metaphysical questions. David is
partly a hypocrite. Tomas has chosen to take orders
out of consideration for his parents. He has wished
for a God who would give him security. But in the
moment of examination which constitutes the film he
realizes failure. It does not matter whether God
exists or not. The world is easier to explain without
Him. Man is freer. To learn to love is to learn the
possibilities of communion and consolation, and it is
toward these things that the characters are
striving...'If God does not exist, all is permitted.'
This peculiar maxim makes the starting point for both
The Devil's Wanton and Winter Light." Donner, The
Films of Bergman, p. 225.

156It seems to be a situation similar to that in which Archibald MacLeish finds himself in his play J.B. While the major thrust of his play is humanistic, MacLeish includes a Voice which can never be accounted for, one which not everyone hears.

157Wood, Ingmar Bergman, p. 118.

158Bergman, as quoted by Stig Bjorkman, et al., p. 176.

159Simon, Ingmar Bergman Directs, p. 196ff.

160Ibid., p. 196.

161Gibson, The Silence of God, p. 113.

162Ibid., pp. 113-114.

163Ibid., p. 114.

164Simon, Ingmar Bergman Directs, pp. 196-197.

165Ibid., p. 197.

166Ibid.

167Ibid.

168Wood, Ingmar Bergman, pp. 122-123.

169Simon Ingmar Bergman Directs, p. 204.

170Ibid., p. 206.

171"My father, as you probably know, was a clergyman--he knew all the Uppland churches like the back of his hand. We went to morning service in various places and were deeply impressed by the spiritual poverty of these churches, by the lack of any congregation and the miserable spiritual status of the clergy, the poverty of their sermons, and the nonchalance and indifference of the ritual.

"In one church, I remember--and I think it has a great deal to do with the end of the film--Father and I were sitting together. My father had already been retired for many years, and was old and frail. No one was there but him and me, well I suppose the clergyman's wife was sitting there too-no, she wasn't, it was the churchwarden; and I suppose a few old women had turned up too. Just before the bell begins to toll, we hear a car outside, a shining Volvo: the clergyman climbs out hurriedly, and there is a faint buzz from the vestry, and then the clergyman appears before he ought to--when the bell stops, that is--and says he feels very poorly and that he's talked to the rector and the rector has said he can use an abbreviated form of the service and drop the part at the altar. So there would just be one psalm and a sermon and another psalm. And goes out. Whereon my father, furious, began hammering on the pew, got to his feet and marched out into the vestry, where a long mumbled conversation ensued; after which the churchwarden also went in, then someone ran to the organ gallery to fetch the organist, after which the churchwarden came out and announced that there would be a complete service after all. My father took the service at the altar, both at the beginning and the end." Bergman, as quoted by Stig Bjorkman, et al., pp. 173-174.

172Ibid.

173Donner, The Films of Ingmar Bergman, p. 225.

174Ibid., p. 219.

175Barrett, Irrational Man, p. 209.

176Simon, Ingmar Bergman Directs, p. 197.

177Wood, Ingmar Bergman, p. 132.

178Bergman, as quoted by Stig Bjorkman, et al., p. 181.

179Ibid., p. 195.

180Donner, The Films of Ingmar Bergman, pp. 232-233.

181Wood, Ingmar Bergman, p. 123.

182Kaminsky, Essays in Criticism, p. 123.

183Carol Brightman in Essays in Criticism, pp. 242-243. Brigitta Steene is of a similar opinion: "The Silence is a film without any real character development. Rather it is an attempt at an exact expression of a mood of isolation, death, and destruction...." Bergman, as quoted by Steene, p. 109.

[184]Carol Brightman in _Essays_ _in_ _Criticism_, p. 245.

[185]Young, _Cinema_ _Borealis_, p. 214.

[186]Bergman, as quoted by Samuels, p. 124.

[187]Bergman, as quoted by Stig Bjorkman, et al., p. 188.

[188]Wood, _Ingmar_ _Bergman_, pp. 131-132.

[189]Brightman _Essays_ _in_ _Criticism_, pp. 247-248.

[190]Bergman, as quoted by Stig Bjorkman, et al., p. 236.

[191]Gibson, _The_ _Silence_ _of_ _God_, p. 131.

[192]Ibid., p. 122.

[193]Kaminsky, _Essays_ _in_ _Criticism_, p. 10.

[194]Bergman, as quoted by Stig Bjorkman, et al., p. 183.

[195]Ibid.

[196]Ibid.

[197]Gill, _Bergman_ _and_ _the_ _Search_ _for_ _Meaning_, p. 34.

[198]Bergman, written for the presentation of the Erasmus Prize in Amsterdam, 1965, and used as an introductory piece to _Persona_, _Persona_ _and_ _Shame_, trans. Keith Bradfield (New York: Grossman Publishers, 1972.)

[199]Barrett, _Irrational_ _Man_, p. 269.

[200]Bergman, as quoted by Stig Bjorkman, et al., p. 202.

[201]Simon, _Ingmar_ _Bergman_ _Directs_, pp. 224-225.

[202]Bergman, as quoted by Stig Bjorkman, et al., pp. 198-199.

203Simon, _Ingmar Bergman Directs_, p. 215.

204Ibid., p. 239.

205Ibid. p. 253.

206Ibid.

207Ibid., p. 252.

208Ibid., p. 253.

209Ibid., p. 294.

210Bergman, as quoted by Samuels, Kaminsky, p. 111.

211Ibid., p. 267.

212Simon _Ingmar Bergman Directs_, p. 224.

213Ibid., p. 259.

214Brigitta Steene also sees "God" in Elisabet, but not quite the same "God" as Gibson finds: "The image of God finds its psychological correlative in the naked but mysterious self of Elisabet Vogler. She is a being with "severe eyes," according to Alma; she is treacherous, detached and yet at times kind and patient; she allures and repels at the same time. She is half benevolence, half "spider-god." Bergman, as quoted by Steene, p. 118.

215Gibson, _The Silence of God_, p. 150.

216Bergman, as quoted by Samuels, Kaminsky, p. 109.

217Bergman, as quoted by Steene, p. 118.

218Simon _Ingmar Bergman Directs_, pp. 33-34.

219Barrett, _Irrational Man_, p. 276

220Bergman, as quoted by Stig Bjorkman, et al., p. 228.

221Barrett, _Irrational Man_, pp. 226-227.

222Judith Crist, "Bergman's Basic Truth", New York Magazine, 13 January 1969, p. 54.

223Barrett, Irrational Man, p. 137.

224Though doubtful, one still wonders if in this episode Bergman had Amos's judgment on Israel in mind: "For three transgressions of Israel, and for four, I will not revoke the punishment; because they sell the righteous for silver, and the needy for a pair of shoes...." Amos 2:6.

225Wood, Ingmar Bergman, p. 7.

226Bergman, as quoted by Bosley Crowther, "Bergman 'Shame' in Twin Premier," New York Times, 1 October 1968, p. 40.

227Bergman, as quoted by Stig Bjorkman, et al., p. 235.

228Ibid., p. 232.

229In the English version of this film, the title is The Passion of Anna, but because this is so misleading in terms of the intent of the film and the popular connotations of the word "passion," I am following the lead of virtually all reviewers and am using the Swedish title: A Passion.

230Wood, Ingmar Bergman, p. 174.

231Young, Cinema Borealis, pp. 248-259.

232Bergman, as quoted by Stig Bjorkman et al., p. 253.

233Bergman, as quoted by Samuels, Kaminsky, pp. 120-121.

234Kaminsky, Essays in Criticism, p. 110.

235Young, Cinema Borealis, p. 267.

236Perhaps, considering the repetitions that do occur, a case could be made for believing that Bergman is employing Frederick Nietzsche's understanding of "eternal return"--that because of the limitation of time and man's possibilities, all things (events) must eventually repeat themselves--yet the changes indicated by Bergman make it hard to accept this as a conscious effort on Bergman's part.

237Bergman, as quoted by Stig Bjorkman, et al., p. 255.

238Ibid., p. 257.

239Ibid., p. 285.

240Ibid., p. 255.

241Italics mine.

242Bergman, as quoted by Stig Bjorkman, et al., p. 257.

243Young, Cinema Borealis, p. 278.

244Ibid., pp. 273-277.

245Ibid., p. 280.

246Ibid.

247Ibid., p. 283.

248Ibid., p. 281.

249Barrett, Irrational Man, p. 31.

250Bergman, Four Stories by Ingmar Bergman, Alan Blair, trans. (Garden City, New York: Anchor Press, 1976), p. 59.

251Ibid., p. 60.

252Ibid., p. 61.

253Ibid., pp. 88-89.

254Ibid., p. 61.

255Ibid., p. 88.

256Ibid., pp. 60-61.

257Ibid.

258Ibid., p. 86.

259Bergman, "Preface," Face to Face, trans. Alan Blair (New York: Pantheon Books, 1976), p. v.

[260]It is interesting to see how far Bergman has come to incorporate all of us in his scheme for involvement. The heroine in the present film is a long way from the sick Karin of Through a Glass Darkly; she is the epitome of successful middle-class Western culture, with woman's liberation thrown in for good measure (an improvement--one of many--over Bergman's film The Touch). In answer to the Doctor's query in Cries and Whispers: "Are there no extenuating circumstances for people such as you and I?", Bergman wants to be able to answer "No!" to us all.

[261]It is reassuring to note this (unintentional, I'm sure) paraphrase of the two-fold nature of Buber's I-Thou and I-It: Reality begins in the two-fold ontology of Being.

[262]Bergman, "Preface", Face to Face, pp. vi-vii.

[263]Ibid., pp. 63-65. Of all the exclusions, this is the most puzzling and inexcusable. Without this explanation the suicide attempt in the film loses much of its plausibility and, consequently, force.

[264]Ibid., p. 10.

[265]Ibid., pp. 19-20.

[266]Ibid., p. 32. Stromberg is "gay," and the film seems to dwell on that. Too bad, for the lack of exposure of this aspect of his personality turns Stromberg of the film into a stereotypical homosexual, which then reflects poorly on Tomas who was once his lover.

[267]Ibid., p. 33.

[268]Ibid., p. 115.

[269]Ibid., p. 117.

[270]Ingmar Bergman, Autumn Sonata, trans. Alan Blair, (New York: Pantheon Books, 1978), p. 53.

[271]The text refers to the grave itself rather than the nursery, but the place of location is incidental to the point Eva is making.

272Bergman, <u>Autumn</u> <u>Sonata</u>, p. 30.

273Ingmar   Bergman,   as   quoted   by   Michiko
Kakutani, <u>The</u> <u>New</u> <u>York</u> <u>Times</u> <u>Magazine</u>, June 26, 1983,
p. 24.

274Pauline   Kael,   "Wrapping   It   Up,"   <u>The</u>   <u>New</u>
<u>Yorker</u>, June 13, 1983, pp. 117-121.

275Ingmar   Bergman,   <u>Fanny</u>   <u>and</u>   <u>Alexander</u>,   trans.
Alan   Blair,   New   York: Pantheon   Books,   1983,   pp.
31-32.

STUDIES IN ART AND RELIGIOUS INTERPRETATION